The Quilters Hall of Fame

42 Masters Who Have Shaped Our Art

Edited by Merikay Waldvogel,
Rosalind Webster Perry,
and Marian Ann J. Montgomery, Ph.D.

Voyageur Press

First published in 2011 by Voyageur Press, an imprint of Quarto Publishing Group USA Inc., 400 First Avenue North, Suite 400, Minneapolis, MN 55401 USA

Voyageur Press titles are also available at discounts in bulk quantity for industrial or sales-promotional use. For details write to Special Sales Manager at Quarto Publishing Group USA Inc., 400 First Avenue North, Suite 400, Minneapolis, MN 55401 USA.

To find out more about our books, visit us online at www.voyageurpress.com.

ISBN: 978-0-7603-4705-8

The Library of Congress has cataloged the hardcover edition as follows:

The Quilters Hall of Fame : 42 masters who have shaped our art / edited by Merikay Waldvogel, Rosalind Webster Perry, and Marian Ann Montgomery.
    p. cm.
Includes bibliographical references and index.
ISBN 978-0-7603-3635-9 (plc)
1. Quiltmakers--United States--Biography. 2. Quilts--United States. I. Waldvogel, Merikay, 1947- II. Perry, Rosalind. III. Montgomery, Marian Ann J.
NK9197.Q55 2011
746.46092'273--dc22
[B]
                    2011009835

Editor: Melinda Keefe
Design Manager: LeAnn Kuhlmann
Layout by: Danielle Smith
Cover designed by: Lois Stanfield

Printed in China

On the frontispiece:

Windows Quilt | Made by Jinny Beyer | 2001 – 2002 | 92 × 92 inches | Hand-pieced and quilted. This 4,777-piece quilt is Jinny's response to the tragedy of September 11, 2001. She visualized looking down from the top floors of the towers and the Windows of the World restaurant at the Statue of Liberty standing proudly below. She selected faded reds, whites, and blues tinged with smoke and ash as well as the occasional vibrant tones . . . representing strength, courage, and spirit. *Photo by Steve Tuttle, courtesy of Jinny Beyer*

On the title page:

Star of Bethlehem (or Lone Star) | Circa 1880–1900 | 85 × 82 inches | Cotton. A tour de force of the exuberant colors and forms that characterize many Pennsylvania quilts and that first attracted Gail van der Hoof and Jonathan Holstein in the late 1960s, this quilt displays energy reminiscent of some contemporary American paintings of the period. *Courtesy of the International Quilt Study Center and Museum (2003.003.0139)*

Additional selected readings, a full timeline of events from the honorees' lives, and information about exhibitions at the Quilters Hall of Fame can be found at www.quiltershalloffame.net or www.voyageurpress.com.

A Note from the Editor

IT HAS BEEN AN HONOR to work with those passionately committed to preserving the history of the inductees of the Quilters Hall of Fame. Those who coordinated the original edition were generous and incredibly helpful on this revised edition, particularly Hazel Carter, Rosalind Perry, Joyce Hostetler, and Merikay Waldvogel.

Marian Ann J. Montgomery, Ph.D.
Photo by Brad Flowers

The original manuscript of this book was created by an extensive cadre of volunteers passionate about preserving quilt history. Updating such a book, created primarily by so many different people, was a challenge. Many of the authors have moved on to other research projects and felt they had said all there was to say the first time around. But this provided a silver lining, giving me the opportunity to work with the families of the honorees and, in the case of those still living, the honorees themselves so that this edition would be up to date with their latest work. As a career historian, the opportunity to talk with family members who seek to preserve the legacies of their loved ones as well as those who have made history in the world of quilting themselves was a unique and wonderful experience. I want to thank especially those family members and living honorees who were open to my inquiries and patient throughout revisions, and I hope that this volume is an apt reflection of their incredible work. Thank you also to the many individuals, organizations, and museums who generously gave permission to use the images that illustrate this book. Thank you especially to editor Melinda Keefe, who came to this project part of the way through, picked up the work without missing a beat, and was a joy with which to work.

Although introduced to embroidery as a child and working as a home economics teacher before earning my master's degree and a position in the museum field, I came to quilting in my twenties as the historic site manager of the eighteenth-century Pennsylvania site Graeme Park. The eighteenth-century inventory of the property indicated that there was at least one quilt in the mansion. A local woman wanted to teach quilting at the site and offered to teach board members of the Friends of Graeme Park and me, so I started on a lap quilt. Since that time, I began my Ph.D. studies at New York University and the Metropolitan Museum of Art, where I met the Texan who married me and whisked me away from the northeast first to Texas, then to Tennessee, where I worked as the curator of fashion and textiles for the Tennessee State Museum, and where I had the good fortune to send part of the collection to Patsy Orlofsky for conservation and to meet Bets Ramsey and Merikay Waldvogel, who had just finished *The Quilts of Tennessee*. They introduced me to the Southern Quilt Symposium, the American Quilt Study Group, and the statewide quilt documentation projects.

My return to Texas found me working with the Bybee Collection of quilts at the Dallas Museum of Art and becoming a member of the Quilter's Guild of Dallas. Geography placed me close enough to the International Quilt Festival in Houston to attend for the past twenty years, to attend the festival in Paducah, Kentucky, once, and to have the opportunity to be part of the largest volunteer-run quilt festival in Dallas, learning from the nationally known teachers a guild that large was able to draw. I am proud that during my service on the Endowment Committee of the Quilter's Guild of Dallas, Inc., the guild funded many quilt research, documentation, and storage projects. My professional work, my support of the work of the American Quilt Study Group, and my love of making quilts have intersected in this project, giving me the opportunity to work with and honor so many who mentored and taught me over the years.

Many aspects of quilt history have been documented, but this book focuses exclusively on the honorees of the Quilters Hall of Fame. Hazel Carter's vision filled a gap in knowledge that would otherwise have continued causing much precious information about these leaders to have been lost. Each of those honored on these pages brought their unique talent and perspective to further this art form that I have come to love and devote so much of my life to studying, exhibiting, and creating. I hope their stories serve as inspiration to quilters and quilt historians of the future.

Marian Ann J. Montgomery, Ph.D.
Dallas, Texas, February 2011

Contents

Preface

by Hazel Carter,
founder of the
Quilters Hall of Fame

Photo by Cook's Photo-Art Studio

THE QUILTERS HALL of Fame evolved from my personal study of quilting, beginning with the techniques I learned from my mother and grandmother while growing up in Iowa. In 1972, I attended a quilting bee in Virginia, where I have lived since 1958. At this quilting bee I was introduced to *Quilters Newsletter Magazine.* Immediately, I became a subscriber and obtained every back issue to broaden my knowledge of quilting.

By December 1972, the quilting bee had grown to such an extent that we formed a guild, which became Quilters Unlimited. During the development of this organization, my sights turned to larger possibilities that could educate quilters from afar on what was happening in their regions. That idea became the Continental Quilting Congress, a quilt convention held at the Sheraton Hotel in Arlington, Virginia, July 13 to 15, 1978. Registrations came in from all areas of the United States and included twenty quilters from Canada.

The success of this first undertaking led to a second convention in 1979, at which I founded the Quilters Hall of Fame. It had become apparent at the first convention that quilters were ignoring our quilting heritage. In 1979, we inducted six individuals to recognize "their accomplishments, and thereby to establish documentation of a part of quilting history." Honorees are not necessarily quilters but include authors, curators, collectors, editors, historians, researchers, and quilt artists from around the United States and in the United Kingdom. A selection committee reviews nominations entered by the public and then submits its choices to the board of directors for approval.

In the pivotal year of 1991, the Quilters Hall of Fame found a home. Rosalind Webster Perry, a granddaughter of Marie D. Webster, was present at her late grandmother's induction. Perry asked if the Quilters Hall of Fame might be located in her grandmother's house in Marion, Indiana, explaining that it would have to be renovated. I immediately said yes.

People often say there is "more to a house than bricks and mortar." That is so true in this instance. Dedicated townspeople formed the Friends of the Quilters Hall of Fame, and along with quilters from across the nation and a dedicated board of directors, the Friends became the backbone of the twelve-year renovation project. The Friends organization, now known as the Marie Webster Quilt Guild, has worked tirelessly in coordinating the Quilters Hall of Fame Celebration, sponsoring National Quilting Day and other exhibits and educational activities, raising funds to renovate and maintain the Marie Webster House, and promoting fellowship in the art of quilting. The Quilters Hall of Fame Celebration, an annual program in Marion, Indiana, honoring new inductees, began in 1992 with the exhibition *Marie Webster Quilts: A Retrospective.*

In July 2004 we celebrated the house's grand opening. Now the public can visit the Quilters Hall of Fame in Marion, Indiana, to view changing exhibits and learn more about the honorees. We have a website with information for visitors, dates and hours of operation, a schedule of exhibits and classes, and merchandise from our museum store: www.quiltershalloffame.net.

Not everyone is able to visit our home in the Marie Webster House; thus this book is intended to tell of the outstanding contributions our honorees have made over the years. The first book about the Quilters Hall of Fame and its honorees, coedited by Merikay Waldvogel and Rosalind Webster Perry, was unveiled at our grand opening in 2004. Research associates volunteered in the endeavor and wrote the essays for each honoree. This group is to be commended for its accomplishments.

I now serve as an honorary board member and, after thirty years, have retired as chair of the selection committee. My interest has not waned for documenting the lives of the present honorees and those who will be inducted in the future, and I am delighted that our book, now edited by Dr. Marian Ann Montgomery, will be in hardcover with the essays updated, including more pictures for everyone's enjoyment.

The Founder of the Quilters Hall of Fame

by Karen B. Alexander, quilt historian
and past president of the Quilters Hall of Fame

A S THIS NEW EDITION OF A BOOK about the Quilters Hall of Fame goes to press, it seems appropriate to share the story of its remarkable, productive founder.

Hazel Carter (née McDowell), born in Salem, Iowa (she moved to Mt. Pleasant, Iowa, at age five), was taught to quilt as a child by her mother, Grace McVey McDowell, and her maternal grandmother, Elsie Long McVey. In 1958, Carter moved to Washington, D.C., to work in the office of Iowa congressman Fred Schwengel, and she continued to quilt. In 1964, she married Joseph G. Carter, and by 1971, she was the busy mother of two small children, who eventually gave her three grandchildren.

In December 1972, Carter, along with two others, was instrumental in founding Quilters Unlimited of Northern Virginia, a guild that would eventually grow into an eleven-chapter, 1,300-member nonprofit that has left its mark in many ways throughout northern Virginia.

In 1978, Carter founded yet another organization: the Continental Quilting Congress, an educational nonprofit based in Vienna, Virginia. It was one of the earliest quilt conferences held in a hotel setting. The first "congress" attracted more than five hundred delegates, with additional attendees who came just to shop at the special vendors' mall, which offered fabrics, notions, and antique quilts, raising the final attendance total to more than one thousand quilt enthusiasts. Previous generations had learned to quilt from a family member or in a church-affiliated group. Hundreds of quilters spending several nights in a hotel to take quilt classes was a trendsetting event in the quilt world. "Who had ever heard of staying overnight at a hotel in order to learn how to quilt!" one husband was heard to exclaim. Ten Continental Quilting Congresses were held over a thirteen-year period.

As Carter analyzed all the comments and feedback she received from that first Continental Quilting Congress, she became aware of the need to educate quilters about their quilting heritage. After careful discussions with her fellow quilters, Carter's insightful solution was to create the Quilters Hall of Fame. The souvenir book for the first induction ceremony in 1979 stated, "The Quilters Hall of Fame has been established to recognize the people behind the quilting renaissance, to pay tribute to their accomplishments and thereby establish documentation of an important part of quilting history."

Carter's interest in quilt history also inspired her to organize one of the earliest series of international quilt tours, with tours in 1981, 1982, 1985, and 1986.

Star of Bethlehem Revisited | Made by Hazel Carter | 1990–1997 | 84½ × 81½ inches. This quilt was selected for a card, *Quilt Cards by the Quilted Page,* and exhibited at the American Quilt Study Group Annual Seminar in Williamsburg, Virginia, October 2001. *Photo by Khoury and Latil, courtesy of Hazel Carter*

As a natural outgrowth of the Continental Quilters Congress and the Quilters Hall of Fame, Carter created the Northern Virginia Quilt Search. On May 13, 1985, the first of twelve Northern Virginia Quilt Discovery Days was held. In July 1987, Carter published the project's findings under the umbrella of the Continental Quilting Congress in a forty-page book, *Virginia Quilts: First Search for Virginia-made Quilts, Beginning in Northern Virginia 1987*. That same year, Carter was instrumental in assisting the historic Decatur House in Washington, D.C., with the creation of its annual Tactile Architecture exhibit, and she served as an adviser to the museum from 1987 to 1991. Today, this same juried exhibit continues as part of the Houston International Quilt Festival. Carter began appraising quilts in 1979 and became an Accredited Senior Appraiser (ASA) with the American Society of Appraisers in 1994.

In 1992, when supporters of quilting discovered the Smithsonian's intention to use a Chinese manufacturer to reproduce five quilts from its collection, the quilt world took note and protested. As a result of her previous professional contacts in Washington, D.C., Carter was contacted by the Smithsonian director and asked to help set up a meeting with members of the American quilting community so that all parties concerned could discuss the issues. Because of their work in the American quilting industry, Carter included Bonnie Leman, founder and publisher of *Quilters Newsletter Magazine*; Karey Bresenhan, founder of the Houston International Quilt Festival; and Jinny Beyer, an internationally known quilt teacher and author living in northern Virginia, in that important gathering. Presidents of local guilds in the Washington, D.C., area were also included. Leman had already begun to write about imported quilts in the pages of *Quilters Newsletter Magazine*, and as a result of this first meeting with the Smithsonian, she wrote a two-page editorial in April 1992 addressing the matter.

Another significant date in Carter's work for the Quilters Hall of Fame occurred in July 1991, when Carter and Rosalind Webster Perry met for the first time. The history of the Quilters Hall of Fame was forever altered as a result of this meeting.

Never one to let grass grow under her feet, in September 1995 Carter cofounded one of the earliest quilt-dating clubs in the nation with her business partner, Bunnie Jordan. The Antique and Vintage Fabric Dating Club of Northern Virginia came about largely as a result of numerous requests for more information from the students of Carter and Jordan's quilt-dating classes. The group is still going strong today.

Over the many years of her active participation in the quilt world, Carter has authored one book and numerous articles in various quilt-related publications, including "New Revelations About the Garden Quilt" (*Blanket Statements*, Winter 2004), "Strippy Quilts in the United States" (*Blanket Statements*, Spring 2007), and a series about editors in the quilt world—Joyce Gross, Jonathan Holstein, Carter Houck, and Bonnie Leman—in the newsletter of the Quilters Hall of Fame. She has also curated numerous exhibits, not the least of which are many of the honoree exhibits of the Quilters Hall of Fame. Hazel Carter has designed patterns, taught many classes, and made many quilts. Thus has this gifted entrepreneur shared her numerous talents with all of us, as quilters tend to do, and kept her childhood Iowa quiltmaking traditions alive and well at the same time.

This image conveys a sense of Quilters Hall of Fame founder Hazel Carter's amazing energy and joy of life.

History of the Marie Webster House

by Rosalind Webster Perry

Photo by Wm. B. Dewey

ALTHOUGH built in 1901, the Marie Webster House's story actually begins in 1887, with the discovery of natural gas just a few blocks away from the home's future location on South Washington Street in Marion, Indiana. The gusher's flames burst thirty feet into the air, while the sound of hissing gas could be heard in the Courthouse Square ten blocks away.

This dramatic event shaped the history of Marion, for it ushered in the "Gas Boom," marking a period of rapid development and great prosperity. Marion became known as the "Queen City of the Gas Belt," with gaslights left burning night and day. Free land and free gas were offered to lure new businesses to the area.

In 1891, the York Inn, a magnificent new four-story hotel, was built on the western edge of town to cater to the industrialists brought in by special trains from the East. However, the heyday of the inn lasted only a few short years. The gas soon petered out, the entrepreneurs moved on, and the hotel went bust. It enjoyed a brief rebirth as a seventy-room sanitarium, or "alcohol cure clinic," before being torn down in 1901. However, the construction materials, including the lumber and foundation stones, were purchased by a Marion businessman for three new houses he was planning to build in the fashionable neighborhood just south of the town center. According to the local paper in April 1901, each of the houses would be "a modern and handsome structure and will add greatly to the beauty of that part of Washington Street, which now has a number of beautiful homes."

Marie and George Webster moved into one of the newly completed houses and hosted a memorable housewarming on April 21, 1902. The *Marion News Tribune* reported, "Two hundred of the city's most representative people figured as guests of the Webster home during the afternoon and evening and the many beautiful gowns worn by the women presented a gorgeous spectacle."

Special features of the colonial revival home included a gambrel roof, dormer windows, and a two-story gabled bay window. Colonial details were added: a porch with Tuscan colonnettes, a modillion cornice, and leaded glass windows. The back porches sported Victorian columns recycled from the York Inn. Inside, the stairhall was the central focus, with a double parlor, dining room, and kitchen beyond. Tiled fireplaces provided heat to the main rooms. Upstairs, four rooms and a bathroom opened off a central hallway. The two north-facing rooms were connected to form a bedroom and sitting room suite. It was this sitting room that would become Marie Webster's sewing room and studio when she started designing and selling quilt patterns. Here, she made her quilts, produced patterns for sale, welcomed customers, and wrote the first book of quilt history, *Quilts: Their Story and How to Make Them*, published in 1915.

The house was furnished in a mixture of Victorian and Arts and Crafts styles. A wicker settee and chairs stood in the entrance hall, and oriental rugs covered the oak floor. Dark green drapes hung at the windows and across the doorways. Various floral wallpapers decorated the upstairs bedrooms, their styles changing along with changing fashions, from Victorian, to Arts and Crafts, and then to Art Deco in the 1920s.

Marie and George Webster made their home here for the next thirty-six years. In 1922, they were joined by Marie's sister, Emma Daugherty. For several years in the 1930s, their son, Lawrence, and his wife, Jeanette, lived in the third-floor "penthouse" before their children were born. George died in 1938, but Marie and Emma continued to live in the house until 1942, when they moved to New Jersey to be with Lawrence and his family. At that time, they sold the house to their next-door neighbors, who converted it into five apartments.

Our family knew nothing of the fate of the house until 1988, when I returned to Marion for the first time since our family had moved away. What inspired me to go back after such a long time? I had recently learned that Marie Webster was well known to quilters for her book and for her floral appliqué quilt designs, which were still appearing in quilting magazines thirty years after her death. I decided to publish a new edition of her book, which would feature her biography. I realized how important it would be to visit Marion to seek out information about my famous grandmother.

My delight at seeing the old family home still standing was eclipsed when I saw the dreadful condition of the house and yard. Before I even reached the front door, the porch gave way, and, much to my surprise, I found myself sprawled out with one leg trapped between the rotten floorboards. As I extricated myself, luckily uninjured, I was determined to find out who owned the property and how it had come to this sorry state.

The Marie Webster House, home of the Quilters Hall of Fame, after restoration.

I managed to locate the owner, who showed me the inside of the building, which had been vacant for about five years. After I returned to California, we kept in touch. She sold the house to a family who planned to fix it up. But in the fall of 1990, the new owner informed me that it had been condemned by the City of Marion as a public nuisance. He had changed his mind about repairing it; would I like to buy it? Otherwise, it would have to be torn down. The drive-in restaurant next door wanted to acquire the land to enlarge its parking lot.

Marie Webster had been nominated to the Quilters Hall of Fame, and her quilts were appreciated as never before. What

a shame if her home were to be torn down! Since the price was very low, I was able to purchase it, preventing its demolition. To remove it from the list of condemned properties, I was required to bring it up to code. At that point, I had no plan of how to fulfill that pledge. I contacted several community groups, hoping to find one that would be able to fix up the house and use it.

Shortly after I acquired the deed for the house, I traveled to Sacramento, California, in July 1991, for the West Coast Quilters Conference, where the induction of Marie Webster into the Quilters Hall of Fame would take place. I had a sudden thought: The Quilters Hall of Fame—perhaps they could use the home of an honoree? When I met Hazel Carter for the first time, at the conference, I exclaimed, "Would you like to put the Quilters Hall of Fame in Marie Webster's house in Indiana?" Much to my amazement, her reaction was enthusiastic. And thus began our collaboration on this challenging project.

But what a herculean task lay ahead! It would be expensive to do all the necessary renovation, and we would need plenty of expert advice. I contacted a historic preservation consultant, Craig Leonard, who recommended applying for listing on the state and national historic registers to provide some measure of protection. He researched and prepared the necessary documentation.

On April 22, 1992, the George Jr. and Marie Daugherty Webster House was entered in the Indiana Register of Historic Sites and Structures, and on June 17, 1992, it was listed in the National Register of Historic Places. With the historical significance of the building officially recognized, I transferred the deed to the Quilters Hall of Fame on October 8, 1992.

We soon learned that the National Park Service was conducting a survey of structures related to women's contributions. We were delighted when the Marie Webster House was selected as a Landmark of Women's History and was officially declared a National Historic Landmark, the highest designation bestowed by the United States government.

It was important to find people in the local community who would support this project. Phebe Smith, a quilter and longtime resident of Marion, spearheaded a new group, the Friends of the Quilters Hall of Fame, now known as the Marie Webster Quilt Guild. The dedication and hard work of this stalwart band of volunteers is largely responsible for the successful completion of the restoration work on the Marie Webster House and for

maintaining and staffing the Quilters Hall of Fame to the present. Meeting monthly, they also sponsor many quilting and fundraising activities, including the annual National Quilting Day event. Together with the Hall of Fame's board of directors, these volunteers work tirelessly throughout the year to plan and host our major Quilt Celebration and Induction Ceremony, with exhibits, workshops, and classes, held each July.

Renovation

Prior to its recognition for its importance in women's history, the Marie Webster House had been condemned as a safety hazard and clearly needed a major overhaul. As work began in 1994 and progressed over the next thirteen years, just how much help it needed became clear. The highest priority was to replace the original roof, in order to stop the leaks that were continuing to damage the interior. Then we received several grants to repair all the ornamental trim, brackets, cornice, siding, and—my nemesis—the sagging front porch. Next, the exterior was painted in the original color scheme, yellow with cream trim.

This initial phase of the project was completed on July 15, 1994, when a large group gathered beside the front porch to view the unveiling of the National Historic Landmark plaque and to hear several dignitaries speak, including the mayor of Marion.

In 1995, historic preservation consultant Craig Leonard undertook a study of the wallpapers in the house, with a Preservation Services Fund grant from the National Trust for Historic Preservation. His goal was to accumulate a complete set of papers—wall, frieze, and ceiling—for every room in the house. This task was complicated by years of roof leaks that had ruined many of the interior walls and by alterations made to the

George Webster Jr., Lawrence Webster, and Marie Webster, about 1905. *Courtesy of Rosalind W. Perry*

house when it was divided into apartments. Fortunately, many wallpapers survived underneath the additions. Working with a handheld steamer and a tiny surgical scalpel, Leonard was able to recover samples of styles ranging from delicate florals and Art Nouveau designs to textured solid-color "oatmeal" papers.

In 1996, we received a grant from the National Park Service to renovate the windows, and matching funds were provided by donors to our capital campaign and by grants from several foundations. Most of the windows were repaired or replaced, including the two elegant leaded-glass windows beside the front door. Members of the building committee helped take down, bundle, and store much of the original woodwork, which was eventually reinstalled and refinished in 2004. All the old lath and plaster, damaged beyond repair by many winters without heat, was removed by the Grant County Jail Work Release crew. Consultant Leonard coordinated these difficult and messy jobs.

Some changes were made to the floor plan to accommodate the building's new role as the Quilters Hall of Fame. An accessible restroom occupies the former kitchen, while the original dining room is now the museum store. The third floor serves as the collections area and archives. Marie's studio was restored as a period room of the early 1900s, when she was actively designing quilt patterns, and the remaining rooms hold exhibits, an office, and a library.

The architect for the interior work was George Morrison of Morrison Kattman Menze, Inc., in Fort Wayne, Indiana.

His investigations showed that the house was not structurally sound and that new beams were needed to support the sagging floors in several rooms. This work was completed in 1997, while he prepared plans for all the mechanical systems: new plumbing, new wiring, a new heating system, a fire protection sprinkler system, and, for the first time, air-conditioning! Fundraising for all these expensive improvements kept everyone busy until 1999, when this phase of the work got underway. In 2001, the house, with its array of modern systems in place, was finally ready for the interior walls to be replaced. When it came time to refinish the old woodwork, a surprising discovery was made. As the dark stain was stripped from the pocket doors leading to the grand parlor, the words *Hotel Office* appeared in ghostly silhouette—a reminder of the original use of these pocket doors in the 1890s, in the grand old York Inn.

Absolutely essential to this long restoration process was the building committee, under its chairman, Scott Shepler, and secretary, Madonna Fowler. Other hardworking members included Jean Chambers, Frieda Faulk, Joe Musser, Richard Fowler, Rex Chambers, Mary and Norm Cheek, Craig Leonard, Liz Dolgner, and Margaret Thomas. Madonna Fowler served as site manager, working closely with the contractor to complete all the complex tasks involved in rescuing this historic structure and transforming it into a state-of-the-art museum. For her dedication to turning dreams into realities, those involved with restoring the Marie Webster House will always be grateful.

Marie Webster House in the 1920s at the time she had her quilt business. *Courtesy of Rosalind W. Perry*

The National Historic Landmark plaque was unveiled on the front porch of the Webster House on July 15, 1994. Hazel Carter, founder and president of the Quilters Hall of Fame, is flanked here by Katherine Webster Dwight (left) and Rosalind Webster Perry, the granddaughters of Marie and George Webster.

The Grand Opening

Gathered on the lawn in front of the Quilters Hall of Fame, more than three hundred enthusiastic guests celebrated the long-awaited ribbon cutting on July 16, 2004. The Grand Opening Celebration, coordinated by Hazel Carter and Karen Alexander, was a festive and historic weekend, thanks to the presence of so many quilt-world legends, including eleven honorees: Cuesta Benberry, Jinny Beyer, Georgia Bonesteel, Barbara Brackman, Karey Bresenhan, Joyce Gross, Jeffrey Gutcheon, Jonathan Holstein, Jean Ray Laury, Yvonne Porcella, and Donna Wilder. Each honoree participated in a special event—a lecture, workshop, or panel discussion. The Marie Webster House hosted its first quilt show, *Pioneer Influences*, and additional exhibits of the honorees' quilts and collections were displayed at other venues. The event was memorialized on film by Georgia Bonesteel, who interviewed the honorees for her documentary *The Great American Quilt Revival*, featuring highlights of twentieth-century quilt history, available on DVD.

Now that the Quilters Hall of Fame is open to the public, you are cordially invited to come and see for yourself this beautifully restored historic home, which was witness to the writing of the first quilt book and the designing of so many influential quilts. Today, Marie Webster's studio recreates the time, a hundred years ago, when her customers came to select their favorite patterns. Now, changing exhibits featuring the honorees and other outstanding quiltmakers fill the house. We hope you will visit and be inspired.

Please visit our website, www.quiltershalloffame.net, for up-to-date information on opening times and current exhibits.

Marie Webster was inspired to create her beautiful quilts by the flowers growing in her garden. The Grant County Evening Garden Club replanted the yard with a lush and inviting garden, including many of her favorite flowers, such as tulips, dogwood, roses, and sunflowers. Zelkova trees that were planted in front of the house in 1994 are now stately trees, similar in appearance to the elms that shaded the yard many years ago. Leading to the garden, a pathway of commemorative engraved bricks honors loved ones. The work of many volunteers and master gardeners has brought about the amazing transformation of an overgrown, weedy lot into a beautifully restored historic garden for the enjoyment of our visitors and the enhancement of the community.

A new ramp leading up to the front porch was added just in time for the Centennial Housewarming Party on July 19, 2002. The first temporary exhibit to be installed was *Dressed to Quilt*, a selection of Marie Webster's clothing and accessories from the nineteenth and early twentieth centuries. A musical event recreated the entertainment of the Websters' housewarming party of April 21, 1902, with many of the same songs performed by a talented ensemble. The renovation work continued apace: Period light fixtures, track lighting, and carpets were selected; the woodwork reinstalled; and lovely period reproduction wallpaper hung in Marie Webster's studio. At last, all the final touches were in place for the Grand Opening.

The grand opening of the Marie Webster House after restoration on July 16, 2004.
Courtesy of Rosalind W. Perry

Introduction

by Merikay Waldvogel

Photo by Deb Rowden

THE QUILTERS HALL of Fame honorees, whose careers span the past one hundred years, devoted their lives to the preservation of quiltmaking, quilts, and their history. These men and women never aimed to be honorees. They were simply captivated by quilts and fabrics. For some, quilt work began as a hobby and evolved into a career, but in the end, their lives were transformed. Reading about these people and their accomplishments, one travels a colorful and fascinating road through twentieth-century quilt history.

The century opened with a renewed interest in America's preindustrial heritage. *Aunt Jane of Kentucky*, written by Eliza Calvert Hall in 1898, included a nostalgic account of quiltmaking that soothed Americans concerned about sweeping changes caused by the Machine Age. In 1915, Marie Webster wrote *Quilts: Their Story and How to Make Them*, the first published attempt to reconstruct an authentic history of American quiltmaking.

The opening of the American Wing at the Metropolitan Museum of Art in 1924, following on the heels of the first issue of the publication *Antiques* magazine in 1922, reflected the growing interest in honoring America's material past. Ruth Finley's book *Old Patchwork Quilts and the Women Who Made Them* (1929) drew attention to quilts at a time when collectors of American antiques wrote mainly about ceramics, coverlets, furniture, and silver.

The 1930s found a growing cadre of quilters hungry for new and old patterns. Newspapers and farm magazines carried regular quilt features including Ruby Short McKim's patterns in block and series formats. McKim's book *One Hundred and One Patchwork Patterns* (1931) has become a classic, as has *The Romance of the Patchwork Quilt in America* (1935) by Carrie Hall and Rose Kretsinger. Both books served as references for traditional quiltmaking and pattern identification in the mid-twentieth century. Anne Orr, needlework editor of *Good Housekeeping*, designed modern quilts and kits, hoping to raise the aesthetic standards of American quiltmaking.

Shortages of fabric and paper during the 1940s due to wartime demands led to a decline in quiltmaking and publishing. Following World War II, however, three important quilt histories appeared. In 1946, Dr. William Rush Dunton Jr. wrote and published *Old Quilts*, an in-depth study of chintz appliqué and Baltimore album quilts. Florence Peto, well known for her book *Historic Quilts* and her articles in *Antiques* magazine, published her second quilt book, *American Quilts and Coverlets*, in 1949. Marguerite Ickis, whose career was devoted to crafts education and recreation, wrote *The Standard Book of Quilt Making and Collecting*, also in 1949.

In England, quilt historian Averil Colby wrote *Patchwork* in 1958, the first of three books documenting the relationship between English and American quilts. Amy Emms, known for reviving the North Country whole-cloth medallion quilting style, began to teach quilting in the 1950s. In the early 1960s, Shiela Betterton signed on as a volunteer docent at the American Museum in Bath, England, a decision that led to her position as textile adviser and curator of the museum's collection of American quilts, today considered the finest outside the United States.

During the 1960s and 1970s, exhibits of quilts shown by established museums awakened an appreciation of quilts outside the circle of traditional quiltmakers. The 1965 *Optical Quilts* exhibition at the Newark Museum and the 1971 exhibition *Abstract Design in American Quilts* at the Whitney Museum of American Art, organized by collectors Jonathan Holstein and Gail van der Hoof, opened up the study of quilts as art and design sources. Newspaper articles about the Whitney exhibition, in particular, resulted in a groundswell of interest in American quilts that was reinforced by the United States bicentennial's use of quilts as emblems of America's past.

Reconciliation | Made by Lucinda Ward Honstain in Brooklyn, New York | 1867 | 97 × 84½ inches. This quilt shows scenes from national life related to the Civil War that had ended two years before, references to the end of slavery, and images of particular interest to Lucinda's family. Her remarkable ability to create compelling images that interweave personal and national history makes this one of America's great folk art documents and a jewel of the collection. *Courtesy of the International Quilt Study Center and Museum, Ardis and Robert James Collection (2001.011.0001)*

In 1973, Bostonian Lenice Bacon's *American Patchwork Quilts* was published, with full-color photos of family and historic quilts. It was perfectly timed to coincide with the bicentennial and provided her with new opportunities for lecturing and travel. The husband-wife team of art historians and quilt collectors, Myron and Patsy Orlofsky, modeled their landmark book *Quilts in America* (1974) on lavish exhibition catalogs and reference volumes on folk art, silver, and furniture.

The late twentieth-century quilt revival was supported by quilt periodicals devoted to both the contemporary quilt world and quilt history. In 1969, Bonnie Leman founded *Quilters Newsletter Magazine* to provide patterns, quilting advice, book reviews, and articles on quilt history. The magazine became a showcase for quilt exhibits, new businesses, and state quilt survey findings. Barbara Brackman's first article was published in *Quilters Newsletter Magazine* in December 1977. Jeffrey Gutcheon wrote a regular column in the 1980s for the magazine called "Not for Shopkeepers Only." Jean Ray Laury wrote two columns: "Keeping It All Together" (May 1982 to March 1984) and "Talking It Over," which began in 1984. Helen Kelley's column "Loose Threads" lasted from 1983 until her death in 2008.

Lady's Circle Patchwork Quilts, edited by Carter Houck, designed each issue around a trip to a particular state, visiting

Patterns, doll quilt, and doll clothes made by Marie Webster, part of the exhibition shown during the 2009 induction weekend. *Courtesy of Rosalind W. Perry*

quiltmakers, collectors, museums, and quilt guilds to showcase their quilts and quilt history. Joyce Gross's *Quilters' Journal* (1977 to 1987) published original quilt research articles, many featuring the Quilters Hall of Fame honorees, with articles by Cuesta Benberry.

During the 1970s quilt revival, quilt groups organized symposia that introduced individuals to quilts, quilt research, and quilters from different regions of the country. In 1974, Bets Ramsey of Chattanooga, Tennessee, organized the first public seminar devoted to quilts, known as the Southern Quilt Symposium, which would serve as a meeting place for several honorees. In the early 1980s, Merikay Waldvogel was introduced to both Barbara Brackman and Cuesta Benberry at a Southern Quilt Symposium meeting. Merikay Waldvogel would go on to conduct research and publish books with Quilters Hall of Fame honorees Bets Ramsey and Barbara Brackman and would, along with many honorees, develop a reputation for solid quilt history scholarship.

In the Northeast, the 1976 Bicentennial Finger Lakes Conference was held in Ithaca, New York. Future honorees Virginia Avery, Jeffrey Gutcheon, Michael James, Jean Ray Laury, and Patsy Orlofsky were teachers and lecturers. This cadre of artists and writers soon found themselves in demand at Midwest symposia in Lincoln, Nebraska, in 1977 and in Lawrence, Kansas, in 1978.

In 1978, Hazel Carter organized an East Coast quilt gathering in Northern Virginia known as the Continental Quilting Congress. At the second meeting, in 1979, she established the Quilters Hall of Fame with the induction of Lenice Bacon, Dr. William Rush Dunton Jr., Ruth Finley, Jonathan Holstein, Marguerite Ickis and Gail van der Hoof.

In 1980, the American Quilt Study Group (AQSG) was founded by Sally Garoutte, becoming the first organization in the world devoted to the study of quilting and quilt history. Since its initial meeting, AQSG has regularly published annual seminar papers in its journal *Uncoverings*, including biographies of several Quilters Hall of Fame honorees.

Even as quilt researchers were expected to produce more academically strong papers, the longstanding tradition of "round robin" pattern collecting continued unabated. Both Cuesta Benberry and Mary Schafer were active in the round robins and, in the process, accumulated extensive collections of quilt research materials, which have been donated to the Michigan State University Museum.

Mary Barton used her extensive collection of fabrics, patterns, and early publications for a workshop called "The Dating Game" at the 1978 Kansas Quilt Symposium. At the 1983 Heirloom to Heirloom conference in Ames, Iowa, Joyce Gross of California

Helen Kelley leading a tour of the exhibition of her quilts during her induction weekend, July 2008. *Courtesy of Rosalind W. Perry*

saw Mary Barton's "quilt study center" and was inspired to do something similar for West Coast guilds. The Barton collection was donated to the State Historical Society of Iowa, and the Gross collection resides at the Dolph Briscoe Center for American History at the University of Texas at Austin

In the early 1980s, state quilt documentation projects were initiated in Kentucky and Texas. Following a model set forth by the Kentucky Quilt Project, other states formed volunteer survey teams that chose a group of representative quilts, organized a quilt exhibit, and wrote a catalog. Several honorees were closely involved in the state projects, including Bets Ramsey and Merikay Waldvogel in Tennessee, Barbara Brackman in Kansas, Jean Ray Laury in California, and Helen Kelley in Minnesota.

It may surprise the general public that not all honorees have been accomplished quiltmakers and not all honoree researchers were academically trained as writers and curators. When one looks for common traits that might elevate a quilt person to the national stage to be considered as a Quilters Hall of Fame honoree, however, it is obvious the person must be passionate about quilts, skilled, assertive, and resilient. They are not afraid to reinvent themselves.

Bertha Stenge, trained as a stained glass artist in college, took up quilting at age fifty, but at first did not win prizes. She changed her original designs often, entered many national contests, and eventually gained national recognition for her original appliqué and trapunto designs.

Bets Ramsey followed a similar path of art training that led to her quiltmaking and later quilt scholarship.

Nebraska quiltmaker Grace Snyder used commercial patterns to make quilts, but she achieved national prominence when her *Flower Basket Petit Point* quilt won a major award in the Storrowton National Quilt Contest.

In the 1958 Storrowton Contest, Jean Ray Laury, a recent graduate of Stanford University with an M.A. in design, failed to win an award for her quilt entitled *Tom's Quilt*, but judge Roxa Wright, editor of *House Beautiful*, was impressed with her contemporary design and referred her to magazine editors for freelance design and writing projects.

At the urging of Hazel Carter, novice quilter Jinny Beyer entered a red, white, and blue center star medallion quilt in the 1976 *Quilters Newsletter Magazine*'s Bicentennial Contest and won a top prize. In 1978, she entered another quilt, *Ray of Light*, in *Good Housekeeping*'s Great American Quilt Contest and won first prize out of ten thousand entries, which led to her own long career in writing, teaching, and fabric design.

Nancy Crow and Michael James both completed master's degree programs in art, though neither made quilts before graduation. The art quilt movement allowed them both to experiment with traditional formats, and both achieved national and international status as artists working in the medium of quilts through exhibits, commissions, and publications.

Marie Webster's quilt designs were inspired by the flowers in her garden, which has been restored by the Grant County Evening Garden Club. *Courtesy of Rosalind W. Perry*

Karey Bresenhan opened her own quilt shop, Great Expectations, in Houston, Texas, in 1974. By 1979, Bresenhan had established the first Quilt Market exclusively for quilt shop owners and the International Quilt Festival for the general public. Her new enterprise allowed for all sorts of innovative ideas. At the 1979 International Quilt Festival, she premiered the Fairfield Fashion Show. When Donna Wilder, vice president of marketing for Fairfield Processing Corporation, proposed the idea for a competition and fashion show for quilted clothing, it was considered a "far-out" idea, but it became so popular that the show was the featured event on Thursday evening at the International Quilt Festival from 1979 into the twenty-first century.

Bresenhan also has a deep appreciation for antique quilts. As the end of the twentieth century approached, she suggested that a panel of distinguished quilt experts choose their favorite one hundred quilts of the century. Seventeen honorees' quilts were chosen, including quilts made by Mary Barton, Jinny Beyer, Nancy Crow, Michael James, Helen Kelley, Rose Kretsinger, Jean Ray Laury, Florence Peto, Yvonne Porcella, Grace Snyder, Bertha Stenge, and Marie Webster.

Quilt historians often divide the twentieth century into revivals followed by declines, but our honorees' lives and accomplishments blanket nearly every decade beginning with 1911, when Marie Webster's quilt designs were first published in *Ladies' Home Journal.*

Marie Webster is shown here with her family in 1899. *Courtesy of Katherine W. Dwight and Rosalind W. Perry*

Originally a weaver and ethnic clothing designer, Yvonne Porcella met quilt artists Virginia Avery and Beth Gutcheon at the 1979 West Coast Quilters' Conference in Portland, Oregon, where Michael James was teaching. She was so inspired she soon finished her first art quilt, *Takoage*, which is now in the collection of the Renwick Gallery, part of the Smithsonian Institution, in Washington, D.C.

In 1978, Georgia Bonesteel was teaching quilting at a local community college when she decided to contact North Carolina Public Television about a quilting program. Her first series aired locally in 1979. The program, now distributed internationally, launched her career of travel, writing, and teaching.

When Jean Wells and her family moved to the small town of Sisters, Oregon, in 1975, she opened a quilt shop, the Stitchin' Post. Her business success became an inspiration to other quilt entrepreneurs throughout the nation. Her shop staff hosts classes and workshops, as well as the famous Outdoor Quilt Show held the second Saturday of July, which attracts tens of thousands of visitors each year.

Quilters Hall of Fame honorees Joyce Gross, Cuesta Benberry, and Barbara Brackman gather for a panel during induction weekend.

Without a central steering committee or a master plan, the quilt world as we know it has blossomed and grown and still attracts a broad range of people producing fabulous quilts. No one is yearning for this story to end. New quilt personalities will enter the scene, and improved tools and fabrics will thrill both new and old quiltmakers. We are already witnessing new communication networks to share patterns, sell items, and showcase individual ideas. What wonderful, colorful, bold quilts will quiltmakers create? What will future quilt historians write about all of us?

The Quilters Hall of Fame thanks the research associates who wrote the following essays. They interviewed living honorees and descendants of deceased honorees. They spent hours in libraries and quilt research centers, compiling an essay, timeline, and bibliography for each honoree. These documents have been deposited in the archives of the Quilters Hall of Fame. As editor of the original volume, I had the pleasure of working with all the research associates and even interviewed some of the honorees myself. Personally, the project offered me an opportunity to reexamine twentieth-century quilt history from one end to the other.

I commend our founder, Hazel Carter, for initiating this project. I want to thank Rosalind Webster Perry for the final editing of the original volume published in 2004. Without her vision for a permanent building and her enthusiastic support, the Quilters Hall of Fame might still just be a list of honorees and their accomplishments.

Dr. Marian Ann Montgomery has gallantly taken on the task of updating the original articles for republication as well as securing new images and patterns for this edition. I salute her for her patience, good judgment, and kindness toward all of us.

Rhythm/Color: Bacchanal | Designed and made by Michael James | 1986 | 72¾ × 71¾ inches | Cotton, silk, cotton batting; machine-pieced and machine-quilted. A later piece in the series that included *Rhythm/Color: Improvisation 2* (see page 120), this quilt reflects the artist's concern with formal elements of the quilt surface. Here, he employs diagonal stripes and curved shapes that break free from the underlying grid of blocks. *Photo by David Caras, © 1986 Michael James*

Virginia Avery

"As we all get deeper and deeper into quilting, our approaches become so innovative, so experimental, so inventive, that we wonder if in time we will sever the thread of continuity which leads to the past and our quilt heritage. I think the answer is 'no way.' No way at all."

—Virginia Avery, "Florence Peto: Pathfinder," *Lady's Circle Patchwork Quilts*, no. 30 (Summer 1983), p. 14

Virginia Avery was inducted into the Quilters Hall of Fame in Marion, Indiana, on July 15, 2006. © *2006 Terry Pommett*

by Donna Wilder

VIRGINIA, KNOWN AS JINNY, is the "grand dame extraordinaire" of the quilt world. Not only is she highly respected, but students and friends often describe her as creative, energetic, humble, innovative, charming, and smart. Nobody hosts or enjoys a party more than Jinny, and she is a wonderful friend to all who are lucky enough to call her such.

As a young child growing up in a small town in Indiana, Jinny taught herself to sew on her mother's treadle sewing machine. She has always loved colorful fabrics and the process of designing and making her own clothing. After graduating from DePauw University in Greencastle, Indiana, with a B.A. in liberal arts, she took a job in Detroit. There she met her husband, a writer for United Press International.

As a young woman, Jinny had dreamed of living in New York. Shortly after she married, her husband was transferred—to New York! They raised four children in their lovely mid-nineteenth-century antiques-filled home in Port Chester.

Jinny has been consistently at the forefront of the quilting industry, and her early success at teaching and writing have helped to validate quilting as a profession. Jinny's career began when she taught sewing and tailoring at local fabric shops. It was during the early preparations for the country's bicentennial celebration—when quilting experienced a grand renaissance—that Jinny began to think about teaching quilting classes.

It didn't matter that she had no idea how to quilt; her sewing skills and creative instinct were all she needed to give herself a crash course in quilting. She began to teach her students with great success, although she often admits she had to stay up half the night to keep one step ahead of her classes, which surely none of her students would have ever suspected.

An early influence on Jinny's interest in quilts was her long friendship with Florence Peto, whom she met in New York City in the early 1950s while Florence was demonstrating quilting at a McCall's needlework exhibit. (For more information about Florence, see her profile on page 157.) They met frequently for lunch and maintained their friendship until Florence's death in 1970. Jinny then wrote two articles about her friend for quilting magazines.

Another pivotal event in Jinny's life occurred when she attended the Finger Lakes Bicentennial Quilt Conference in Ithaca, New York, in 1976. There she met many of the leaders of the burgeoning quilt world, including future Hall of Fame

Mostly Koos and Red Squared | Reversible coat and accessories made by Virginia Avery, using a Geoffrey Beene design from Vogue | 2003. Here, a model displays one side, made of fire-engine-red flannel appliquéd with Thai silk log cabin squares. The cummerbund and handbag both reverse to echo the coat's two innovative faces. The outfit was named for Dutch designer Koos Van den Akker's appliqué technique. *Photo by Perrault Studios, courtesy of Bernina and Quilts, Inc.*

23

Virginia Avery points out features of her quilted garment *A Hot Time in the Old Town Tonight* at the *Fabrics and Fabrications* exhibit in Southport, Connecticut, March 4 and 5, 2011. *Photo by Mike Lauterborn*

honorees Jean Ray Laury, Jeffrey Gutcheon, Bonnie Leman, and Michael James. When she saw some of the attendees wearing patchwork clothing, she was inspired to begin teaching classes in quilted fashions.

Jinny has always been a strong advocate for wearable art. One needs only to see her to know she believes women can and should

WONDERFUL WEARABLES

A CELEBRATION OF CREATIVE CLOTHING

VIRGINIA AVERY

Virginia Avery's *Don't Shoot the Piano Player, She's Doing the Best She Can* appeared on the cover of her book, *Wonderful Wearables*.

wear their art. Her typically black, red, and white patchwork garments, accessorized with colorful accents and her "It's OK" rhinestone pin, are worn with panache and have become her trademark style. Jinny's influence has given credibility to quilted and embellished clothing and has raised this art form to a high level of professionalism.

When the Fairfield Fashion Show was started in 1978, Jinny was the first person invited to make a garment. The show's organizers needed only to enlist Jinny to convince other designers to participate. In all, Jinny was featured in eighteen of the twenty-two Fairfield Fashion Shows and continued to dazzle audiences with her one-of-a-kind garments, which were also featured in four of the Bernina fashion shows that followed. In 1994, Jinny curated a wearable art exhibit at the Museum of the American Quilter's Society.

Teaching is important to Jinny. By sharing her talents, she ensures continuity of her creative heritage. Not only is her quilting an inspiration to her students, but Jinny herself is an inspiration. Through her classes, she cultivates quilters' imaginations and encourages beginners to stretch their creativity. Her extensive knowledge, great sense of humor, and incredible patience have contributed to her extraordinary teaching ability. I can't tell you how many times I've heard quilters tell me, "It all began when I took a class from Virginia Avery." Students praise Jinny as one of the best quilt teachers they have ever experienced.

Jinny was probably one of the first to teach quilting outside the United States, and her work has been exhibited extensively in both the United States and abroad. Her one-woman shows have been mounted at the Rye Art Center, Rye, New York; Port Chester Public Library, Port Chester, New York; DePauw University Art Center, Greencastle, Indiana; and Textile Museum of the Smithsonian Institution, Washington, D.C.

Jinny is also a prolific writer. *The Big Book of Appliqué*, published by Scribner in 1978, introduced a whole new generation of quilters to the joys of appliqué. She has written numerous quilting- and clothing-related articles for quilt and needlework magazines, including *Quilters Newsletter Magazine*, *Fiberarts*, *Threads*, *Country Journal*, *McCall's Needlework*, *Lady's Circle Patchwork Quilts*, and many others.

Her books, *Quilts to Wear* (published by Scribner in 1982 and later reprinted by Dover) and *Wonderful Wearables: A Celebration of Creative Clothing* (published in 1989 by the American Quilter's Society) were largely responsible for an increased interest in quilted and embellished clothing that began at that time. Jinny also wrote *Hats: A Heady Affair* and *Nifty Neckwear*, which proved to be real primers for her classes on accessories.

For "expanding horizons and creating new opportunities for other quiltmakers," Jinny received the prestigious Silver Star Award at the International Quilt Festival in 1996. Hundreds of students, friends, and family were there to celebrate and enjoy this important award. At the ceremony, she was praised for "devoting her own creative genius to foster the creativity of other quilters

Selected Reading

Avery, Virginia. *The Big Book of Appliqué*. New York: Scribners, 1978.

———. "Quilts to Wear." *Quilter's Newsletter Magazine*, no. 146 (October 1982): 28–29.

———. *Wonderful Wearables: A Celebration of Creative Clothing*. Paducah, KY: American Quilter's Society, 1989.

"Presenting Virginia Avery." Online web portrait in *Quilt Treasures: Documenting the 20th Century Quilt Revival*. Alliance for American Quilts. www.centerforthequilt.org/treasures/va.

and wearable art designers . . . but her real legacy will be the thousands of quilters throughout the world who have learned to love quilting and wearable art in the classes presented by this enthusiastic master teacher."

Festival director and Quilters Hall of Fame honoree Karey Bresenhan later noted, "Virginia is not only one of the most creative and talented people in the world of quilting, she is also one of the most sharing with both her time and knowledge."

Jinny's sphere of recognition extends far beyond the quilt world. *Mirabella* magazine recognized Jinny's contributions by naming her one of "the 1,000 Most Influential Women in the United States" in 1996. Jinny was one of only two women known primarily as a quilter among these 1,000 women. (The other was honoree Nancy Crow.) In addition, Jinny was awarded a Distinguished Alumnus Citation from DePauw University.

On a slightly different creative note, Jinny has played piano in a jazz group she formed more than fifty years ago. Known as the King Street Stompers, the group meets monthly at Jinny's home to jam and entertain an enthusiastic audience of friends and friends of friends. What fun it is to listen to Jinny and the eight other musicians, all men, playing familiar old standards and lively Dixieland tunes. The group has appeared on the *Today Show* and played for delegates of the United Nations. Jinny has often said that the common thread between her love of quilting and jazz is the improvisation, and no one is better at improvisation than Jinny.

Jinny is truly a legend in the quilting world, never afraid to venture into new territories or experiment with new techniques. Her witty quilts and wonderful wearables have had a tremendous impact on today's quilters. Everyone who has been touched by her humor, passion, and generosity would certainly agree that Virginia Avery's induction into the Quilters Hall of Fame is well deserved.

Virginia Avery with *Fabrics and Fabrications* event co-founder Cecily Zerega. Proceeds from the two-day show were donated to the Make-a-Wish Foundation, Emerge, Inc., and Project Learn. *Photo by Mike Lauterborn*

Lenice Bacon

1895–1978

*"There surely is a quilt revival today
and perhaps with it a revival of concern
for tradition and craftsmanship
and the special beauty of handmade things."*

—Lenice Bacon, *American Patchwork Quilts* (1973), p. 24

Lenice Ingram Bacon was inducted into the Quilters Hall of Fame at the Continental Quilting Congress, Arlington, Virginia, on October 27, 1979. *Photo by Bradford Bachrach, courtesy of Joyce Gross*

by Susan Fiondella

KNOWN NATIONALLY AS A QUILT AUTHOR and scholar, Lenice Bacon's fascination with quilts and quilt lore began during her childhood in Tennessee. She was intrigued by the patterns and colors of her family's quilts, which seemed to speak to her of stories from another time and place.

Lenice was born on January 28, 1895, in Rockwood, Tennessee. During her youth, quilts were always a part of her family's life. Their custom was to send cloth scraps collected from sewing projects to women who pieced tops "on the half," piecing half of the scraps for the Ingrams and the other half for themselves. After these tops were finished, the Ingrams sent them to another woman to be quilted.

The Ingrams enjoyed a very comfortable lifestyle, encouraging Lenice, a progressive young woman for her time, to pursue her education at Ward-Belmont College in Nashville, Tennessee, where she studied elocution under the renowned Pauline Sherwood Townsend. Lenice continued her studies in speech and drama at the Curry School of Expression in Boston, graduating in 1915.

In 1921, Lenice married Frederick Sayford Bacon and moved to Newton, Massachusetts. Her husband, a chemical consultant, was a graduate of Harvard University and owned his own firm. The Bacons were prominent people in the Boston community, where Lenice was active in political, collegiate, and literary associations while raising two children, Bessie Rilla and William Elisha.

In 1926, after a trip back home to Tennessee, Lenice was inspired by her cousin Rebecca's beautiful Rose of Sharon quilt. Lenice decided to make a copy for her daughter's Bride's Quilt, following an old custom. For her son, she chose the traditional Randolph family pattern for his Freedom Quilt, completed in 1930. These were the only two quilts from her hand. She made the tops, then sent them to expert quilters for the quilting.

Lenice's career as a lecturer began when she was working on these quilts at sewing circle meetings near her home. Lenice later wrote in her book *American Patchwork Quilts*, "I suppose I presented an unusual sight—a young woman working on something as old-fashioned as a quilt. It certainly aroused interest in spite of the fact that quiltmaking was no longer a popular pastime, and

Diamond in a Square | Anonymous | 1850–1880 | 72 × 70 inches | Silks and satins, tufted. This quilt from Lenice Bacon's collection was described in *American Patchwork Quilts* as follows: "In October 1789, when President George Washington paid his visit to Salem, Massachusetts, a ball was given in his honor. The central square in this quilt is said to be a memento—a piece of the gown worn to the ball by Sally Crowninshield where she danced with the honored guest." *Courtesy of the New England Quilt Museum, gift of Bessie Rilla Milne (1984.01)*

Lenice Bacon displaying the quilt she made for her son, using a traditional family pattern. The original quilt belonged to the family of her ancestor, William Randolph, who migrated from Virginia to Tennessee. *Photo by George Dixon, courtesy of Joyce Gross*

served her well for lecturing. She dressed in colonial costume and used her quilts and quilt blocks to illustrate her talks. A management agent handled contracts for her engagements. Her publicity portfolio contained her photos and a sample press release giving a brief description of her lectures, their venues, and glowing reviews from local newspapers.

The *Rockwood* (Tennessee) *Times* had this to say: "Mrs. Bacon has lost none of the charm of the South and her talk was beautifully expressed, the many poems she quoted and the stories told in dialect adding greatly to her hearer's enjoyment of the subject."

During her speaking career, she presented at least fifty-five lectures in sixteen states and gave one lecture at the American Museum in Bath, England. Many of her audiences were women's clubs, but after the publication of *American Patchwork Quilts* in 1973, she was also invited to speak to quilt groups.

In the fall of 1974, Joyce Gross arranged for Lenice Bacon to speak to quilters in California. Joyce remembered that Lenice rehearsed her presentations "with all the dramatics" and recalled, "At dinner she charmed the ten of us with her quilt anecdotes, delivered in her unique way and all the time her eyes twinkled

people appeared eager to hear about it. I was asked to speak before groups of club and church women. Thus my vocation began." The aspect of quiltmaking that interested her most was "how the quilt seemed to have served not only as a means of providing necessary warmth, but also as an outlet for an inherent longing for beauty and decoration." It was her premise "that the making of quilts was the most universal of all the folk arts in early America, appealing to women everywhere and in all walks of life."

Since Lenice's experience with quilts revolved around middle- and upper-class women, she wondered if her theory applied to women from all backgrounds. While World War II raged, Lenice traveled to the mountain regions of West Virginia, North Carolina, and Tennessee to gather the information that would strengthen her belief "that the quilt served as an outlet for artistic longings." While there, she found that the women who were still quilting were very proud of their quilts. Making quilts was one of the most stimulating and satisfying parts of their lives.

During her travels, Lenice collected several quilts as well as their stories, which became material for her entertaining lectures on "Quilts and Quilt Lore." Her training in speech and drama

A brochure advertising Lenice Bacon's club programs featured this photo of her in costume with the caption, "Mrs. Bacon might just have stepped from the porch of an old Southern home." *Courtesy of Joyce Gross*

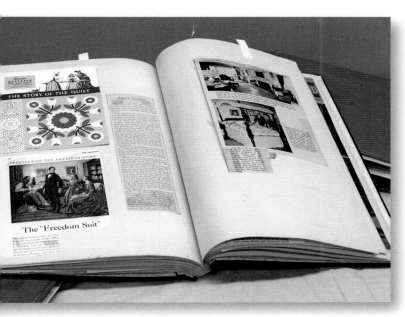

Scrapbooks of quilt materials assembled by Lenice Bacon. *Courtesy of the New England Quilt Museum*

and her lovely face was full of smiles," (*Quilters' Journal*, Winter 1977). Nancy Halpern, a nationally known quilt artist living in the Boston area, assisted Lenice during her East Coast lectures.

The first books on quilting were written by Marie Webster in 1915, Ruth Finley in 1929, Carrie Hall and Rose Kretsinger in 1935, and then Florence Peto in 1939. Lenice Bacon was not only a contemporary but also a student of these women, to whom she acknowledged her indebtedness in *American Patchwork Quilts*. She visited both Ruth Finley and Florence Peto in their homes. Florence wrote to a friend in 1947 after meeting Lenice, "She had my book under her arm and it was almost worn out—said she used it all the time and recommended it to others. . . . She was so interested in what I had to say about textiles telling the story of the age of a quilt."

Lenice also corresponded with Dr. William R. Dunton Jr. When his book *Old Quilts*, appeared in 1946, Lenice was lecturing in Baltimore, Maryland. "On the very day his book *Old Quilts* was released," she said, "I went to his home in Catonsville, Maryland, where he autographed my copy," and delighted her with his rare sense of humor (*Quilters Newsletter Magazine*, no. 73, Nov. 1975).

Nearly thirty years later, in 1973, when she was seventy-eight years old, Lenice Bacon's own book on quilt history, *American Patchwork Quilts*, was published. The book jacket described it as "a concise and knowledgeable history . . . with forty-eight full-page plates (thirty-two colored) of quilts . . . [it] gives sound advice on buying, collecting, caring for and repairing old quilts." Reviewer

Lee Hale wrote in *Quilters Newsletter Magazine*, "She knows quilts and quilt lore from personal experience and her knowledge and love of quilts is obvious. . . . For quilt history and romance this is one of the best of the new books on the market." It was included in the *Philadelphia Inquirer*'s list of "Best 100 Books of 1973."

The publication of *American Patchwork Quilts* coincided with an upsurge in interest in quilts following the landmark exhibit at the Whitney Museum of Art in New York City and leading up to the United States bicentennial celebration. The tempo of Lenice's life accelerated, with frequent lectures on "The Historical Significance of Quilts," television appearances both local and national, and participation in bicentennial events in her native state of Tennessee as well as in Massachusetts.

Lenice summed up her excitement in her 1975 Christmas letter to friends and family: "That the Bicentennial of our country and the nation wide revival of interest in quilts should have coincided has made for a happy combination of events, with enthusiasts, young and old, male and female, individually and in groups, going on a huge 'Quilting Bee' binge."

She died in May 1978 and was inducted into the Quilters Hall of Fame in 1979. In 1983, an exhibit of the *Lenice Bacon Quilt Collection* was held in conjunction with the New England Images Show in Topsfield, Massachusetts. Most of her collection is in private hands, but the New England Quilt Museum owns several pattern blocks used by Lenice in her lectures, as well as a silk quilt in the Diamond in a Square pattern.

Lenice's curiosity about quilts lasted a lifetime. What began as a child's fascination with quilt colors, patterns, and stories led Lenice as a young mother to make quilts for her own children. Later still, quilts enabled her to embark on a career of lecturing and writing. While fulfilling her "creative longings" in the performance of her lectures, she also made a major contribution to public awareness of the remarkable heritage of our quiltmaking tradition.

Selected Reading

Bacon, Lenice Ingram. *American Patchwork Quilts*. New York: William Morrow & Co., 1973.

———. "Recollections of a Quilt Lover." *Quilter's Newsletter Magazine*, no. 73 (November 1975): 19–21.

Gilbert, Jennifer. "Researching the Collection: The Lenice Bacon Silk Crazy Quilt." *New England Quilt Museum News*, Fall 1996, 5.

Gross, Joyce. "Lenice Ingram Bacon." *Quilters' Journal* 1, no. 2 (Winter 1977): 1–2.

Mary Barton
1917–2003

"I just try to preserve material which will be useful to future historians."

—Mary Barton, *Quilter's Newsletter Magazine*, no. 141 (April 1982), p. 29

Mary Pemble Barton was inducted into the Quilters Hall of Fame at the Continental Quilting Congress, Arlington, Virginia, on September 29, 1984. *Courtesy of State Historical Society of Iowa*

by Pat L. Nickols

COLLECTOR, HISTORIAN, QUILTMAKER, and *generous friend* are some of the terms used to describe Mary Barton, a woman who had a mission: to collect historically important Iowa quilts and related material for others to study and enjoy. Soft-spoken, she modestly stated, "I prefer to call my work independent research, conservation, and preservation."

Mary's desire to collect, understand, and share resulted in one of the most comprehensive collections of quilts, costumes, and fashion plates ever assembled and donated to public institutions. Mary was one of the first to collect both clothing and women's magazines as a means to provide a reliable way of documenting and dating quilts by the fabrics they contained. Her meticulous notes and countless scrapbooks have made important comparative studies possible.

Mary Alice Pemble was born June 9, 1917, in Indianola, Iowa. Mary enjoyed her tomboy years with her equally active brothers and sisters harvesting fruit in the orchard or weeding in the garden or the strawberry patch. The family had cows, chickens, four ponies, and a large garden, so there was always home activity.

For the girls, the afternoons were a time to play with their dolls or to play dress-up with costumes a neighbor had given them.

Both of Mary's grandmothers were quiltmakers and made quilts for Mary when she was young. Mary began sewing and embroidering her own clothes at an early age and kept fabric swatches and pictures showing herself wearing these garments as a record of changing styles. And she won prizes with her outfits—which, in addition to dresses, included suits and coats—at the Iowa State Fair.

Mary was an outstanding athlete in high school, and in 1935 she was Representative All-Around Girl Athlete and on the winning volleyball team. She started college at Simpson, then transferred to Iowa State College (now Iowa State University), where she earned her B.S. in landscape architecture, a very unusual field for women at that time. In July 1942, she married Tom Barton, a classmate. Shortly after their wedding, they moved to the Washington, D.C., area, where they both worked in the Hydrographic Office of the Navy Department as engineering draftsmen, making air navigation maps. She was the only woman in the department.

Heritage Quilt | Designed, pieced, and appliquéd by Mary Barton | Quilted by the Quilters of St. Petri Lutheran Church, Story City, Iowa. | 1976 |
100 × 102 inches. With insight gleaned from diaries and family letters written on their pioneer journey west, Mary Barton created this masterpiece quilt, which was selected as one of *America's 100 Best Quilts of the 20th Century. Courtesy of the State Historical Society of Iowa (1987.44)*

In 1946, Mary became a full-time homemaker when their first child was born. Her husband's career took them from Washington, D.C., to Iowa, to Michigan, and back to Ames, Iowa, in 1955 when he joined the faculty and later became head of the department of landscape architecture at Iowa State University.

In 1949, at the time of her grandmother's death, Mary's mother gave her some family quilts; this was the start of Mary Barton's quilt collection and her interest in the textiles they contained. In 1967, she purchased her first quilt at a local farm auction. Concerned about some fine Iowa quilts bringing high bids at auction and leaving the state for distant eastern museums, she recognized the need to save as much as she could of Iowa's heritage—and "save" she did. She collected quilts, quilt tops, quilt fragments, blocks, fabric scraps, quilt patterns, periodicals, fashion illustrations, books, newspaper articles, mail-order catalogs, family record books, diaries, and photographs. The numerous notebooks she compiled are now housed in Iowa public institutions to be used and enjoyed.

Mary Barton with the *Heritage Quilt* she made depicting the migration path of her ancestors. Mary used narrow tape and threads to show the routes her ancestors traveled in the corner of the quilt, inspired by a quote from a newspaper article of October 28, 1869, which described the wagon trains passing through town on their way to Guthrie County, Iowa: "Long lines of emigrant wagons passing through . . . coming from points further east to settle in this county or farther west. . . . Large trains sometimes numbering wagons by the dozen pass through each containing a family, household goods, and extra stock suggestive of permanent settlement." *Courtesy of Pat L. Nickols*

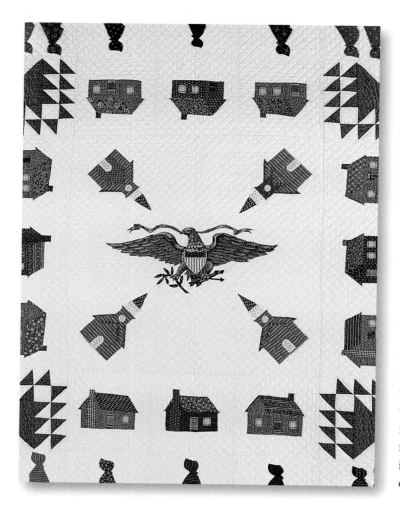

Mary was an active member of the Faculty Women's Club at Iowa State University and took part in a special interest group called the Heritage Division. In 1968, Mary suggested a program about quilts. When she was asked to develop the program, she began her thorough research about quilts and quilt history using the few books then available on the subject. Her play *Aunt Mary's Quilting Party* acted out the age-old American custom of a quilting bee. On January 8, 1969, this play was performed to an enthusiastic audience of the Faculty Women's Club.

In 1968, inspired by her research and her collection of antique fabric, Mary began her *Heritage Quilt*, showing the immigration of her ancestors from England and Germany and their migration trail from North Carolina, Pennsylvania, and New York westward to Iowa. An original design, this quilt features a symbolic eagle in the center with four churches in the corners, to show religious freedom, and rows of houses and log cabins—their new homes in Iowa. The pioneer women and children wear dresses made of antique fabric and walk among a variety of miniature quilt

New honoree Mary Barton proudly displays her Quilters Hall of Fame engraved box at her induction in 1984. *Photo by Henry French*

patterns. After seven years, the finished top was quilted by a group at St. Peti's Lutheran Church in Story City, Iowa, in time for the 1976 bicentennial celebrations.

Mary Barton stepped onto the national stage that year, receiving honorable mention at the National Bicentennial Quilt Contest held in Warren, Michigan. In addition, this masterpiece won a blue ribbon at the Iowa State Fair and was later selected as one of *America's 100 Best Quilts of the 20th Century*. She later made a number of other quilt tops, often reproductions of her favorite antique quilts.

Mary was soon invited to lecture at some of the earliest quilt conferences, including the Kansas Quilt Symposium in 1978 and the Missouri Quilt Symposium in 1980. She served on the planning committee for Iowa's first statewide quilt gathering, the 1983 Heirloom to Heirloom Quilt Conference, where she set up an innovative Study Center, which she described as "the largest collection of comparative dating helps ever opened to a quilt conference group." The Study Center included quilts and tops as well as scrapbooks, fabrics, and quilts arranged by decade from 1800 to 1940. In 1984, Mary Barton installed a similar study area at the Continental Quilting Congress in Arlington, Virginia, where she was honored by induction into the Quilters Hall of Fame.

While Mary Barton found her many accomplishments rewarding, she knew that the lasting legacy of her work was the preservation of quilts and historic textiles and the information she had collected about them. Beginning in the 1970s, she donated items from her collection to various organizations in her home state, including the Farm House Museum and the textiles and clothing department at Iowa State University, Simpson College in Indianola, and the First United Methodist Church in Ames. The Department of Special Collections of Parks Library at Iowa State University now houses several hundred fashion plates from magazines that Mary collected.

In 1987 and 1988, she presented her famous *Heritage Quilt* to the Iowa State Historical Museum, along with a major gift of sixty-seven quilts and tops, her numerous fabric sample muslin panels, and countless notebooks about nineteenth-century textiles. Thanks to Mary Barton, researchers can now study these items in a climate-controlled room in their new building. These materials were also featured in the museum's 1993 exhibit *Patterns for Learning: Selections from the Mary Barton Collection*.

Mary also donated more than one hundred quilts to the Living History Farms near Des Moines. These gifts form the core of their exhibits, showing quilts and other textiles in their historic settings. In all, she donated more than two hundred quilts and quilt tops that will be preserved by Iowa organizations as an enduring record of women's artistic and creative endeavors. As Mary herself put it, "I'm just trying to save things for future historians."

Mary Barton passed away on December 7, 2003. At her funeral service, her family displayed some of the quilts she had made—a fitting tribute to Mary's quilt-filled life.

Selected Reading

Austin, Mary Leman, ed. *The Twentieth Century's Best American Quilts: Celebrating 100 Years of the Art of Quiltmaking.* Golden, CO: Primedia Special Interest Publications, 1999.

Benberry, Cuesta. "The Meetin' Place: Cuesta Benberry Introduces Us to Mary Barton of Ames, Iowa." *Quilter's Newsletter Magazine*, no. 141 (April 1982): 29.

Houck, Carter. "Meet Mary Barton." *Lady's Circle Patchwork Quilts*, Spring 1984, 16–17, 63.

Kiracofe, Roderick. *The American Quilt: A History of Cloth and Comfort 1750–1950.* New York: Clarkson Potter, 1993. Photographs of Mary Barton Collection dresses, quilts, and quilt blocks on pp. 34–35, 39, 86, 87, 131, and 216.

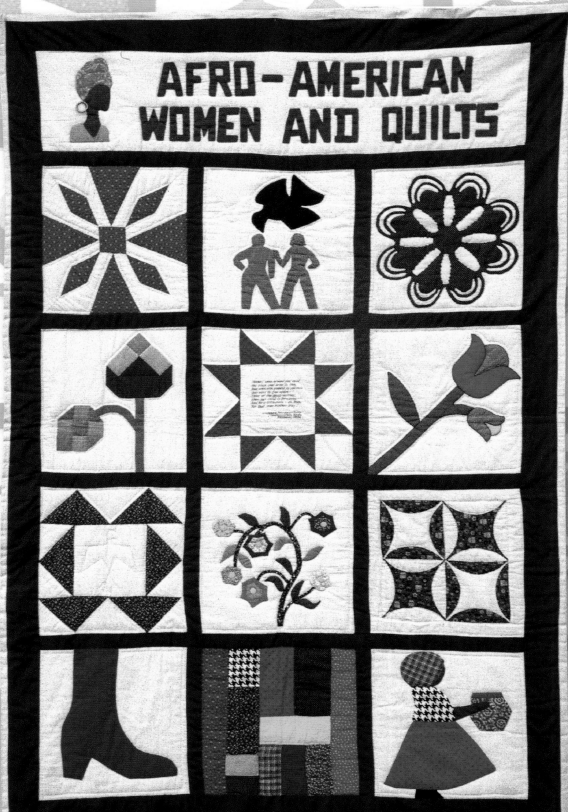

AFRO-AMERICAN WOMEN AND QUILTS

Cuesta Benberry
1923–2007

"It seems I may be standing alone, like St. John in the wilderness, exhorting the cause of the individual African-American quilter's creativity, a recognition of the diversity of African-American quilting, and most of all, an abandonment of the en-masse 'cookie cutter approach' to the investigations and research of African-American quilt history."

—Cuesta Benberry, *Piecework*, January/February 1995

Cuesta Ray Benberry was inducted into the Quilters Hall of Fame at the Continental Quilting Congress in Arlington, Virginia, on November 5, 1983.

by Mary Sue Hannan

CUESTA RAY BENBERRY'S DILIGENT SEARCH for accuracy and truth, coupled with her generous support of other researchers, has endeared her to quilt enthusiasts for decades. Described by *Who's Who in America* as "a quilt historian, archivist, and consultant," she is known to the quilt world for her expertise on quiltmakers, quilt pattern history, and African American quilts. Her exhaustive research and her enormous collection of patterns and quilt ephemera are legendary.

Born in Cincinnati, Ohio, Cuesta was raised in St. Louis, Missouri, by her father, Walter Ray, and grandmother following the death of her mother, Marie. She was educated in the St. Louis public schools before attending Stowe College (now Harris-Stowe State College), where she received a B.A. in education in 1945. After graduation, she embarked on a career as a teacher, reading specialist, and school librarian that lasted forty years. Cuesta also earned an M.A. in library science from the University of Missouri at St. Louis, enabling her to broaden the scope of her quilt research with a historical perspective.

She first took an interest in quilts not because she was born into a quiltmaking family but because she married into one. George Benberry's family made quilts; the young couple received one from his mother as their wedding present in 1951. When they visited George's relatives in Western Kentucky, Cuesta was immediately captivated by their quilts—the colors, patterns, and quilting stitches. Cuesta, the researcher, began asking questions. "Who made them, when, how, where?" and, most important, "May I photograph them?" Her curiosity about those Kentucky quilts launched a lifelong quest to fully understand quilt pattern history.

Cuesta arrived on the national stage by a circuitous route. Despite her busy life as mother, wife, and school librarian, she always maintained a wide network of quilt correspondents. Starting in the 1950s, she actively participated in several round robins—a popular means of pattern exchange in the days before the photocopying machine. Patterns were carefully hand copied onto tissue paper and circulated to each participant to copy in turn.

Afro-American Women and Quilts | Made by Cuesta Benberry and friends in St. Louis, Missouri | 1979 | 53 × 73 inches | Printed and plain cottons; pieced, appliquéd, embroidered, and ink-inscribed. Each block of this historical sampler quilt replicates a design made by an African-American quiltmaker. The date of the original design is quilted on each block. In all her years of quilt research, this is the one quilt that Cuesta made, "with lots of help!" *Courtesy of Michigan State University Museum, Cuesta Benberry African and African-American Quilt and Quilt Ephemera Collection*

One round robin friend, Dolores Hinson, was writing for the highly regarded publication *Nimble Needle Treasures*, edited by Pat Almy. After receiving Cuesta's long letters filled with fascinating pattern information, Dolores suggested that Cuesta write for the magazine on a regular basis. As its research editor for five years, Cuesta had a vehicle to share her findings with a wide audience.

Soon after *Nimble Needle Treasures* ceased publication in 1975, Bonnie Leman invited Cuesta to write for *Quilter's Newsletter Magazine*. For nearly twenty years, Cuesta contributed countless book reviews and articles on quilt history, pattern history, and little-known quiltmakers and designers. She was also a regular contributor to *Quilters' Journal*, a magazine concentrating on quilt history, published and edited by honoree Joyce Gross from 1977 to 1987.

Cuesta announced her interest in African American quilt history with a query published in *Quilter's Newsletter Magazine* in the mid-1970s, asking readers to send her information about quilts made by African Americans. She began a new file that filled rapidly with the missing information, and she became a voice for the overlooked African American quilters. Her studies became a passion; she decided to make a quilt from patterns significant to the story of African American women and their quilts. The center block, in the Evening Star pattern, included an inked poem referring to the plight of a black mother whose child was sold into slavery.

Cuesta's findings clearly proved that quilts made by African American quilters were as varied as those made by other American quilters. She discovered that the quilts were products of talented, creative needlewomen and artists and did not necessarily reflect a cultural memory of African designs, a theory fostered by some researchers.

In 1980, Cuesta traveled to California to attend the first meeting of the American Quilt Study Group, where she made a special presentation entitled "Afro-American Women and Quilts," which was published in the first volume of *Uncoverings*. Cuesta later served on the group's board of directors and presented two other papers at the annual seminars.

In 1985, Cuesta retired from her full-time position with the St. Louis Public Schools to devote more time to her own research and writing. She often contributed articles to *The Women of Color Quilters' Network Newsletter* and other publications.

Cuesta served as a consultant for several state quilt projects, often writing the forewords for the catalogs. Requests for her slide lectures increased, and she found herself in demand as a speaker throughout the United States and Europe.

The Kentucky Quilt Project asked Cuesta to curate an exhibition of African American quilts and write a book to accompany it. The exhibit and book, entitled *Always There: The African American Presence in American Quilts*, gave Cuesta an opportunity to present her findings regarding the diversity, originality, and importance of African American quilts and quiltmakers. The exhibit was shown in Louisville, Kentucky, in 1992, and also at the Anacostia Museum of the Smithsonian Institution.

In November 1983, Cuesta Benberry was inducted into the Quilters Hall of Fame. In her acceptance speech, she declared,

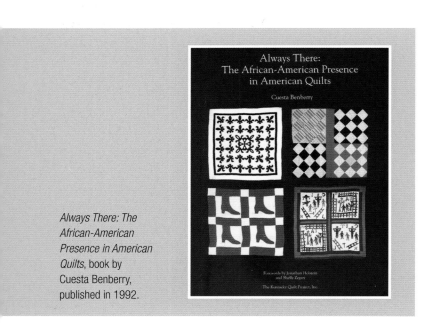

Always There: The African-American Presence in American Quilts, book by Cuesta Benberry, published in 1992.

Cuesta Benberry and Hazel Carter at Cuesta's induction in 1983 in Arlington, Virginia. In the background is the quilt block *Cuesta's Choice*, which Hazel created in her honor.

Hazel Carter designed and made this block the year Cuesta Benberry was inducted into the Quilters Hall of Fame, 1983. Cuesta had sent Hazel a block called *Hazel's Choice* and said she knew there would never be a *Cuesta's Choice* block, no doubt because people did not know how to spell "Cuesta" and probably did not often pronounce it correctly.

Selected Reading

Benberry, Cuesta. "The 20th Century's First Quilt Revival." Parts 1, 2, 3. *Quilter's Newsletter Magazine*, no. 114 (July 1979); no. 115 (September 1979); no. 116 (October 1979).

————. "Afro-American Women and Quilts: An Introductory Essay." *Uncoverings 1980*. Mill Valley, CA: American Quilt Study Group, 1981.

————. *A Piece of My Soul: Quilts by Black Arkansans*. Fayetteville: University of Arkansas Press, 2000.

————. "White Perspectives of Blacks in Quilts and Related Media." *Uncoverings 1983*. Mill Valley, CA: American Quilt Study Group, 1984.

"Quilt Treasures Presents: Cuesta Benberry." www.allianceforamericanquilts.org/treasures/main. php?id=5-16-3. Accessed December 6, 2010.

"What I see as the quilt investigator's obligation is the explanation and enrichment of quilt information undergirded by accuracy and truth in a form of serious scholarship." She also called for "the documentation of all quilts in retrievable form for future scholars and for posterity."

Cuesta later served on the board of directors and as advisor to the selection committee for the Quilters Hall of Fame, and in 1995, she lectured at the organization's annual celebration on "America's Cherished Quilts: The Harriet Powers Bible Quilts." In 1999, she gave the Hall of Fame her extensive collection of some 800 quilt blocks, 200 of which were featured in the exhibit *Evidences of Friendship: The Quilt Block Collection of Cuesta Benberry*. Cuesta's love of children also led her to establish an African-American quilt archive at the Vaughn Cultural Center in St. Louis, where groups of schoolchildren come on field trips to learn about quilting traditions.

In 1997, Cuesta joined Joyce Gross in curating a landmark exhibit, the meticulously researched *20th Century Quilts 1900–1970: Women Make Their Mark*, at the Museum of the American Quilter's Society in Paducah, Kentucky. The exhibit represented the combination of nearly eighty years of quilt scholarship on the part of the two quilt historians. In 2000, Cuesta curated *A Piece of My Soul: Quilts by Black Arkansans* for the Old State House Museum in Little Rock and wrote the accompanying volume.

Cuesta's work on pattern history, quilt documentation, and African American quiltmakers has greatly enriched the understanding of the American quilt experience. To paraphrase her own 1983 Quilters Hall of Fame acceptance speech, Cuesta has "given it her best shot" by "minding her P's and Q's"—her patterns and her quilts—for nearly fifty years. Quilters and historians everywhere are the beneficiaries.

The results of Cuesta's research fill 150 scrapbooks of newspaper and magazine clippings, pattern booklets, paper patterns, tracings, and related materials that form the nucleus of a much larger quilt archive. In the middle of the 2000 decade, the American Folk Art Museum became the custodian of Cuesta's large quilt archive until 2009 when, with Cuesta's son's permission, the property was transferred to the Michigan State University Museum in East Lansing. Prior to this transfer and following Cuesta's death, the remainder of her quilt collection and her black history archive were donated to the Michigan State University Museum. "We were . . . honored that Cuesta Benberry's collections have come to the museum," said Marsha MacDowell, MSU Museum curator and professor of art and art history. "Research-based collections like hers are critical to still under-studied but important aspects of quilt history and of African American art and cultural history. We know this collection of primary materials will enable scholars on campus and around the world to benefit from Cuesta's trailblazing work and to carry it forward."

Shiela Betterton
1920–2008

Shiela Betterton was inducted into the Quilters Hall of Fame in Wabash, Indiana, on July 16, 1999.

"Making patchwork became so much part of a woman's life that by the middle of the nineteenth century, designing patchwork quilt patterns had become one of the major forms of domestic folk art."

—Shiela Betterton, *More Quilts and Coverlets from the American Museum in Britain* (1989), p. 8

by Suellen Meyer

SHIELA BETTERTON looked like everyone's favorite English grandmother. With her apple cheeks, curly auburn hair, and ready smile, she immediately put others at ease. But her charm cloaked an incisive and encyclopedic mind, one that had studied quilts for more than thirty years.

Perhaps better known in England than in America, Shiela was widely recognized as an authority on American quilts. She lived in Bath, England, where from 1963 to 1993, first as steward and later as textile adviser, she developed the outstanding textile collection of the American Museum in Britain. During her career, she also curated textile shows, lectured widely, wrote four books on quilting, and published numerous scholarly articles.

When Shiela joined the museum in 1963, she found a small quilt collection there. Under her direction it grew to 165 quilts, all of which are fine examples of American quiltmaking, and some of which are truly extraordinary pieces. Shiela developed the collection thoughtfully; she understood what examples she needed to fill the collection's holes, and based on her study and her finely honed eye, she recognized the finest examples when she saw them.

The director of the museum, William McNaught, wrote to the Quilters Hall of Fame: "At the American Museum in Britain she has created what is considered the most distinguished collection of American quilts that exists outside of the United States." But this accolade did not come without enormous effort on Shiela's part.

As a young woman in the early 1960s, she lived in Bath with her husband, Ernest, and their two small daughters. At this time, Shiela had no interest in quilts, although she had discovered the American Museum, which lay at the base of her hill, Combe Down. Regularly, she popped her two little girls into their pram and walked the several miles so she could admire the museum's furnishings and art. Soon she found herself so drawn to the museum that she volunteered to work as a docent. After a training period, she found herself explaining the textiles to visitors, and before long she was hired to care for the textiles.

Shiela quickly became interested in the quilts because she noticed that some had the same quilting patterns as her mother's whole-cloth Northumberland quilts that she had slept under as a child. As she traced the cables and feathers on the American quilts, she wondered how these designs got to America. That curiosity began a lifelong study of quilts that resulted in numerous publications and exhibitions as well as international travel to study quilts.

Chalice Quilt | Believed to have been made by slaves on the Mimosa Hall Plantation, Marshall, Texas | Circa 1980 | 87 × 75 inches | Cotton.
Shiela Betterton was very proud to have been instrumental in the acquisition of this quilt for the museum. It is believed to have been made by slaves on the Mimosa Hall Plantation for the visit of the Bishop of New Orleans to the plantation. *Courtesy of the American Museum in Britain (1983.172.01)*

Shiela's enthusiasm for the history of quilts led her to make firm friends with other researchers who admired her careful research and generosity. Helen Kelley, a close friend, said Shiela regularly sent her information typed on onionskin paper—a reference to a quilt or wall hanging, a quote alluding to a quilt in a novel, or some hard-to-find bit of history. Helen described Shiela as a "tremendous manager" with "enormous energy."

Shiela drew upon these qualities as she searched for quilts to add to the American Museum's collection. She used not only her

The *Classic American Quilts* exhibition at the American Museum in Britain from March to October 2010 was presented by Laura Beresford, curator. An exhibition catalog, *Classic Quilts from the American Museum*, accompanied the exhibition and is a wonderful resource regarding the many quilts Shiela Betterton added to the museum's collection during her service as curator. *Courtesy of the American Museum in Britain*

Exterior of Claverton Manor, Bath, England, home of the American Museum in Britain. The mansion was designed by Sir Jeffry Wyatville, architect to King George IV, in 1820. It stands in 126 acres of park and woodland, high above the valley of the River Avon. *Courtesy of the American Museum in Britain*

Shiela Betterton with Dr. Frank E. Lodge, chairman of the Wisbech Society at the National Trust property Peckover House, Wisbech, September 23, 1977. The property had an exhibition that featured twelve of the museum's quilts. *Courtesy of the American Museum in Britain*

knowledge but also her considerable charm and wit to develop the collection. For years, she paid close attention to comments about who might want to sell or donate a quilt. Following up on her information, she contacted the owners, recruited quilts for the museum, and, when successful, sometimes took them home to be washed in her bathtub and prepared for exhibit.

She followed all leads. Whenever she heard about an old quilt in an English stately house, she would write to the lady of the manor, who invariably would invite her to tea. Shiela and her husband, Ernest, would appear at the proper time to study the quilt, with Ernest taking photographs and Shiela writing notes, before having tea with the duchess. Even though the quilt would often stay in its ancestral home, Shiela would gather photographs and documentation to add to her considerable store of quilt history.

To share this history, Shiela curated many shows, including the 1976 exhibition with the Commonwealth Institute in London, in conjunction with the American bicentennial; the 1980 British Council Exhibition in St. Louis, Missouri; and the 1997 exhibit *Crazy for Quilts: 200 Years of American Quilts*, held at the American Museum in Britain, for which she acted as consulting curator and which, to her great surprise, was dedicated to her.

To take the history of quilts to people who could not attend the exhibitions, Shiela added lectures to her schedule and informed audiences not only in England but also on the European continent and in the United States. Even at the end of her life, although officially retired, Shiela would choose a lecture topic, research it thoroughly, prepare it meticulously, and present it flawlessly to her audience, and never give it again.

People who did not hear Shiela speak can still benefit from her deep knowledge by reading one of her many scholarly articles or books. To illustrate and interpret the quilts in the American Museum's collection, she wrote *Quilts and Coverlets from the American Museum in Britain* (1978) and *More Quilts and Coverlets from the American Museum in Britain* (1988). In addition, she wrote *American Textiles and Needlework* (1971) and *The American Quilt Tradition* (1976). Her books and articles are now widely regarded as standard reference works.

While Shiela is rightfully known as a pioneer in England for her study of American quilts, she had many other interests. She wrote about rugs and about Navajo weaving and textiles of the American Southwest.

Shiela Betterton was inducted into the Quilters Hall of Fame in 1999. England also recognized her great contributions by electing her Fellow of the Royal Society of Arts and appointing her an Honorary Life Member of the British Quilters Guild and the Bath Quilters Guild. Her English colleagues agree that her tireless efforts to educate others about quilts, American quilts in particular, earned her this recognition, for she is acknowledged as the foremost British specialist on American quilts.

Selected Reading

Betterton, Shiela. *American Textiles and Needlework*. Bath, England: The American Museum in Britain, 1971, 1977.

———. Introduction. *Folk Art Quilts: 20 Unique Designs from the American Museum in Britain* by Anne Hulbert. Great Britain: Anaya Publishers Ltd., 1992.

———. *More Quilts and Coverlets from the American Museum in Britain*. Bath, England: The American Museum in Britain, 1989.

———. *Quilts and Coverlets from the American Museum in Britain*. Bath, England: The American Museum in Britain, 1978.

———. Royal Connections: Quilting and the British Monarchy." *The Quilt Journal: An International Review* 4, no. 1 (1995): 5–8.

Mariner's Compass | Pieced and appliquéd in Pennsylvania | Circa 1820–1850 | 103 × 103 inches | Cotton. As textile and needlework specialist for the American Museum in Britain, Shiela Betterton was instrumental in building its outstanding collection of American quilts. *Mariner's Compass* was featured in her book, *Quilts and Coverlets from the American Museum in Britain* (1978). The materials are mainly those of the 1820s and 1830s, but some fabrics date from as late as 1850. *Courtesy of the American Museum in Britain, gift of George G. Frelinghuysen*

Jinny Beyer

*"A quilt is a piece of art, and for me,
there can be no compromise.
I want to be proud of it and I want my children
and their children to be proud of it."*

—Jinny Beyer, *Quilters' Journal*, vol. 1, no. 1 (Fall 1977)

Jinny Beyer was inducted into the
Quilters Hall of Fame at the Continental
Quilting Congress, Arlington, Virginia, on
September 29, 1984. *Courtesy of Jinny Beyer*

by Pamela Neiwirth

JINNY BEYER lives on a 250-year-old Virginia farm, tucked away in the woods outside our nation's capital. The location suits her many interests as artisan, athlete, gardener, writer, and, yes, quilter.

Jinny's success is well known within the quilt world, but she has also received awards in debating, Little Theater, and running, which she took up at age forty, writing *How to Run a Six-Minute Mile* in 1984. Surprisingly, she also knows Morse code, operates a ham radio, and plays the sitar. John, her husband of more than forty-five years, comments, "If Jinny is sitting on the couch doing nothing, she must be sick!"

Jinny juggles many professional duties as designer, author, teacher, quilter, and lecturer. Perhaps that is why it is so amazing that Jinny has exclusively pieced and quilted her creations by hand since the early 1970s. "This is my quilt to last a lifetime. I am in no hurry. I can catch my breath," explains Jinny. Of course, many have advised Jinny to use a machine to be more prolific, but she has never wavered in her commitment to handwork. She recommends that people always have one hand-piecing project to carry with them for those inevitable waits at doctors' offices, airports, car repair shops, or soccer fields.

In fact, Jinny mentions, "I don't remember not having a project going even when I was very small." Her mother, Polly Kahle, an artist, taught Jinny and her three sisters how to sew and knit when they were quite young. At the age of five, Jinny would sit quietly sewing or knitting while her mother shopped for groceries. A very creative family, the Kahle women spent hours together doing crafts and needlework. This handwork, which kept Jinny busy while growing up in Colorado and California, gave her a firm foundation for her future success.

Jinny also has a love of gardening and cares for a variety of flowers, fruits, and vegetables. In her yard, she designed a formal "quilt" garden laid out like a medallion quilt, with each flowerbed serving as one point of a large star. There is a fountain in the middle with a mosaic star as the central focus. Nature's shapes and colors have a great influence on her work as a designer.

Daylilies Quilt | Designed and made by Jinny Beyer | 1998 | 79 × 88 inches | Hand-pieced and hand-quilted. Jinny Beyer created this quilt as an example of a tessellated design for her book *Designing Tessellations: The Secrets of Interlocking Patterns.* Beautifully shaded red, brown, and purple flowers swirl across the quilt.
Photo by Steve Tuttle, courtesy of Jinny Beyer

Often, the inspiration for her textile designs begins in her garden, where she selects leaves and flowers to scan into her computer, then manipulates their dimensions and colors to create the final designs for her fabrics.

Born Geraldine Elizabeth Kahle in Denver, Colorado, Jinny later moved to California with her family. In 1962, she married John Beyer, and the following year, she graduated with a B.A. in Speech and French from the University of the Pacific in Stockton, California. In 1964, she earned an M.A. in special education at Boston University. With this credential, she offered to volunteer with the Malaysian Department of Education and, through their assistance, began a program for the deaf in Kuching, Sarawak, one of the many places where Jinny, her economist husband, and their three children have lived.

Wherever they lived abroad—Borneo, Nepal, India, and South America—Jinny would sew clothes for the family with local fabrics. In India, she became fascinated by the dark, richly colored hand-blocked prints sold by the piece. Each piece always had a border on it. Shortly before leaving India in 1972, Jinny was seeking a new project. When a quilter gave her a Grandmother's Flower Garden quilt pattern, she began her first quilt by cutting out 600 hexagons of Indian fabrics in reds and blues. Jinny considers herself lucky to have started quilting in India, because she was not influenced by American fashions or rules.

When she returned to the United States, she had to learn how to quilt the top and bind it. But she was unable to locate other quilters until she was fortunate to discover Hazel Carter's quilt meeting near her home. When Jinny brought out her unusual

The Quilter's Album of Patchwork Patterns: More than 4,050 Pieced Blocks for Quilters by Jinny Beyer was published in 2009.

Indian Grandmother's Flower Garden quilt top with the navy background, the other quilters were very surprised at her color choices, but it was well received.

The "Jinny Beyer look" was born, first with her quilts, and later with a line of fabrics featuring prints in rich, dark colors, border prints, and geometric patterns, made with textiles that still evoke an Indian influence.

Hazel Carter encouraged Jinny to enter the 1976 *Quilter's Newsletter Magazine*'s Bicentennial Quilt Contest. Her red, white, and blue *Bicentennial Quilt* became a top prizewinner. The center star medallion contains fifty five-pointed stars, surrounded by an outer border consisting of eighteen blocks with historical significance.

In 1978, Jinny entered *Good Housekeeping* magazine's Great American Quilt Contest, winning first prize for her *Ray of Light* quilt, which catapulted her to national fame. This stunning quilt with an intricate Mariner's Compass design was named for her daughter's Indian name, Kiran, which means "ray of light." Jinny hand-pieced the quilt with unusual American and batik prints and heavily hand-quilted it. This magnificent medallion quilt was photographed on the lawn in front of the Governor's Palace in Williamsburg, Virginia, and was featured in *Good Housekeeping*'s March 1978 issue.

Reflecting on the creation of *Ray of Light*, Jinny remembers that she was hand-quilting it right up until the UPS man knocked on the door. She had worked on it for ten months straight to meet the contest deadline.

Jinny soon became an author, writing *Patchwork Patterns* in 1979 and *The Quilter's Album of Blocks and Borders* in 1980. All of the attention bestowed upon *Ray of Light* revived the antique medallion style quilts. Jinny's third book, *The Art and Technique of Creating Medallion Style Quilts*, was published in 1982, inspiring others to create their own masterpieces. *The Scrap Look*, published in 1985, was followed by a book of her original designs, *Patchwork Portfolio* in 1989. One of her most widely read books is *Color Confidence for Quilters*, published in 1992. *Soft-Edge Piecing* followed in 1995, *Christmas with Jinny Beyer* in 1996, and *Designing Tessellations: The Secrets of Interlocking Patterns* in 1998. There was a small break between books before *Quiltmaking by Hand: Simple Stitches, Exquisite Quilts* was published in 2004. This book was published during the development in the quilt world of long-arm quilting and the increase of two-person quilts, and it was a call back to hand piecing, a wonderful "how-to" for beginning hand piecers and a validation for those who were hand piecing. This book was followed by *Patchwork Puzzle Balls* in 2005, the encyclopedic *The Quilter's Album of Patchwork Patterns: More than 4050 Pieced Blocks for Quilters* in 2009, and *The Golden Album Quilt* in 2010.

Ray of Light | Designed and made by Jinny Beyer | 1977 | 80 × 91 inches | Indonesian batiks and American cottons, hand-pieced and hand-quilted. Named in honor of her daughter Kiran (Kiran is an Indian name meaning "ray of light"), this quilt won the Great American Quilt contest sponsored by *Good Housekeeping*, the U.S. Historical Society, and the Museum of American Folk Art in 1978. It was chosen to be in the exhibit of *America's 100 Best Quilts of the 20th Century* at the International Quilt Festival in 1999. *Courtesy of Jinny Beyer*

Fabrics in the Jinny Beyer Palette line. Frustrated with fabric colors coming in and going out of fashion, Jinny created an ongoing line of fabrics with RJR Fabrics in 1990. Designs in her 150-fabric Quilter's Palette collection change periodically, but the color range is always available. *Courtesy of Jinny Beyer*

In 1982, Jinny became the first quilter to have her own line of fabrics when she began designing for V.I.P. by Cranston fabrics, including the border prints for which she is now famous. In 1985, she introduced her signature Jinny Beyer Collection for RJR Fabrics. The Jinny Beyer Studio near her home in Great Falls, Virginia, features her fabric line and other specially designed needlework items.

Jinny has received many honors. She was inducted into the Quilters Hall of Fame in 1984, and in 1995, she received the International Quilt Festival's Silver Star Award, "to honor a person who is active in the quilt world today, and whose work represents a lasting influence on today's quilting and the future of the art." In 1996, she received the Michael Kile Lifetime Achievement Award from the International Quilt Market, "honoring commitment to creativity and excellence in the quilting industry." The American Quilter's Society honored Jinny as its American Quilter, voted on by the readers of *American Quilter* magazine in the 2004 summer issue.

Beyer has also completed several videos, including *Palettes for Patchwork*, *Mastering Patchwork*, and *Color Confidence*.

Jinny's sons, Sean and Darren, recall her teaching quilting classes at home, with neighborhood women coming and going on a regular basis. As her reputation grew, Jinny was asked to teach classes farther away. She is now sought after as an international teacher, making several foreign trips each year. She has taught in Asia, Australia, New Zealand, Europe, Canada, and even Iceland. In 2000, she lectured in Stockholm at a convention of mathematicians and artists on the topic of symmetry. As of 2010, Jinny had been invited to teach at a quilt seminar in Australia every year for five years and in the Ukraine for three years. Recently, she has been the guest quilt teacher on a tour to see quilt-inspiring aspects of India, with trips to Morocco and Ireland planned in the future.

The Jinny Beyer Seminar on Hilton Head Island in South Carolina was an annual event for twenty-nine years from 1981 until 2009. Many of Jinny's innovative techniques, such as Soft-Edge Piecing and Tessellated Designs, were born in her Hilton Head brainstorming sessions. Jinny's approach to teaching quilting is unusual. She seldom provides patterns in her classes or in her books because she believes her students must understand the creative process so they can make discoveries of their own.

Television and Internet appearances further extended Jinny's ability to share her methods and her color and design sense with wider audiences. She was the guest on several of Alex Anderson's *Simply Quilts* programs for the Home and Garden (HGTV) network. Jinny also did several Internet shows for Alex Anderson and Ricky Tims's *The Quilt Show* and was named their 2008 Quilt Legend.

Jinny Beyer is a popular quilt teacher and author. Here she is signing a copy of her book *The Quilter's Album of Patchwork Patterns: More than 4,050 Pieced Blocks for Quilters*. *Courtesy of Jinny Beyer*

Jinny's work is appealing and is often reproduced by her students and those who buy her quilt books and videos. The use of these materials to make quilts for personal use is acceptable, but when a friend alerted Jinny that a Chinese company was reproducing and selling versions of her *Ray of Light* quilt, she felt the need to stand up for the protection afforded under the copyright law. The case was settled out of court. Not interested in pursuing the Chinese company for financial benefit but only on principle, Jinny donated the settlement funds, beyond her legal costs, to various organizations that preserve quilt history, including the Alliance for American Quilts, the Virginia Quilt Museum, the San Jose Museum of Quilts and Textiles, the American Quilt Study Group, and the Quilters Hall of Fame.

Jinny continues to be active, writing books, leading tours, sharing her love of quilting with others, and making beautiful quilts.

Selected Reading

Beyer, Jinny. *The Art and Technique of Medallion Quilts.* McLean, VA: EPM Publications, 1982.

———. *Color Confidence for Quilters.* Guala, CA: The Quilt Digest Press, 1992.

———. *Designing Tessellations: The Secrets of Interlocking Patterns.* Lincolnwood, IL: Contemporary Books, 1998.

———. *The Golden Album Quilt.* Elmhurst, IL: Breckling Press, 2010.

———. *Patchwork Patterns.* McLean, VA: EPM Publications, 1979.

———. *The Quilter's Album of Blocks and Borders.* McLean, VA: EPM Publications, 1980.

———. *Quiltmaking by Hand: Simple Stitches, Exquisite Quilts.* Elmhurst, IL: Breckling Press, 2004.

Rhapsody | Designed and made by Jinny Beyer | **1992–1993** | **76 × 98 inches.** Inspired by the cover she created for her book *Color Confidence for Quilters*, Jinny created a tessellating design for this quilt. *Courtesy of Jinny Beyer*

Georgia J. Bonesteel

"Many of the quilters explain that before, quilting had seemed such an overwhelming task, but lap quilting has made it both possible and plausible.*"*

—Georgia Bonesteel, introduction to *More Lap Quilting with Georgia Bonesteel*, 1985

by Amy V. Bonesteel Smith

GEORGIA BONESTEEL HAS BEEN MAKING QUILTS for more than forty years. She first learned to sew by watching her mother, who said, "In those days, I had to sew in order to save money dressing two daughters." Georgia's father worked as an attorney with the U.S. Department of Justice, and the family moved often. "Always being the new girl made me more outgoing and helped me conquer shyness," Georgia recalls.

After attending Iowa State University in Ames, Iowa, and Northwestern University in Evanston, Illinois, Georgia earned a degree in home economics. Upon graduating, she started work in merchandising at Marshall Field & Co. in Chicago. She had the opportunity to utilize her creativity and strong sense of color by designing store window displays at the Old Orchard store and preparing fashion models for runway shows. Marriage in 1959 and children took priority until a move to New Orleans in 1969. With three children in school, Georgia was finally able to concentrate on her favorite pastime, sewing.

"I had studied textiles at Iowa State, but I'd probably have to say the adventure with piecing and patchwork began when we lived in New Orleans," Georgia told the *Quilters Hall of Fame Newsletter* in 2003. "I was mostly just making home projects and

clothes for my daughter at the time, but I remember a particular McCall's pattern for neckties that I was making for my husband, too. Those ties must have been about four inches wide, geometric, terrible designs. I'm surprised he wore them. I used to sew a small label, 'Home-made by Georgia,' in them," she recalls. "There was always some fabric left over.

"Being frugal," she continued in the article, "I wanted to do something with the leftover patchwork triangles. I found a little book with about 12 patterns, and I tried them all. It was called *Modern Patchwork* and was published by Countryside Press Farm Journal Inc. and had a 1970 copyright date. I made pillows with those leftovers."

Little did Georgia know that her job in the fabric section of a New Orleans department store in 1972 would lead to a professional quilt career. After winning an audition for a television wardrobe assistant, she went on to guest star in several segments of an educational series called *Sewing Is Fun*. During this filming, she discovered that remnant silk tie fabric could be recycled into charming crazy-patch-quilted handbags. She didn't learn to "properly" quilt until several years later, by sitting with the senior citizens' quilt group at the Opportunity House in Hendersonville,

Stars Over the Smokies | Designed and made by Georgia Bonesteel | 1984 | **74 × 92 inches.** *Stars Over the Smokies* is based on sixteen-inch star blocks set with single borders and square corner inserts. However, two rectangles make an interesting break in the repetition. Discovering the flexible curve prompted this new curvy approach to machine patchwork and led to creative circles inside a square. "A curved line is a line of beauty, and a straight line is a line of duty." *Courtesy of Georgia Bonesteel*

Georgia Bonesteel created this *Beddy Byes* quilt pattern using the printed fabrics she developed based on Marie Webster's appliqué quilts. *Courtesy of Windham Fabrics*

North Carolina, where the family had relocated. As she recalls in her book, *Lap Quilting*, "I learned to sew at my mother's knee; I learned to quilt through serendipity!"

The move to North Carolina launched her interest in full-size quilts and a further step, teaching quiltmaking at the Blue Ridge Community College. Soon she was able to combine teaching and quiltmaking into a PBS television series of her own called *Lap Quilting*, produced by the University of North Carolina Center for Public Television. The first six segments taped in 1976 had limited viewing in North Carolina but were so well received that another seven were taped to create a full thirteen-week series that aired across the country. A companion guide, *Lap Quilting Your Legacy Quilt*, which sold for five dollars, became a top seller.

Soon Georgia's children were collating copies on the dining-room table, and her mother was typing up addresses for the mailings. That little booklet helped to buy a hardware store, and Georgia and her husband began operating Bonesteel Hardware & Quilt Corner. This gave Georgia a base for classes, supplies, and sewing machine sales.

By 2003, Georgia had completed twelve series for television. Each series comprised thirteen thirty-minute shows with a theme, demonstrations, step-by-step methods, and interviews. The exposure Georgia received from her television programs led to more books, workshops, judging of quilt shows, lectures, and even a line of fabric with Wamsutta. Her world of teaching extended from Alaska to Australia to Europe.

In addition to the television series, Georgia has written nine books, the most recent among them *Georgia Bonesteel's*

Quiltmaking Legacy. Featured in each book is Georgia's novel approach to lap quilting, which helped to bring great portability to the marvelous art form. Georgia also authored a three-volume continuity program (basically a series) for Oxmoor House entitled *Spinning Spools.*

Working with fabric and all the paraphernalia that accompany quiltmaking has led Georgia to develop several useful quilting products. She likes a supported lap hoop that accommodates a busy lifestyle and an indented thimble that helps quilters master the quilting stitch in a hoop. Georgia had a wood crafter make supported lap hoops that sold in her store until the postage became prohibitive. She never made but did carry the indented thimbles in her shop. Georgia also created a portable light box as a solution for transferring patterns, but she is most proud of her product that combines a graph pad and template in one tool—a continuous grid printed on freezer paper, Grid Grip.

Georgia has been honored with several awards: the Silver Star Salute at the International Quilt Festival in 2000, the Bernina of America Leadership Award in 2002, a North Carolina Quilt Symposium Yearly Scholarship Award in 2003, and induction into the Quilters Hall of Fame, also in 2003. In 2005 she and her quilts starred in the documentary *The Great American Quilt Revival*, which aired on several PBS television stations. This film, produced by her son Paul Bonesteel of Bonesteel Film, Inc., is the story of how quilts came to be recognized as works of art and how the craft of quilting has exploded into popular culture.

Promotional card for Georgia Bonesteel's public television quilting program (produced by University of North Carolina Public Television). *Courtesy of Georgia Bonesteel*

Through negotiations with Baum Textile Mills, Georgia was able to produce more than twenty-five cotton fabrics based upon Marie Webster's designs. The fabrics, along with a panel interpreting Marie's quilts, became best sellers and earned more than $3,000 for the Quilters Hall of Fame. Georgia has also been the subject of a profile in *Sophie* magazine, and her quilt *Moon and Stars* was chosen as the cover art for a children's CD, *Celeste Sings, Kids Dream* (Romantic Realist Records).

Teaching remains Georgia's passion, and she gives seminars at weeklong retreats at John Campbell Folk School in Brasstown, North Carolina, and Nine Quarter Circle Ranch in Gallatin Gateway, Montana, as well as a two-week session at the William Black Lodge in Montreat, North Carolina. Each of these venues requires a new and original quilt project for students to learn. "Learning and sharing over a longer period of time at these venues has very positive results," says Georgia. "The interplay of students is invaluable. That is how quiltmaking has thrived and grown from hand to hand and mind to mind."

Locally, Georgia remains active with several quilting groups and continues to produce art quilts and designs (in between traveling with her husband, raising chickens, and visiting with her eight grandchildren). She is also a master gardener, volunteers regularly, maintains a plot in a community garden, and constantly updates and cares for her lakefront property.

Over the years, her philosophy and drive have not changed; she still believes making something handmade is always worth the time and expense, and its even better when not perfect. "When it comes to creating quilts, making a mistake is the truest form of creativity."

Masks, Moose and Qupak | Designed and made by Georgia Bonesteel. | 1988 | 82 × 102 inches | Machine-stitched with Qupak accents on the side panels; hand-quilted, machine-quilted, and tie-tacked with beads. Georgia created a totem pole effect using motifs inspired by her Alaskan journeys. She is shown here with the quilt, which appeared in *Bright Ideas for Lap Quilting*. Photo by Oxmoor House, courtesy of Georgia Bonesteel

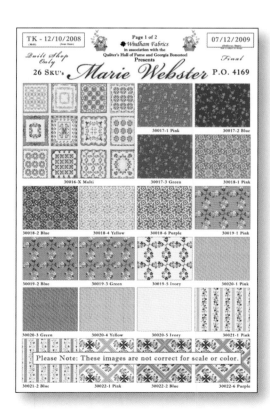

Printed fabric line designed by Georgia Bonesteel for Windham Fabrics in 2009 based on the appliqué quilts designed by Marie Webster. A portion of the sales from these fabrics was donated to the Quilters Hall of Fame. *Courtesy of Windham Fabrics*

Selected Reading

Bonesteel, Georgia. *Bright Ideas for Lap Quilting*. Birmingham, AL: Oxmoor House, 1990.

———. *Lap Quilting Lives*. Bothell, WA: Martingale/That Patchwork Place, 1999.

———. *Lap Quilting with Georgia Bonesteel*. Birmingham, AL: Oxmoor House, 1982.

———. *Patchwork Potpourri*. Chapel Hill: University of North Carolina Press, 1997.

———. *Spinning Spools*. 3 volumes. Birmingham, AL: Oxmoor House, 1990.

Barbara Brackman

*"My interest in computers and visual perception
may have influenced the way I look at quilts,
but I must confess my childhood fascination
with girl detective Nancy Drew may have influenced me more.
Each undated quilt I see as an unsolved mystery
that summons the quilt detective in me."*

—Barbara Brackman, *Clues in the Calico*, 1989, p. 10

Barbara Brackman was inducted into the
Quilters Hall of Fame in Marion, Indiana,
on July 21, 2001. *Photo by John Gary Brown,
courtesy of Barbara Brackman*

by Karen B. Alexander

BARBARA BRACKMAN'S first introduction to quilts came in the early 1960s through her college roommates at the University of Kansas. Even her boyfriend had quilts. "It was the personal value they placed on those quilts that first caught my attention," remarked Barbara when interviewed by the author in 2001. Though Barbara saw no quilts during her early childhood, she nevertheless was taught to sew and embroider, which she enjoyed very much. She was born in New York City and only moved to Overland Park, Kansas, when she was entering high school.

"My real introduction to quilt research seems almost fortuitous when I look back," Barbara said. "I was taking an art history class in 1964 at the University of Kansas. One day I got to poking around in drawers at the back of the classroom at the University of Kansas Art Museum and came upon the Carrie Hall block collection. Hall had donated the collection to the University in 1935. I was immediately drawn to them because I loved the elements of pattern. The blocks had languished there for some time. . . . I immediately became interested in cataloguing them. Carrie Hall had also donated a lot of paper ephemera to the University. This was my next discovery. It was like my own little playground."

This chance encounter with the Carrie Hall collection eventually changed the course of her life. "I began recording quilt patterns on index cards from day one," stated Barbara, "starting with the Carrie Hall Block Collection and the paper ephemera accompanying her collection, but I didn't try to make a quilt until 1966. I tried using Rose Kretsinger and Carrie Hall's book, *The Romance of the Patchwork Quilt in America*, as my guide. Not the best 'how-to' book for a beginning quilter, but it was the only book about quilts that I was aware of at the time."

Barbara soon began to comb libraries for books and old magazines that might carry quilting designs and added a new index card every time she found another pattern. "My card index file continued to grow steadily," she said. "Once I had the information and pattern sketched on the index card, I could sort the cards. I am so visually oriented that I very quickly began to intuitively see the interconnections of the vast number of patterns."

In the early 1970s, another major milestone occurred in her slowly evolving second career as a quilt historian: Barbara received a gift subscription to *Quilter's Newsletter Magazine*. Her immediate reaction was to realize that she could write pattern history articles.

Emporia Rose | Designed and machine-appliquéd by Barbara Brackman, hand-quilted by Anne Thomas and the St. Joseph's Church group | 1999 | **87 × 87 inches.** Inspired by the twentieth-century masterpiece quilts of Emporia, Kansas, Barbara designed a sampler using several of their traditional designs in an updated color scheme. *Photo by Jon Blumb, courtesy of Barbara Brackman*

When she contacted Bonnie Leman, founder and editor of *Quilter's Newsletter Magazine*, Barbara was invited to submit some articles. The two met face to face in Denver in 1975, launching Barbara's long and productive relationship with the magazine, which continues to this day. Her very first article—on the history of airplane patterns—was published in December 1977.

In 1976, while living in the Chicago area, Barbara began teaching classes on basic quilting, with the emphasis on design, at evening continuing education classes. During the day, however, she continued to teach within her career field, developmental education. About this time she also began lecturing on the history of quilt patterns. Returning to Lawrence, Kansas, at the end of the teaching year, Barbara joined the Kaw Valley Quilt Guild and delved ever deeper into her fabric and pattern studies.

From the late 1970s on, Barbara would play a remarkable number of roles within the quilting world: author, lecturer, teacher, curator, researcher, scholar, pattern collector, and quiltmaker. Her expertise in pattern and fabric identification would have a profound impact upon quilt history nationally and internationally. Quilt historian Merikay Waldvogel commended Barbara for sharing her discoveries by publishing what she found: "My twentieth-century quilt research built upon Brackman's findings, and her advice and counsel was always forthcoming and welcomed," she says. This theme of Barbara's unfailing generosity in encouraging others, of sharing her ideas and knowledge as well as her time and practical assistance, is echoed again and again by those who have worked with her.

As the demand for access to her research increased, in 1979 Barbara translated her index card pattern identification system

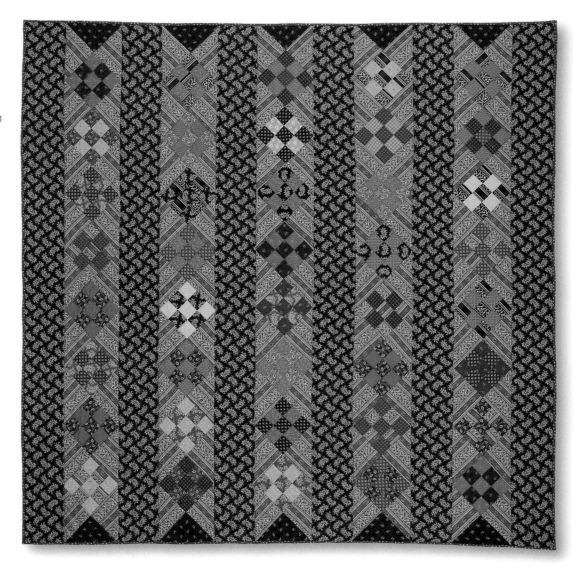

Sorghum Taffy Strip | Designed and made by Barbara Brackman, quilted by Lori Kukuk | 2010 | 84 × 84 inches | Made from a reproduction fabric line Barbara Brackman designed for Moda called *Civil War Homefront.* This strip quilt with the striped setting triangles was inspired by an antique quilt Barbara Brackman saw in an online auction. *Courtesy of Barbara Brackman*

Facts and Fabrications: Unraveling the History of Quilts and Slavery by Barbara Brackman was published in 2006 and was based on two years of reading first-person accounts and looking at photographs on slavery and African-American history.

into a self-published photocopied series. The many state quilt documentation projects that began in the mid-1980s would draw upon this research extensively. In fact, so frequently was Barbara's pattern identification system referred to that patterns simply became known by their "Brackman Number."

Barbara credits three other Quilters Hall of Fame honorees as highly influential mentors: Cuesta Benberry for her emphatic advice, "Do your own original research"; Sally Garoutte for setting high standards for accurate history; and Joyce Gross for her tireless encouragement and razor-sharp questions. Barbara presented her research on patterns and on World's Fair quilts in four papers at American Quilt Study Group seminars, from 1980 to 1983.

Fabric dating became a logical extension of Barbara's interest in quilts, and in 1985 she decided to educate herself in a field with a scarcity of published material. Four years later, her book *Clues in the Calico: A Guide to Identifying and Dating Antique Quilts* was published. Her own self-published pattern identification work, *Encyclopedia of Pieced Quilt Patterns*, was published in a new hardcover edition in 1993 and has become probably the most referenced book in the study of quilt history along with its companion volume, *Encyclopedia of Appliqué*.

As a freelance writer specializing in history and folk arts, Barbara's research has never simply been limited to quilt history. She also writes and consults about women's history, visionary art, cowboy costume, and Civil War history, and she has written for a variety of publications, including *Country Living*, *Fiberarts*, the *Clarion*, *Kansas!*, the *Christian Science Monitor*, *Americana*, and

Fine Homebuilding. She has served as a curator and consultant to numerous museums as well.

Barbara shared a studio space with business partner and friend Terry Clothier Thompson in Lawrence, Kansas, from 1997 to 2001. Their classes in textile history attracted students from around the nation; they offered these same classes as far afield as Germany and Japan. In 1999, their first of many reproduction antique fabric lines with Moda of United Notions of Dallas was released at the spring Houston Quilt Market.

In 1999, Barbara began to publish her first mini-newsletter series *Material Pleasures*, focusing on the history of nineteenth-century fabric production and dyes. This series formed the basis of her later book *America's Printed Fabrics 1770–1890*. Her 2002 series *Making History: The Twentieth Century* focused on pattern designers of the early twentieth century. The subsequent book *Making History: Quilts & Fabric from 1890–1970* made the 2009 Kansas Notable Book List. In 2008, she received the Lawrence Cultural Arts Commission Phoenix Award.

These latest honors simply reinforce the significance of Barbara Brackman's lifetime achievements. The Quilters Hall of Fame recognized her many pioneering contributions to the study of quilt and textile history by selecting her as the 2001 honoree.

Selected Reading

Brackman, Barbara. "A Chronological Index to Pieced Quilt Patterns, 1775–1825." *Uncoverings 1983*. Mill Valley, CA: American Quilt Study Group, 1984.

———. *Clues in the Calico: A Guide to Identifying and Dating Antique Quilts*. McLean, VA: EPM Publications, 1989.

———. *Encyclopedia of Appliqué*. McLean, VA: EPM Publications, 1993.

———. *Encyclopedia of Pieced Quilt Patterns*. Self-published, 1979. Reprinted by American Quilter's Society, 1993.

———. *Patterns of Progress: Quilts in the Machine Age*. Exhibit catalog. Los Angeles: Autry Museum of Western Heritage, 1997.

———. "Quiltmaking on the Overland Trails: Evidence from Women's Writings." *Uncoverings 1992*. San Francisco, CA: American Quilt Study Group, 1993.

Brackman, Barbara, et al. *Kansas Quilts and Quilters*. Lawrence: University Press of Kansas, 1993.

Waldvogel, Merikay, and Barbara Brackman. *Patchwork Souvenirs of the 1933 World's Fair*. Nashville, TN: Rutledge Hill Press, 1993.

Karey Bresenhan

*"Today, quilts old and new—
the products of an artistic tradition and heritage—
continue to touch American lives,
regardless of economic or ethnic differences.
In this century, it can truly be said that quilts
have become America's collective memory bank."*

—Karey Bresenhan, preface of *The Twentieth Century's Best American Quilts*, p. 3

Karey Bresenhan was inducted into the Quilters Hall of Fame in Marion, Indiana, on July 22, 1995. *Photo by Richard Cunningham*

by Robert Ruggiero

THROUGHOUT HER EXTENSIVE and varied experience in the quilt world, Karoline Patterson Bresenhan has often heard words like *no*, *can't*, and *impossible*, but with determination and a drive inherited from her Texas pioneer ancestors, the founder of Quilts, Inc. and its numerous shows and affiliated organizations has helped to spread the art and craft of quilting across the United States and all over the world. "I certainly had no grand plan," Bresenhan says today, "but I rarely give up on anything I think is a good idea."

Though Karey is descended from a long line of quilters, her initial exposure to quilting did not come until 1963, when she joined her grandmother, mother, aunt, great-aunts, and cousin in a round-the-clock quilting bee to finish her wedding quilt in time for her marriage to Maurice Bresenhan Jr. This Touching Stars quilt had been pieced by Karey's great-grandmother Karoline when her namesake was born.

"Now learn to take pretty little stitches," her grandmother admonished during this initial quilting foray, "because you're going to have to wake up every morning of your life and look at them." It proved to be sound advice that Karey still follows today.

She learned through her quilting how important it is to do a good job in the small steps that lead to life's finished projects.

After graduating from Sam Houston State University in 1962, Karey held a series of positions in teaching, editing, and public relations. In 1969, she received a master's degree in journalism from the University of Texas, and from 1970 to 1974, she served as vice president of a large public relations firm. In 1974, she turned her efforts to politics, running as a Democrat for the Texas legislature and funding much of her campaign by selling antiques and quilts in friends' homes. Although she lost the election, she has continued to be involved with civic, political, and health issues, particularly those centered on women.

In 1974, Karey, along with her mother-in-law, Mary Kelly Bresenhan, opened Great Expectations, a retail antique shop in Houston. She hung family quilts to camouflage the bare areas where they lacked enough merchandise to fill the store, but when customers began to inquire more about the quilts than the antiques, Karey realized that a surprisingly large number of people held an interest in quilts, quilting, and quilt history—and she found her niche.

Star of Bethlehem | Unknown quiltmaker, Mennonite, made in Pennsylvania | Circa 1880 | 80 × 80 inches | Cotton; pieced and hand-quilted using seven stitches per inch. A striking Star of Bethlehem, or Lone Star, from the collection of Karey Bresenhan, this pieced quilt has stars and half-stars appliquéd on the setting. Cable wreaths are quilted in the corners with an inner feather wreath, and feathers and baskets are quilted in the border. *Courtesy of the International Quilt Festival Collection*

Positive responses from customers led to her first Quilt Fair in 1974—a thank-you to the city of Houston for a great first year in business—an event that attracted thousands of eager aficionados and was the precursor of the famous International Quilt Festivals to come.

In 1976, Karey and her mother, Jewel Patterson, founded the Quilt Guild of Greater Houston. Karey converted her antique shop into Great Expectations Quilts, which grew into one of the nation's largest quilt stores. It closed in 2003, following the death of her mother, who had been the senior quilting teacher at the shop for two decades.

The Houston guild decided to sponsor the annual Quilt Fair—with Karey as chairperson—to capitalize on the excitement created by the inaugural event. When the guild stopped running the fair, Karey stepped in to see that the popular show continued. Today, the International Quilt Festival in Houston is the largest annual show, sale, and quiltmaking academy in the world, attracting more than 50,000 visitors each year. Some 5,000 quiltmakers participate in the festival's 350 classes and lectures, and it has become Houston's largest convention.

In 1979, Karey held the first Quilt Market exclusively for quilt shop owners, to give them direct access to wholesalers of fabrics, books, and quilting supplies from around the country. In the same year, she formed Quilts, Inc., which is still the parent company for her shows and projects.

Also in 1979, she cofounded the South/Southwest Quilt Association with her mother, her aunt Helen O'Bryant, and her cousin Nancy O'Bryant Puentes. This group evolved into

Karey P. Bresenhan. *Photo by Haney Whipple Portraits, courtesy of Quilts, Inc.*

the International Quilt Association, a nonprofit organization dedicated to advancing quiltmaking throughout the world.

A deep love for her home state of Texas, a desire to celebrate the 150th anniversary of Texas independence, and the opportunity to focus attention on the contributions of female quiltmakers provided the impetus for the first Texas Quilt Search—just the second quilt documentation project in America. Karey and her cousin Nancy traveled to big cities and tiny towns, documenting Texas's unknown quilt treasures and the stories behind them. Their efforts, and those of many other volunteers and nonprofit organizations, led to an exhibit in the statehouse rotunda and the two volumes of *Lone Stars: A Legacy of Texas Quilts*, coauthored by Karey and Nancy. An adjunct effort, the Great Texas Quilt Roundup, showcased contemporary Texas quiltmaking.

Soon Karey found herself exploring a new market—Europe. While writing *Hands All Around: Quilts from Many Nations*, she made many contacts in Europe and realized that there was enough interest to support a sister consumer show and trade show. In 1988, the Patchwork & Quilt Expo and the European Quilt Market were first held in Salzburg, Austria. The expo regularly attracted nearly 20,000 visitors from more than thirty countries and was held in Holland, France, Austria, Denmark, Germany, and Spain. The final Quilt Expo was held in France in 2006.

I Remember Mama by Karey Patterson Bresenhan was published in 2005 as part of the three-year I Remember Mama Project, which was created in memory of Karey's mother, Jewel Pearce Patterson. For the project, quilts were made in honor and in memory of the mothers of the quilt artists.

Karey's next challenge was an issue very close to her heart and to the hearts of quilters around the nation. When the Smithsonian Institution licensed some of its rarest quilts for reproduction overseas, many American quilters felt betrayed, believing that this showed a lack of understanding of the iconic status of these quilts. Karey was also convinced that the practice would harm the economic status of the U.S. quilting industry, and indeed, sales of American-made quilts dropped precipitously. Karey initiated a nationwide petition drive that collected 25,000 signatures. Karey and others took the battle to Congress, presenting the petitions and testifying before a U.S. House of Representatives Appropriations Subcommittee. The Smithsonian ultimately decided not to renew the licensing agreement that allowed copies of the quilts to be made in China.

The International Quilt Festival in Houston is the largest ongoing convention in America's fourth largest city. This aerial view of the festival floor provides some feeling of the hundreds of vendors who participate. *Courtesy of Quilts, Inc.*

Kells: Magnum Opus | Made by Zena Thorpe | 2001 | 82 × 92 inches. This spectacular quilt was recently added to the Corporate Collection of Quilts, Inc., founded by Karey Bresenhan. The quilt has won many prestigious prizes, including the Founders Award at the 2001 International Quilt Association judged show; Best of Show at the American Quilter's Society show in Paducah, Kentucky, in 2001; Best in World at the Mancuso Bros. World Quilt and Textile show in 2001; and Best of Show in the Road to California show in 2002. It was also awarded masterpiece status by the National Quilting Association. *Courtesy of the Quilts, Inc., Corporate Collection*

This experience prompted Karey Bresenhan, Nancy O'Bryant Puentes, Eunice Ray, and Shelly Zegart to found a nonprofit organization, the Alliance for American Quilts, to preserve and make accessible information about American quilt history. Their projects include the Center for the Quilt Online, Boxes Under the Bed (to promote the preservation of quilt documentation), Quilters S.O.S. (Save Our Stories, a project to collect oral histories of quilters), Quilt Treasures, and the International Quilt Index. "The alliance is an umbrella organization under which all elements of the quilt world can unite to achieve these goals," Karey says.

As a quilt historian who specializes in the dating of fabrics, Karey has a deep appreciation for antique quilts. One of her proudest accomplishments was the creation of a remarkable exhibit at the Houston Quilt Festival: *America's 100 Best Quilts of the 20th Century*. The exhibit succeeded in bringing to Houston seventy-five of these incredible quilts, which had been selected by representatives of five major quilt organizations.

After the tragic events of September 11, 2001, Karey curated another exhibit, *America: From the Heart*. "We had no idea how many quilts would be sent in," she says. "And oh, how many splendid quilts they made—so many beautiful, heartfelt quilts that served not only to help the quilt artists deal with their own sorrow and anger over what had happened, but also helped viewers come to grips with the horror and yet realize that despite everything, our nation would go on."

A silent auction raised more than $25,000 for the Families of Freedom Scholarship Fund, for the education of family members of the terrorists' victims. And from the exhibit came a book, *America: From the Heart*, which Karey edited, with all of the profits earmarked for the same fund.

Karey Bresenhan's collection of quilts, which began with pieces inherited from both sides of her family, now numbers more than 250 quilts, in her personal collection and in the corporate collection of Quilts, Inc. She has one important criterion for adding a work to her collection: "I collect a quilt only if it speaks to my heart," she explains. "It can be a wonderful, valuable quilt . . . but if I don't love it, then none of that matters." She has recently collected more contemporary art quilts because she believes it's essential to support quilt artists working today.

In 2003, Karey created a second International Quilt Festival—a spring show in Chicago, Illinois (since moved to Cincinnati, Ohio), which has enjoyed tremendous success. She then started a summer edition in Long Beach, California, in 2006. With Nancy O'Bryant, she coauthored a book about the festival and its quilts, *Celebrate Great Quilts!* published in 2004 to mark the thirtieth anniversary

of the show. Other books that she either wrote or edited include *I Remember Mama*, *Creative Quilting: The Journal Quilt Project*, and *500 Art Quilts*.

Also during this period, Karey opened the Great Expectations Creativity Center in La Grange, Texas. Featuring a fully functional classroom, studio, and dormitory, the center regularly offers seminars and workshops from many top instructors from all over the world, as well as hosting an artist in residence program. Quilting groups have also used the facility to hold retreats, and Quilts, Inc. conducts business meetings in the scenic surroundings as well.

The year 2011 will see the publication of the third volume in the *Lone Stars* series, *Lone Stars III: Texas Quilts Today (1986–2011)*, written with Nancy O'Bryant. It will also see the opening of the Texas Quilt Museum in La Grange, Texas. The museum, a lifelong ambition of Karey's, will feature both permanent and rotating exhibits of quilts, with an emphasis on quiltmakers and artists from the Lone Star State. Both projects will also celebrate the 175th anniversary of Texas independence. Finally, Karey is spearheading the Texas Barn Quilt Trail program, with the goal of having a large "quilt block" on display in every county in the state.

Many honors have come her way. In 1995, she was inducted into the Quilters Hall of Fame. She has received the Distinguished Alumni Award of Sam Houston State University and also was the first recipient of Bernina's annual Quilt Leadership Award. Innovative businesswoman, quilt historian, and industry advocate, Karey Bresenhan has been one of the prime catalysts for the growth of quilting in America for nearly forty years—and she's not finished yet!

Selected Reading

Bishop, Robert, Karey P. Bresenhan, and Bonnie Leman. *Hands All Around: Quilts from Many Nations*. New York: E. P. Dutton, 1987.

Bresenhan, Karey, and Nancy O'Bryant Puentes. *Celebrate Great Quilts!* Lafayette, CA: C&T Publishing, 2004.

———. *Lone Stars: A Legacy of Texas Quilts 1836–1936*. Austin: University of Texas Press, 1986.

———. *Lone Stars II: A Legacy of Texas Quilts 1936–1986*. Austin: University of Texas Press, 1990.

———. *The New American Quilt Shop Series: Great Expectations*. Bothell, WA: Martingale/That Patchwork Place, 1995.

Averil Colby
1900–1983

*"Possibly this book may be the means
of finding unknown work . . . and perhaps the patterns,
and in many cases the humour, of the best work we possess
may stimulate the present generation to do likewise
for the future ones. I hope so."*

—Averil Colby, *Patchwork* (1958), p. 9

Averil Colby was inducted into the Quilters
Hall of Fame at the Continental Quilting
Congress in Arlington, Virginia, on
October 15, 1980. *Courtesy of the Quilters'
Guild of the British Isles*

by Tina Fenwick-Smith

AVERIL COLBY was the eldest of three girls and two boys, whose father was a North Country doctor in Yorkshire, England. As a young woman, she was educated at Cheltenham Ladies College in Gloucestershire and then studied horticulture at Studley Agricultural College in Warwickshire from about 1917 to 1920. On leaving college, she teamed up with a fellow graduate and together they rented the Old Court House with forty acres in Somerset County in the West of England. This smallholding supported a milk delivery route with a pony and cart and a butter- and cheese-making enterprise.

For about ten years, Averil enjoyed country life, transforming the Old Court House garden from a wilderness into a spectacle of great beauty. In the early 1930s, there was a parting of the ways, and Averil moved to live with her widowed mother in North Devon and then Hampshire, but she yearned to return to the Old Court House. Her brother Richard remembered, "She was never happier than when her fingers were delving in the earth tending her plants."

Averil joined the local branch of the National Federation of Women's Institutes, where she became involved in making a group quilt and quickly became hooked on patchwork. Averil and patchwork were made for each other, as her natural flair and horticultural training had sharpened her designer's eye.

After a short time, Averil returned to the Old Court House, the home she so dearly loved. With just a spell in the Women's Land Army during World War II, when she filled in for farmers who were off to war, she was able to spend the rest of her life in this much-loved home.

Having set the stage, what of her as a person? Her stern Yorkshire upbringing meant that Averil did not suffer fools gladly. She was immensely practical, full of common sense, and a marvelous cook. When her youngest brother stayed with her, they took in turns cooking, she teaching him.

She had a warm personality and enjoyed her many nieces and nephews, who had great affection for her, assuming the role of grandmother after her own mother died. She was fun to be with, a lively, energetic little lady who took her family completely by surprise when, at nearly sixty, she took up writing. Batsford, a London publishing firm, asked her to write a book on patchwork, since up to then nothing had been published in such depth on the subject in England.

Hexagon Banner | Maker of pieces unknown; assembled by Averil Colby | 1960 (assembly date; pieces created circa late nineteenth or early twentieth century) | 35⅝ × 70¾ inches | Silk, satin, velvet; hand-pieced. This banner was made from 81 hexagons of silk and satin stars joined together by brown velvet lozenges, mounted on a pole with a silk cord for hanging. The hexagons are hand-pieced, and the papers are still intact. The banner is finished on the back with a coarse netting. © *The Quilters' Guild of the British Isles*

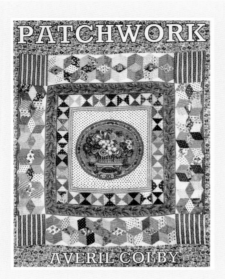

Patchwork by Averil Colby was published in 1958 and was an early book on the quilts of Great Britain and Canada.

Averil Colby meets Queen Elizabeth, the Queen Mother. The date and place of this encounter is unknown. *Courtesy of Richard Colby and the Quilters' Guild of the British Isles*

A tireless researcher, she traveled throughout the country looking for material for her books. Her first book, *Patchwork*, published in 1958, described the early history of quilts. The use of all the geometric shapes, other patterns, and different techniques of appliqué are discussed, as well as the importance of design and color placement in quilts. A chapter is given to finishing, in which she points out that "however well the patchwork is executed, the whole can be spoilt by a bad finish." The illustrations of quilts dating back to 1708 were gathered from museums and private individuals. Since its publication, *Patchwork* has been reprinted many times.

Four other books by Averil Colby followed: *Samplers* (1964), *Patchwork Quilts* (1965), *Quilting* (1971), and *Pincushions* (1975). *Patchwork Quilts* included detailed documentation of thirty-three quilts, describing their origins and characteristics, with instructions. A reviewer of *Patchwork Quilts* in a British newspaper called Averil "a Virtuoso of Patchwork" and "Britain's main authority," but "the odd thing is that once she could not sew, and even now she seems surprised by her own knowledge and finds it rather funny: 'I'm really only a farmer, you see.'"

It is in her book on pincushions that her sense of humor is best shown. Her brother remembered, "She liked to sit in the evening, never still, always working at something and often suddenly a pincushion would materialize from scraps of fabric that were to hand." Quite often, departing guests would be presented with a pincushion that had been made while they sat and chatted.

Averil Colby was a meticulous worker and abhorred slovenly work. Although she maintained that she could not sew before she

Averil Colby paper-pieced the six 1-inch hexagons and the two tiny ⅜-inch hexagons in the center. On the right, we see the back of the same hexagons, showing the basting stitches. *Collection of the Quilters Hall of Fame*

became hooked on quilts, excellence in needlework was part of a girl's education in the days of her youth. Feeling that quilting is a craft demanding greater needle skills than she possessed, she never became a quilter. Her work, usually without batting, employed only a little quilting around some of the blocks to unite the two layers and invariably relied on discreet knotting.

She was emphatic that quilts were for use and should always be washable. Equally emphatically, the right fabric for the job was of great importance to her. The contents of her scrap bag spanned nearly two hundred years, so that when she was asked to dress a nineteenth-century doll's bed, she could use a fabric of the appropriate date and suitable small design.

Rosettes, swags, trails, and wreaths of flowers, all executed in hexagons, some as small as one-half inch across, are the hallmark of Averil Colby's patchwork. Background also played a great part in her quilts. Instead of using a plain white background, she cut hexagons from a wide variety of white fabrics, such as dimities, piques, twills, and sateens, to construct the background. This gave the finished quilt a vivacity and richness that was both subtle and extremely pleasing.

She might have remained an unknown enthusiast but for Muriel Rose, the Craft Officer to the British Council, who borrowed some of Averil's work for an exhibition of English needlework to travel abroad. As well as promoting the work of leading craftsmen and craftswomen, Muriel Rose was instrumental in revitalizing patchwork and quilting in Wales. Orders were taken at her shop in London and passed through the Rural Industries Bureau to the Welsh quiltmakers. It is thought that Averil executed designs for several of these orders.

She was a frequent visitor to the American Museum in Britain at Bath, to evaluate quilts new to the museum's collection or to research quilts for one of her books. Honoree Shiela Betterton, until recently the Keeper of Textiles at the museum, was Averil's friend for many years.

Averil Colby remained a faithful member of the Women's Institute, working diligently at local and district levels to promote patchwork and quilting crafts. From 1956 to 1961, she was chairman of the Handicrafts Committee, where she arranged classes and organized exhibitions on a national scale. With her substantial designing ability and very high standard of execution skills, she made an excellent judge.

In 1979, Averil Colby was named the first honorary member of the Quilters' Guild of the British Isles and was inducted into the Quilters Hall of Fame in 1980. She kept the engraved box she had received when inducted on a table beside her favorite chair, with her cat, Hobo, a onetime stray who had somehow lost his tail, sitting nearby. She died just three weeks short of her eighty-third birthday, on January 5, 1983.

Blue Diamond Honeycomb Coverlet | Designed by Averil Colby, pieced by many hands | 1959 | 84 × 106 inches | Cottons; lined with white calico and tied. This quilt is pictured and described in Averil Colby's *Patchwork Quilts*: "The coverlet was made in the traditional manner by a number of workers, from the Somerset villages of Broadway and Horton, each being responsible for sections made in their homes—the double rosettes, small triangular units, and strips of white and dark blue pieces, were so prepared . . . the edges are finished with a red covered piping cord." © *The Quilters' Guild of the British Isles*

Selected Reading

Colby, Averil. *Patchwork*. London: Batsford, 1958.

———. *Patchwork Quilts*. London: Batsford, and New York: Charles Scribner's Sons, 1965.

———. *Quilting*. New York: Charles Scribner's Sons, 1971. London: Batsford, 1972.

———. *Samplers*. London: Batsford, 1964.

———. "Two Early Nineteenth-Century Bedspreads." *America in Britain* Bath, England: American Museum in Britain, 1969.

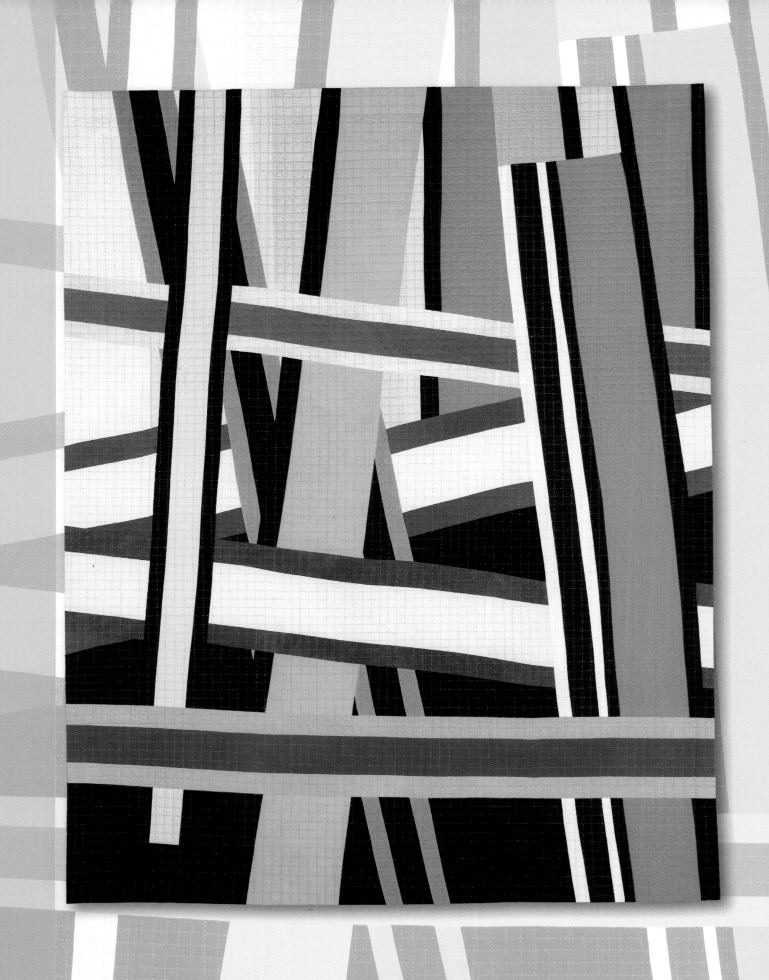

Nancy Crow

"No time to waste.

Just feel the joy and liberation!

Become one with the fabric; feel its rhythms;

understand the medium! Everything leads to freedom!"

—Nancy Crow, *Improvisational Quilts* (1995), p. 3

Nancy Crow was inducted into the Quilters Hall of Fame in Marion, Indiana, on July 11, 1997. *Photo by Nathaniel Stitzlein, courtesy of Nancy Crow*

by Amy Korn and Vickie Douglas

FEW HAVE ACHIEVED THE SUCCESS that Nancy Crow has in the art world. Her graphic, linear quilts are highly desired by museums and private collectors. "I create my own work," says Nancy, "including designing, dyeing, cutting, arranging, and machine piecing."

As an artist, Nancy is a risk taker, always on the edge, never working with a safety net. She produces quilts of stunning originality, with an explosive use of color that is visually demanding and interactive. Nancy began dyeing her own cloth in the late 1980s to achieve the full range of color not readily available in traditionally manufactured fabrics. Working in her studio, she mixes and dyes and achieves her personal interpretation of the richness of color for which her quilts are known.

Nancy's studio, added as a wing to her farmhouse, is an artist's dream. Light spills from multiple windows and, on every available surface, thousands of yards of hand-dyed fabric wait for inclusion in future quilts. Nancy prefers to "work on the wall" without patterns or templates, making many compositions in a series to help focus and refine her ideas. Her goal is to create ten new pieces a year to be hand quilted by several women she employs. She is constantly charged with new ideas, only lacking sufficient time to execute them all.

Her designs come from within her subconscious, which acts as her interpreter of life experiences and of her surroundings.

Nancy says, "My quilt compositions result from how I perceive my reality." Her graphic interpretation of nature depicts design elements from the plowed furrows of the fields, the branches of her favorite crab apple trees, and their timber-frame barn remodeling projects.

Born in Loudonville, Ohio, Nancy was the youngest of eight children. She describes her family as "stoic, straightforward, and direct." Her parents encouraged a love of nature in their children, as well as a respect for the value of a liberal arts education. In 1965, Nancy earned a B.F.A. in ceramics at Ohio State University, and she finished the three-year M.F.A. program with a major in ceramics and a minor in tapestry weaving. She is married to John Stitzlein; they are the parents of two sons, Nathaniel and Matthew.

As a mother, Nancy believes strongly that "a person shouldn't have to give up what she loves in order to raise children." She has instilled in both her sons a love of the arts as well as an appreciation of the multiple roles women play. As a result, both her sons have degrees in fine arts. Matthew is a master carpenter and Nathaniel is working as a graphic designer, artist, and sculptor. Her husband and sons were instrumental in erecting the timber frame barns on their farm.

Nancy is a consummate artist working long hours in her studio yet balancing her virtual isolation by teaching workshops nationally and internationally. Nancy exhorts her students to work

Constructions #93: Yes! | 2007 © Nancy Crow | Designed and pieced by Nancy Crow, hand-quilted by Marla Hattabaugh with pattern denoted by Nancy Crow | 37 × 48 inches | 100 percent cottons hand-dyed and machine-pieced by Nancy Crow *Photo by J. Kevin Fitzsimons, courtesy of Nancy Crow*

Constructions #85: Wrestling with Black Thoughts | 2007–2008
© Nancy Crow | Designed and pieced by Nancy Crow, hand-quilted by
Marla Hattabaugh with pattern denoted by Nancy Crow | 78½ × 81½ inches |
100 percent cottons hand-dyed and machine-pieced by Nancy Crow *Photo by
J. Kevin Fitzsimons, courtesy of Nancy Crow*

Nancy continues to reach out to other quilters through her teaching facility, the Crow Timber Frame Barn. In 1997, Nancy's husband and sons moved an 1848 barn onto their ninety-acre farm. A basement and second story were added. By 2000, the barn was fully renovated, ready to offer five-day retreats on many different topics. The Crow Timber Frame Barn is open each year for a month in the spring and another in the fall. Nancy hires other prominent artists to teach alongside her and refers to this venture as the Crow Barn Workshops.

The Barn hosts in-depth workshops in surface design, fabric dyeing, screen printing, composition, machine piecing and other topics, with each student enjoying an individual eight-by-eight-foot design wall and a large worktable.

Constructions #71 | 2003 © Nancy Crow | Designed and pieced
by Nancy Crow, hand-quilted by Marla Hattabaugh with pattern denoted by
Nancy Crow | 37¾ × 65¾ inches | 100 percent cottons hand-dyed and
machine-pieced by Nancy Crow. "It's all about . . . being alone, in solitude, so
one can think and feel deeply without interruption." (Artist's statement, Nancy
Crow's website.) *Photo by J. Kevin Fitzsimons, courtesy of Nancy Crow*

intuitively and improvisationally, and to learn to cut shapes without the use of templates. She shares her love of color by encouraging experimentation with rich gradations of solid hues.

Nancy's contributions to the quilt world are many and varied. In 1979, along with Harriet Anderson, Virginia Randles, Francoise Barnes, and others, Nancy Crow organized the first biennial *Quilt National*, a professional, juried exhibition that promotes contemporary quilts and is held at the Dairy Barn in Athens, Ohio. Nancy also was instrumental in beginning the Art Quilt Network in 1988, the first large organization of professional quilt artists. In 1990, with codirector Linda Fowler, she organized the Quilt/Surface Design Symposium, which offers in-depth workshops for serious quiltmakers and other craftspeople from around the world.

Nancy is the author of six books: *Nancy Crow: Quilts and Influences, Nancy Crow: Work in Transition, Gradations: From the Studio of Nancy Crow, Nancy Crow: Improvisational Quilts, Nancy Crow,* and *Crossroads.* Lavishly illustrated, her books serve as textbooks on her developing focus and style. Two of her quilts have appeared on the covers of Maya Angelou's books. As a commercial fabric designer, Nancy designed fabrics for John Kaldor from 1993 to 1996. From 1996 to 2002, she designed two fabric collections each year for Westwood, Inc., under the name Nancy Crow for Kent Avery.

In 1997, Nancy Morrison Crow was inducted into the Quilters Hall of Fame. In 1996, she was selected for the National Living Treasure Award by the University of North Carolina (Wilmington) Museum of World Cultures for excellence in a traditional handcraft, and in 1999, she was named a Fellow of the American Craft Council. The Ohio Arts Council has awarded her many fellowships, including a grant for travel in China in 1990 and 1991 as an exchange artist.

Her quilts have been exhibited throughout the United States and worldwide—in South Korea, Japan, Germany, Finland, Ireland, England, France, New Zealand, and South Africa. In 1995, she was the first quiltmaker to be featured in a one-person show at the Renwick Gallery of the Smithsonian Institution. In 2002, her work was included in the exhibit *Six Continents of Quilts* at the Museum of Art and Design in New York City.

Nancy's quilts form part of many corporate and museum collections, including the Renwick Gallery, Smithsonian Institution; the American Museum of Folk Art and the Museum of

Nancy Crow led a tour of the exhibit *Nancy Crow: A Retrospective* at the Marion Public Library and Museum on July 11, 1997, celebrating her induction into the Quilters Hall of Fame. *Courtesy of Rosalind W. Perry*

Art and Design in New York City; Miami University Art Museum in Oxford, Ohio; and the Indianapolis Museum of Art. Two of her quilts, *March Study* and *Double Mexican Wedding Rings #4*, were selected for the Houston Quilt Festival's major exhibit, *America's 100 Best Quilts of the 20th Century* in 1999.

As artist, designer, curator, organizer, and teacher, Nancy has dedicated her life and her talents to establishing quilting as a recognized art form. With creative energy and tenacious determination, she has forced her quilts to be examined with new eyes—not as merely warm bed coverings, but as works of art.

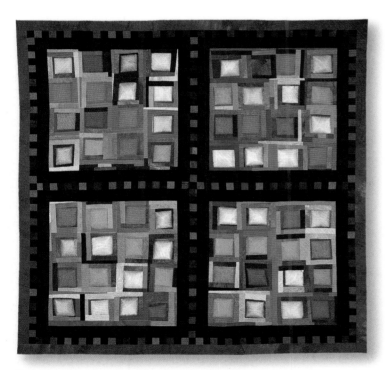

Color Blocks #17 | 1991–1992 © Nancy Crow | Designed and pieced by Nancy Crow and hand-quilted by Brenda Stultz | 71½ × 71½ inches | Cottons hand-dyed by Nancy Crow and Lunn Fabrics. "When I work on a quilt, I put away all thoughts that are not helpful and channel my energies towards relaxing and becoming one with my fabrics. . . . I love being inside my brain and pushing myself to think in ever more complex ways because I know the ideas are there for the taking. . . . I love the work, the experience of making each quilt. It's my life, my life's work!" (Artist's statement, Nancy Crow's website.) *Photo by J. Kevin Fitzsimons, courtesy of Nancy Crow*

Selected Reading

Crow, Nancy. *Crossroads: Nancy Crow*. Elmhurst, IL: Breckling Press Publishers, 2007.

————. *Gradations: From the Studio of Nancy Crow*. Saddle Brook, NJ: Quilt House Publishing, 1995.

————. *Nancy Crow*. Elmhurst, IL: Breckling Press Publishers, 2006.

————. *Nancy Crow: Improvisational Quilts*. Lafayette, CA: C&T Publishing, 1995.

————. *Nancy Crow: Quilts and Influences*. Paducah, KY: American Quilter's Society, 1990.

————. *Nancy Crow: Work in Transition*. Paducah, KY: American Quilter's Society, 1992.

William Rush Dunton Jr.

1868–1966

"It is easily understood that a nervous lady who is concentrating on making a quilt block has no time to worry over her fancied physical ill health or even over wrongs or slights which may be real, so that she is cultivating a more healthy mental attitude and habit."

—William Rush Dunton, Jr., *Old Quilts* (1946), pp. 3–4

William Rush Dunton Jr., was inducted into the Quilters Hall of Fame at the Continental Quilting Congress in Arlington, Virginia, on October 27, 1979. *Courtesy of Henry H. Dunton*

by Eileen Jordan

NOTED PSYCHIATRIST AND AUTHOR Dr. William Rush Dunton Jr. possessed an insatiable curiosity, wide-ranging interests, and a delightful sense of humor. He is best known to quilters for his book *Old Quilts*, which he published himself in 1946. The volume, the result of thirty years of research, remains a valuable source of documentation on Maryland and Baltimore Album quilts. Because he had a great respect for history and needlework skills, he encouraged an appreciation of quilts as valuable records of the past and quiltmaking as a worthy activity for the modern woman.

Born in 1868 in Chestnut Hill, Pennsylvania, William Rush Dunton was named for his bachelor uncle, a prominent Philadelphia physician. His parents, Jacob and Annie Gordon Gemmill Dunton, greatly influenced his path through life; his father was a pharmacist and inventor, and his mother had studied at the Philadelphia School of Art Needlework.

Dunton received his higher education at Haverford College, earning a B.S. degree in 1889 and an M.A. in English literature in 1890. After receiving his medical degree from the University of Pennsylvania in 1893, he became engaged to a nurse, Edna Hogan, and moved to Baltimore to join the staff of the Sheppard Asylum (later known as the Sheppard and Enoch Pratt Hospital) as a psychiatrist. He and Edna were married in 1897 and had two sons and a daughter.

Dunton stayed at the hospital for twenty-nine years, eventually becoming the director of occupational therapy. From 1924 to 1939, he was medical director of Harlem Lodge, a private sanitarium near Baltimore. From 1906 to 1942, in addition to his hospital work, he was an instructor in psychiatry at Johns Hopkins University. A great organizer, he founded several professional organizations, including the Maryland Psychiatric Society and the National Society for the Promotion of Occupational Therapy (now the American Occupational Therapy Association). He is often referred to as the "Father of Occupational Therapy."

Dunton's interests were wide and varied. He enjoyed fishing, gardening, singing, and the production of amateur theatricals,

Washington Monument Baltimore Album Quilt | Collected by William Rush Dunton Jr. | Made by Mary Patten Everist (? –1891), Cecil County, Maryland | circa 1847–1850 | 97¾ × 97⅛ inches | Cottons and braid with wool or cotton embroidery threads. This beautiful example of the Baltimore Album style, formerly in the collection of Dr. William Rush Dunton Jr., is made up of thirty-six signed blocks, each measuring thirteen inches square. The fabrics include glazed chintzes and calicoes, as well as cotton moire. The border is reverse appliqué in a feather design, with a central vein of white tape and stitching added. *Courtesy of the Baltimore Museum of Art, gift of Dr. William Rush Dunton Jr. (BMA 1946.159)*

and he also played the drums, guitar, banjo, and piano. In addition to quilts and quilt patterns, he collected matchbook covers, recipes, nonsense rhymes, and stamps. His professional study of mental illness helped to forge his philosophy that everyone should have at least two hobbies to stay healthy—one indoor and one outdoor. His own hobbies were an integral part of his life, enjoyed in times of stress as well as times of relaxation.

Many of Dunton's boyhood interests continued throughout his life, such as his enthusiasm for writing and printing. His first publication was *Aunt Weampie's Recipes*, which he wrote and printed on his own press at age fourteen. He was a prolific author, writing more than 111 books and articles, mainly on medical topics for doctors, nurses, and occupational therapists. From 1911 to 1923, he was editor of the journal *Occupational Therapy and Rehabilitation*, and from 1935 to 1961, he was associate editor of the *American Journal of Psychiatry*. He was still actively adding to and revising his work in his late eighties, gaining him the title of "Maryland's oldest author."

While Dunton didn't sew—except for the occasional button— he was proud of the fact that his mother attended the Philadelphia School of Art Needlework. He donated to the Baltimore Museum of Art a sample of silk diamonds stitched using the English paper-piecing method. He refers to the eighteen- by twenty-two-inch tumbling blocks pattern as the English Tea Box pattern. In his book, Dunton states that his mother made this before 1880 and the revival of quiltmaking that expressed itself "in those horrible silk things called crazy quilts." He states that to his mother's

Dr. William Rush Dunton Jr. at the quilt exhibit he organized in 1916. *Courtesy of the Baltimore Museum of Art: Dunton Archives*

Dr. Dunton's quilt exhibit at Sheppard and Enoch Pratt Hospital, Towson, Maryland, in September 1916. By showing a variety of antique and contemporary quilts, he hoped to encourage his patients to take up quiltmaking. *Courtesy of the Baltimore Museum of Art: Dunton Archives*

credit, she never made one. He credited Marie Webster's book *Quilts: Their Story and How to Make Them*, published in 1915, with sparking his interest in quilts. He believed that cutting and sewing colorful pieces of cloth would distract his patients from their problems. Working on quilts together would be a socializing measure, combating loneliness and fostering happier thoughts.

He supervised the occupational therapy activities of his patients and was known to mark the cutting and sewing lines and teach the construction process. If patients were not interested in keeping the finished quilt, he retained it for use on hospital beds at Harlem Lodge. He also felt every quilt should be signed and dated because "it will increase the value of the quilt in future years" and "it is a work of art, perhaps not of high order, akin to peasant art, but may represent the fashion of the time or the cravings of the maker" ("Quiltmaking As a Socializing Measure," 1937).

Dunton collected quilt patterns for his patients and organized a quilt exhibit at the hospital in 1916, which included several quilts loaned by Marie Webster. The exhibit was successful in motivating the patients, but it was Dr. Dunton who was most dramatically affected, for this experience launched his lifelong interest in quilt

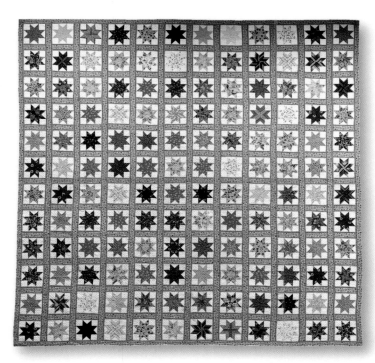

LeMoyne Star | Collected by William Rush Dunton Jr. | Made by Rachel Balderston (1812–1889), Baltimore, Maryland | c. 1825–1830 | 106 × 108 inches | Cotton. Included in an exhibition at the Baltimore Museum of Art held in the 1970s, this quilt was described as follows: "Each of the 144 stars is made from varicolored cotton diamonds, pieced together to form an eight-pointed or Le Moyne Star. . . . Materials used are cotton roller prints, English chintzes, and Indian calicoes. The border and bands separating the star motifs are of a dull rose, printed cotton twill. Quilts of this very large size were made to cover and to extend over the sides of high feather beds." Museum records indicate that Dr. Dunton and his wife, Edna, purchased this quilt in 1932 from Wilton Snowden Surrat, who was given the quilt by Emma Dukehart. *Courtesy of the Baltimore Museum of Art, gift of Dr. William Rush Dunton Jr. (BMA 1947.43)*

study. Later, he curated three quilt shows at the Baltimore Museum of Art, including one in 1944, which focused on his particular interest, Baltimore Album Quilts.

Whenever Dunton located a quilt of historical value, he would borrow it from the owner, make a sketch of the pattern, record details of its history and construction, and have it photographed by his son, Henry, an expert photographer. He amassed a collection of 500 photographs and more than 1,000 sketches. He was aware that quilt owners might be misinformed by family stories handed down. In his effort to accurately date quilts, he also researched indelible inks and calico printing, and corresponded and visited with quilt authorities like Quilters Hall of Fame honorees Lenice Bacon, Ruby McKim, Florence Peto, and Marie Webster.

Based on this extensive research, his book *Old Quilts* was a study of evolving quilt styles of the 1800s, especially the elaborate album quilts. The most significant aspects of the book are its historical documentation of quilts made in Maryland and its 125 photographs. The book also included information about the history of textile weaving and printing, local and social history, inventions and genealogy.

Dunton was not successful in locating a publisher for *Old Quilts* and finally published it himself in 1946. However, the book's sales proved disappointing, and he ended up losing $3,000 on the project. Today, the book is extremely rare and highly sought after by collectors.

A 1956 *Baltimore Sun* article described eighty-eight-year-old Dr. Dunton as "a short, lively, white-topped man whose appetite for dealings with the world remains undulled by the years, rues his book's adventures, and wishes similar projects a more prosperous outcome."

He did not regret his decision to publish *Old Quilts*, but because it was not a financial success, his two other quilt manuscripts, *A Dictionary of Quilt Names and Patterns* and *Pieced Quilts*, have never been published, but remain in the Dunton Archives of the Baltimore Museum of Art, along with his scrapbooks, patterns, photographs, and correspondence. He also donated several quilts that he collected to the museum.

Dr. William Rush Dunton Jr., has been honored for both his professional achievements and his quilt research. In 1957, he was given the Award of Merit by the American Occupational Therapy Association, and in 1979, he was among the first to be inducted into the Quilters Hall of Fame.

Dunton's pioneering quilt studies have had a lasting and very important influence. He generously shared the results of his research, contributing to a wider appreciation of quilts, their history, and their artistic qualities. With the recent heightened interest in quilt pattern history and Baltimore Album quilts, his contributions are even more highly valued today.

Selected Reading

Dunton, William Rush, Jr. "Chintz Work." *Occupational Therapy and Rehabilitation* 25 (February 1946): 14.

———. "How I Got That Way." *Occupational Therapy and Rehabilitation* 22 (October 1943): 244.

———. *Old Quilts*. Catonsville, MD: William Rush Dunton Jr., 1946.

———. "Quiltmaking as a Socializing Measure." *Occupational Therapy and Rehabilitation* 16 (August 1937): 275–78.

Dunton, William Rush, Jr., and Edna Dunton. "Quilts and Quilting." *Occupational Therapy and Rehabilitation* 9 (June 1930): 159–72.

Amy Emms, M.B.E.

1904–1998

"Now all you need for quilting is plenty of time; take things easy,
kind of relax, sit comfortably and no worrying
or else you will make a big stitch or maybe prick your finger
until it bleeds. Of course you are not a 'Quilter'
until you have some sore fingers and especially a sore thumb."

—Amy Emms, M.B.E., *Patchwork and Quilting*, Winter 1986

Amy Emms was inducted into the Quilters
Hall of Fame in Marion, Indiana, on July 19,
1992. *Courtesy of Newsquest North East*

by Dorothy Osler

IN A LIFETIME that almost spanned the twentieth century, Amy Emms made quilts for nearly eighty years. That is a rare and astonishing statistic, but her quilting lifetime should be measured not only in years, but also in the cultural shifts that it spanned. What began within an oral, largely insular, regional tradition, little known beyond the confines of northeast England, has ended with an assured place for a much-loved figure within the world of quilting.

Amy Emms described herself as a Durham quilter: She made whole cloth quilts using the pattern library and characteristic pattern set that came to be known as "Durham quilting." This particular style grew, within the County of Durham, out of the broader tradition of quiltmaking in northern England in the nineteenth and early twentieth centuries, a tradition characterized by the quality of the quilted surface stitchery rather than intricate piecing or appliqué. Mrs. Emms, as she was affectionately known, reflecting the old-world courtesies of her generation and place, became the supreme practitioner of the craft in the second half of the twentieth century.

Her whole cloth quilts, in satin or occasionally silk, with their characteristic centers of "scissors" patterns, "Durham feathers" and "feather twist" borders forming the pattern set that can be regarded as her signature, are now prized pieces in public and private collections. If the pattern library seems limited, the symmetrical arrangements and swirling feathers are testimony to a quilt designer of skill, experience, and confidence who recognized at a young age that she had a particular talent. "We all have a gift of some kind, and mine is quilting," she said.

Amy Emms (née Harrison) was born in 1904 to a mother widowed just before her birth. Like many women in northeast England at that time who found themselves in difficult circumstances, Amy's mother drew upon her skills to increase family income by making quilts for local customers, who paid a small sum on a weekly basis. Many of the whole cloth and "strippy" (Bars) quilts used throughout northeast England in the early years of the twentieth century were produced in just this way. So young Amy grew up in a household where quilting was

A hand-quilted ivory silk cushion by Amy Emms. © *Jacqui Hurst/Alamy*

Quilting the design on this Amy Emms cushion. © Jacqui Hurst/Alamy

the onset of World War II. But the war years were not kind to Amy; her husband had to leave home and join the forces, her mother died in 1940, her eldest child, George, was evacuated, and the family home was destroyed in 1943 by a land mine.

It was in the war years, however, that Amy joined the British Legion, an important step, for the legion encouraged fund-raising and community activities. Soon Amy was leading a quilting group. Annual exhibitions in Sunderland followed, with numerous prizes for quilts and cushions. This led to further evening class teaching, which continued right through the 1950s—a period when quiltmaking of any kind reached a low point in Britain as a whole. It can truly be said that the tradition of Durham quilting was kept alive by Amy Emms and a handful of other quilters in those years.

The evening classes established just after the war continued until 1967, when Amy's husband retired and they left Sunderland to live in a cottage in the country—in the Weardale village of St John's Chapel, in the heart of a region with a strong quiltmaking tradition.

For Amy, encouragement to teach and show her work now came from the Women's Institute and from the North of England Open Air Museum (now renamed Beamish Museum) established in the 1970s. When the revival of quilting in Britain, from the

an everyday activity and quilting frames an ever-present feature: "Frames were like furniture in our house." At seven years of age, she began threading needles; by fourteen she was helping her mother to quilt: "I loved it, for while we both sat quilting, Mother would tell me about her early life and how they quilted at night because there was no entertainment."

Once she left school, Amy's life followed the conventional route of office job and eventual marriage at the age of twenty to Albert Emms, a glassmaker. They set up home with her mother in the house just outside Sunderland, so the mother-and-daughter quiltmaking activities continued despite Amy's motherhood and

Amy Emms' Story of Durham Quilting by Amy Emms focused on the quilts of the Durham area, which was known for its wholecloth quilts.

Amy Emms at her quilting frame.

Wholecloth Quilt (detail) | Made by Amy Emms | 1982 |
43 × 58 inches. This wall hanging was commissioned by the Quilters' Guild of the British Isles and made by Amy Emms, who presented it to Deirdre Amsden in May 1982 to commemorate the end of her term as the guild's first president. It is densely quilted with some of Amy's favorite designs: a large eight-petal rosette in the center, with a feather twist border. *Courtesy of the Bowes Museum, County Durham, England, Collection of Deirdre Amsden*

Selected Reading

"Amy Emms, M.B.E.: A Durham Quilter for 80 Years." *Patchwork and Quilting*, June/July 1997.

"Amy Emms." *Patchwork Quilt Tsushin*, no. 70 (1996).

Emms, Amy, M.B.E. *Amy Emms' Story of Durham Quilting.* Edited by Pam Dawson. Tunbridge Wells, England: Search Press, 1990.

Osler, Dorothy. "A Medal for Her Services to Quilting." *Quilter's Newsletter Magazine*, no. 359 (January/February 2004): 27–29.

———. *North Country Quilts: Legend and Living Tradition.* Barnard Castle, Co. Durham, England: Bowes Museum and Friends of Bowes Museum, 2000.

her quilts that were admired—her pen was praised, too. Amy became a regular and popular contributor to the letters page of the Quilters' Guild magazine, her prose revealing the endearing personality that subsequently captivated audiences at the many quilt shows and exhibitions she was later to attend.

In the late 1970s, Amy Emms began teaching in the Shipley Art Gallery in Gateshead. This particular gallery was establishing its reputation as a leading craft gallery, encouraging both contemporary and traditional crafts. Here, she encountered a new audience of dedicated quilters, eager for knowledge and skill, but also questioning traditional methods. Rising to the challenge, she embraced the new book-learning approach and wrote *Amy Emms' Story of Durham Quilting*, published in 1990 when she was eighty-six years of age. It fulfilled a long-held ambition.

Amy Emms also received a singular honor, of which she was extremely proud. In 1984, she was appointed a Member of the British Empire (M.B.E.) by Queen Elizabeth for her "services to quilting." It was a fitting award for someone who had become a legend in Britain in her lifetime. She was inducted into the Quilters Hall of Fame in 1992.

In a letter published in the spring 1984 issue of the newsletter of the Quilters' Guild of the British Isles, she expressed her devotion to her art: "I have been thinking of retiring from quilting being as I am reaching a good age, but they want me to continue a bit longer. But as for quilting at home or giving any information about it, I shall never give that up. As I tell people it is in the blood, and it is the quilting that keeps me young and keeps me going."

Amy never stopped making quilts or educating others about quilting. In 1998, just a month before her death at the age of ninety-four, she spoke to a group at a quilt show, winning over her audience, as ever, with her humor, dignity, knowledge, and skill.

1970s onward, began as a follow-up to the American revival, it was not long before Amy came to the fore as an established quilter brought up within the oral tradition of a distinctive regional style of quilting and destined to be the last from that lineage.

Her quilting skill and pattern drafting within this tradition were much admired when her work was given a wider platform through exhibitions arranged and promoted by such organizations as the British Crafts Council and the newly established Quilters' Guild of the British Isles in the early 1980s. And it was not only

Ruth Finley

1884–1955

"Yet there is a living reason
for all that human fingers create. . . .
Quilt names tell the story
of both the inner and outer life
of many generations of American womanhood."

—Ruth Finley, *Old Patchwork Quilts and the Women Who Made Them* (1929), pp. 7–8

Ruth Ebright Finley was inducted into the Quilters Hall of Fame at the Continental Quilting Congress in Arlington, Virginia, on October 27, 1979. *Courtesy of William and Margaret Dague*

by Virginia Amling

RUTH FINLEY secured her reputation as a recognized authority in the quilt world with the 1929 publication of her book *Old Patchwork Quilts and the Women Who Made Them*. To the present day, this work is a popular resource for authors and quilt researchers, due largely to its detailed descriptions and pattern diagrams, along with nearly one hundred photographs of quilts and fabrics. Its folksy narrative style gives it a personal appeal.

Ruth was born September 25, 1884, into the socially prominent and well-educated Ebright family of Akron, Ohio. Her father was Dr. Leonidas S. Ebright, a physician who served at various times as surgeon general of Ohio, a state representative, and Akron's postmaster. Her mother, Julia Bissell Ebright, was a graduate of Oberlin College, the first American college to grant degrees to women. Julia's family, with seventeenth-century roots in Connecticut, had two state governors in its lineage.

Ruth used her background advantages as an embarkation point for her own intellectual pursuits and creative undertakings. Lovina May Knight, a family friend of the Ebrights, described Ruth as a young woman who possessed an attractive combination of good health, strength, and femininity, with a perceptive wit and a sense of fun.

In 1902, Ruth enrolled for one semester at Oberlin College in Oberlin, Ohio, and then transferred to Buchtel College (later the University of Akron), where she completed only two terms. Instead of finishing her formal education, she spent a year touring the western United States, writing stories and poems as she traveled.

Her journalistic career began in August 1907, when she accepted a job as cub reporter with the *Akron Beacon-Journal*. She rose through the ranks as society editor, music critic, and special interviewer, earning her first byline when she secured a rare interview with Mrs. Henry Ford. By the time she left the newspaper in 1910, she had become editor of its women's page.

She then moved to Cleveland for a job as feature writer for the *Cleveland Press*. In 1910, her career began to blossom when she assumed the pen name of "Ann Addams" and went undercover to report on the harsh working conditions of women in factories

Liberty Medallion Quilt | **Made by Elizabeth Hobbs Keckley (1818–1907), Washington, D.C.** | **Circa 1870** | **85½ × 85½ inches** | **Silks; pieced, appliquéd, and embroidered.** This quilt was in the collection of Ruth Finley. The maker, Elizabeth Keckley, a former slave, was both dressmaker and confidante of President Abraham Lincoln's wife, Mary Todd Lincoln. The quilt is believed to have been made from fabric used in dresses worn by Mrs. Lincoln. According to Ruth Finley, the quilt was "a personal gift from Mrs. Keckley to Mrs. Lincoln, who used it as a counterpane on her bed at the White House." *Kent State University Museum, gift of Ross Trump in memory of his mother, Helen Watts Trump (1994.79.1); photo courtesy of the University Archives and Records Center, University of Louisville, Louisville, Kentucky*

Roosevelt Rose, designed by Ruth Finley, was illustrated in *Good Housekeeping*, January 1934. *Courtesy of Merikay Waldvogel*

OLD
PATCHWORK QUILTS
AND
THE WOMEN WHO MADE THEM
RUTH E. FINLEY

Old Patchwork Quilts and the Women Who Made Them by Ruth Finley was one of a few books on quilts written during the first half of the twentieth century in the United States.

and households. During this time, she also wrote poems, fiction serials, and short stories for the paper. She met her future husband, Emmet Finley, also a reporter, while she was doing her investigative writing. They were married August 24, 1910.

Ruth grew up with a knowledge of quilts through her family connections. During her years as a newspaper writer and editor, she began to collect antique quilts. From 1910 to 1919, during the first years of her marriage in Cleveland, and after the couple moved to New York in 1920, she would take little motor vacations along the country roads of Ohio, Pennsylvania, New York, and New England. When certain quilts hanging on a clothesline caught her attention, she stopped at the farmhouse and asked for a drink of water. With that simple entrée, she elicited from the owners the pattern names and stories of the quilts. Ruth sometimes purchased these quilts to add to her growing collection.

Ruth also collected patchwork patterns, making diagrams and identifying each by name. If more than one name was given to the same pattern, she recorded all variants and eventually included in her book the one she thought most appropriate. Her meticulous research continued for several years, culminating in the book that was to bring her lasting fame.

The writing of *Old Patchwork Quilts and the Women Who Made Them* began in 1915 and ended in 1929, a fourteen-year effort. The first quilt book published since Marie Webster's *Quilts: Their Story and How to Make Them* appeared in 1915, it includes information on more than three hundred quilt patterns. Her empathy for the women of the nineteenth century is evident throughout the book.

There is no doubt that this book had a profound influence on quilters and designers of the day, as well as on many who came later. For example, Rose Kretsinger wrote to her asking for a pattern of *The Garden* quilt. When Ruth replied that she had no pattern, Rose designed her own, using only the black-and-white picture in *Old Patchwork Quilts*. Several other excellent quilt makers also made versions of *The Garden*, and three were selected as among *America's 100 Best Quilts of the 20th Century*.

Although not a quilter herself, Ruth did design one particular quilt: the *Roosevelt Rose*, named in honor of President Franklin Delano Roosevelt. In a 1934 article in *Good Housekeeping*, she claimed she was reviving "a peculiar and paramount tradition—the creation and naming of new designs in honor of events political, economic, and social." Photographs and descriptions of the quilt portray it as "a rectangular wreath of fantasy flowers appliquéd in gorgeous bas-relief. A great variety of brilliant calicoes were used for the flowers of the wreath against a background of black sateen. The quilt was lined and corded with lipstick red."

Ruth's husband shared her interest in collecting antiques, but in 1916, the two discovered a heretofore unexplored common bond—a keen interest in the occult. While waiting for a snowstorm to subside, the two began playing with a Ouija board. To their great shock and surprise, the board spelled out messages from a young American soldier who had been killed while fighting with the French Army in Alsace. Although they first reacted with disbelief, they continued the activity through much of 1917, with Emmet hastily jotting down the messages as Ruth received them.

While their public careers flourished, Ruth and Emmet wrote a book, *Our Unseen Guest*, published in 1920 under the pen names "Darby and Joan." They kept this facet of their lives a deep secret in order not to jeopardize their careers or offend their families. Until the cover-up was discovered by Lovina May Knight in 1990, only their publisher and their little group of psychic friends shared the knowledge of their true identities.

Ruth also received messages from "the other side" from her friend Betty, wife of Stewart Edward White. Stewart wrote a book called *The Unobstructed Universe* in 1940, based on these communications. Following Stewart's death, the Finleys started writing *Content of Consciousness*, based on messages from Stewart. Emmet became ill and died in 1950, leaving this book unfinished.

Ruth Finley's last known writing was the start of her autobiography. Fourteen typewritten pages, with penciled margin notes, are all that remain of this attempt. After a lingering illness, Ruth died in Glen Cove, Long Island, New York, on September 24, 1955, the day before her seventy-first birthday. In 1979, Ruth Finley was among the first group to be inducted into the Quilters Hall of Fame.

An early feminist, Ruth Finley promoted quilting as women's folk art. Through her personal contacts with the quilters and their stories, she recognized the importance of the art of quilting in the lives of American women. In honoring quilters past, Ruth created a work of lasting value. The patchwork quilts that she thoroughly researched and meticulously described have provided valuable historical information for generations of quiltmakers and researchers. The frequency with which she is cited in recent publications reveals the depth of respect still felt for her in the quilt world.

Ruth Ebright Finley. *Courtesy of William and Margaret Dague*

Selected Reading

Brackman, Barbara. "*Old Patchwork Quilts* and the Woman Who Wrote It: Ruth E. Finley." *Quilter's Newsletter Magazine*, no. 207 (November/December 1988): 36–38.

Clark, Ricky. "Ruth Finley and the Colonial Revival Era." *Uncoverings 1995*. Edited by Virginia Gunn. San Francisco: The American Quilt Study Group, 1995, 33–66.

Finley, Ruth E. *The Lady of Godey's: Sarah Josepha Hale*. Philadelphia: J.B. Lippincott, 1931.

———. *Old Patchwork Quilts and the Women Who Made Them*. Philadelphia: J.B. Lippincott, 1929. Reprint, with introduction by Barbara Brackman, McLean, VA: EPM Publications, 1992.

———. "Patchwork Quilts." *House and Garden*, February 1943, 61–63.

———. "The Roosevelt Rose—A New Historical Quilt Pattern." *Good Housekeeping*, January 1934, 54–56, 100.

Sally Garoutte

1925–1989

"Historical research never ends.
We come to an understanding of our history
only through small steps continually taken. . . .
There is much yet to uncover."

—Sally Garoutte, *Uncoverings 1981*, foreword

Sally Jeter Garoutte was inducted into the
Quilters Hall of Fame in Marion, Indiana,
on July 16, 1994. *Courtesy of the American
Quilt Study Group*

by Robin L. Rushbrook, Ph.D.

IN 1979, SALLY GAROUTTE printed a saying on a cloth block for her friend, Jean Ray Laury: "Who knows what bird will peck at the seed you drop?" Just one year later, Sally was the driving force in organizing the first seminar of the American Quilt Study Group (AQSG). The seed that Sally dropped in 1980 has blossomed into a strong and influential nonprofit organization, the leader in supporting and publishing quilt scholarship. AQSG seminars have continued annually, and the organization is highly regarded for its dedication to quilt research. While Sally had strong hopes for the group's future, one wonders if she could have imagined how firmly this seed would take root.

Sally Jeter Garoutte was an energetic, independent, and accomplished woman. Born to Myrtle and Harry Jeter in Kokomo, Indiana, Sally moved with her family to LaMesa, California, when she was twelve years old. After high school graduation, Sally earned her R.N. degree from the San Diego County Hospital School of Nursing, where she met her future husband, Dr. Bill Garoutte, and they were married in 1948. After the birth of their first child in 1949, they spent Bill's Fulbright Scholarship year in London, England, where Sally studied at the Royal School of Weaving. This was the beginning of her continuing exploration

of textile arts, while raising their four children and pursuing her nursing career. Travel abroad took her to Indonesia in 1956 and to Tokyo in 1963. In 1957, she studied oil painting at the de Young Museum in San Francisco, where twenty-six years later she would lead a discussion on quilt history. In the 1960s, even after she obtained a real estate license and became a community activist involved in Marin County politics, Sally continued her interest in visual arts and took private lessons in stitchery.

Her serious interest in quilts emerged in the early 1970s while she studied silk-screen printing. It was during this period that Sally Garoutte and Joyce Gross founded the Mill Valley Quilt Authority, an organization devoted to the promotion of quilting and the preservation of quilts. In 1972, the Mill Valley Quilt Authority organized a quilt show, *Patch in Time*. This exhibit was a significant event in the West Coast quilt revival of the early 1970s, leading to the collaboration of Joyce and Sally on *Quilters' Journal* and the American Quilt Study Group.

Concurrently, Sally decided to study art and graduated with a B.A. in 1976 from Goddard College, where her senior thesis was on color. She energetically pursued her independent research on quilts and textiles, and traveled across the United States (including

Friends and Relations | Made by Sally Garoutte, Mill Valley, California | 1974 | 74 × 81 inches. A color study, this quilt is composed of seventy-two striped squares, made of folded fabric. The minimal quilting is hidden under the folds. It was published on the cover of *Textile Chemist and Colorist* in March 1978 and is apparently the only quilt, apart from group projects, that Sally ever made. *Courtesy of Kate Garoutte*

Quilt being documented and examined at the first American Quilt Study Group Seminar in 1980. *Courtesy of the American Quilt Study Group*

Hawaii) and Europe, examining quilts and historical documents as well as interviewing quilters and collectors. This investigative style continued throughout Sally's life.

From 1977 to 1982, Sally actively participated in the production of *Quilters' Journal*. With Joyce Gross as editor and publisher, Sally performed the duties of textile editor and contributing editor, writing twenty-one groundbreaking articles for the journal, documenting the lives of individual quilters, and exploring a variety of topics in textile history. She researched subjects such as Turkey red dye, seventeenth-century American textiles, and Hudson Bay blankets. She also wrote an influential analysis of crazy quilt styles.

This cover of *Uncoverings 2006*, the scholarly journal devoted to the publication of quilt history research, features a circa-1850 Polk's Fancy quilt owned by Teri Klaussen and is an example of how the vision of Sally Garoutte continues to be carried forward by the American Quilt Study Group that she founded. *Photo of Polk's Fancy by Michael Cavanagh and Kevin Montague, courtesy of the American Quilt Study Group and Teri Klassen*

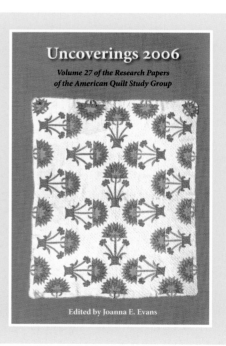

Uncoverings 2006

Volume 27 of the Research Papers of the American Quilt Study Group

Edited by Joanna E. Evans

With so much time devoted to research, writing, and organizational duties, Sally had little time for quilting. In fact, when asked why she took up quilting, she responded, "Can't understand it! Don't like to sew." The only example of her quiltmaking is *Friends and Relations*, made in 1974, which appeared on the cover of *Textile Chemist and Colorist* in 1978. Nevertheless, Sally was a self-proclaimed "fabric freak" with a large fabric collection. Her good friend and colleague Laurel Horton incorporated some of this fabric into several quilts after Sally's death.

From the early 1980s until her death in 1989, Sally Garoutte devoted herself to the development of the American Quilt Study Group and was the guiding force behind that organization. In November 1980, fifty people, whom she regarded as co-organizers, attended that first seminar in Mill Valley, California. Given the strong interest shown, a nonprofit organization with a board of directors was formed, and annual seminars have been held ever since. Sally also edited the seminar papers for the first seven volumes of *Uncoverings*, which is published annually by AQSG.

The American Quilt Study Group provided Sally with the opportunity to combine her talent for leadership, her need for creative expression, and her powerful hunger for historical truths. Directing the group eventually usurped most of Sally's time and, quite literally, most of her home. Initially, Sally's dining room was the location of the AQSG library, seminar presenters were housed with the Garoutte family, and Sally attended to the organization's bookkeeping, correspondence, and publication duties. In addition, she presented four research papers at various seminars on Marseilles quilts, Hawaiian quilts, early colonial quilts, and California's early quilting traditions.

By 1987, AQSG had outgrown the Garouttes' dining room, so the headquarters was moved to San Francisco, but the library remained in their home. Upon Sally's death, her library, textile collection, and quilt ephemera were bequeathed to the American Quilt Study Group, whose seminars continue to expand the knowledge of the history and social context of quilts and textiles. Her books are now in the Sally Garoutte Core Collection of the Archives/Special Collections of the University of Nebraska–Lincoln.

In addition to her work establishing AQSG, she served as a consultant to various quilt projects, such as the Kentucky Heritage Quilt Search and the California Heritage Quilt Project, as well as to Ferrero Films for the company's 1985 production *Hearts and Hands*.

Sally Garoutte's motivation came from her strong desire to discover and share the truth about textile history, an important aspect of women's history. In her foreword to the 1983 volume of *Uncoverings*, she wrote:

> Aristotle observed that "the statements of history are singulars," whereas those of poetry are universals. It is exactly those "singulars" of history that the individual researcher goes out to find. The small and singular bits of the record—carefully gathered from wherever time has scattered them, meticulously inspected for authenticity, and willingly offered for public sharing—will in due time fill those massive gaps in our understanding of the lives of women and the nature of their arts.
>
> As is true for all historians, quilt historians find their subjects from some individual and personal urge deep inside themselves. Often they do not even know what led them to a particular investigation.

Clearly, the desire to document women's arts and a personal urge, whose origin may have been a mystery even to herself, moved Sally Garoutte to devote her heart and intellect to quilt scholarship. In the American Quilt Study Group, Sally left behind a vigorous organization that allows others to continue that work. In recognition of her achievements and influence, she was inducted into the Quilters Hall of Fame in 1994.

A silk-screened repeat designed by Sally Garoutte, circa 1960–1979. This is a reflection of Sally's artistic talents, which were expressed in other textile mediums in addition to the quilt she made. *Courtesy of Bets Ramsey*

The American Quilt Study Group Seminar, 1986, at the Santa Sabina Center in San Rafael, California. Front row: Lucy Hilty, Sally Garoutte, Virginia Gunn. Middle row: Julie Silber, Cuesta Benberry, Flavin Glover, Barbara Brackman. Back row: Sandy Metzler, Bets Ramsey, Dorothy Cozart. *Courtesy of the American Quilt Study Group*

Selected Reading

Garoutte, Sally. "California's First Quilting Party." *Uncoverings 1981*. Mill Valley, CA: American Quilt Study Group, 1982.

———. "Doing Research—Part I." *Quilters' Journal* 2, no. 3 (Fall 1979).

———. "Early Colonial Quilts in a Bedding Context." *Uncoverings 1980*. Mill Valley, CA: American Quilt Study Group, 1981.

———. "The Elusive English Quilt." *Quilter's Newsletter*, no. 50 (December 1973).

———. "Seminole Patchwork." *Quilter's Newsletter*, no. 58 (August 1974).

———. "Turkey Red Dye." *Quilters' Journal* 1, no. 2 (Winter 1977).

———. "Types of Crazy Patch." *Quilters' Journal* 1, no. 6 (Winter 1978).

———. "Uses of Textiles in Hawaii, 1820–1850." *Uncoverings 1985*. Mill Valley, CA: American Quilt Study Group, 1986.

Garoutte, Sally, ed. *Uncoverings: The Research Papers of American Quilt Study Group*. Vols. 1–7 (1980–1986). Mill Valley, CA: American Quilt Study Group, 1981–1987.

Horton, Laurel, and Sally Garoutte, eds. *Uncoverings 1987*. Vol. 8. Mill Valley, CA: American Quilt Study Group, 1988.

Joyce Gross

"*We hope to encourage as many people as possible to get into the act, because there is so much to do in researching and recording. . . . When your story is published, it can be appreciated by and shared by all of us now, and will become part of the quilt story for future generations.*"

—Joyce Gross, *Quilters' Journal*, vol. 1, no. 2 (Winter 1977)

Joyce Gross was inducted into the Quilters Hall of Fame in Marion, Indiana, on July 20, 1996. *Courtesy of Vicki Chase Photography*

by Kathlyn Ronsheimer
with assistance from Nancy Bavor

JOYCE RICHARDSON GROSS is known as a quilt researcher; teacher; lecturer; editor; publisher; collector of quilts, books, and ephemera; curator; and most recently as a quilt "legend." In 1969, when she first became involved with quilts, she brought to that endeavor the vision, enthusiasm, and drive that she had displayed throughout her life as a student activist, boutique owner, school board member, and political campaign manager. As a result of these traits, the history of quilts and the lives of many early twentieth-century quiltmakers have been preserved for others to study and enjoy.

Born in Alameda, California, Joyce graduated with a B.A. in History from the University of California at Berkeley, where she was the first woman manager of the student newspaper. In 1947, she married Edmond Gross, a commercial artist, and they had three children. She also worked for Wells Fargo Bank, managing their magazine and creating historical window displays, which proved to be good preparation for her future work as editor, publisher, and exhibit curator.

How did Joyce become so interested in quilts? She has an early recollection of buying ten cents' worth of blue percale at J. C. Penney's for her grandmother, who was piecing a quilt. Later, while visiting the historic houses and inns of Boston in 1945, antique quilts caught her attention, and she even inherited some family quilts. However, her entry into the world of quilts was one of those events that some people simply call fate.

In 1969, a group of four women in Mill Valley, California, including Joyce and Sally Garoutte (the Quilters Hall of Fame 1994 honoree), frequently worked together on important local school and civic issues. During their weekly meetings, they decided to make an embroidered quilt as a fund-raiser and greatly enjoyed the friendships that developed around the quilting frame.

This group evolved into the Mill Valley Quilt Authority (MVQA), which would make significant contributions to the nationwide quilting renaissance. Throughout the 1970s, under Joyce's leadership, the MVQA would produce several important exhibitions in California including four landmark *Patch in Time* exhibitions. Joyce developed an artists' series and brought many quiltmakers and quilt historians of note, such as Lenice Bacon, Myron and Patsy Orlofsky, Deborah Kakalia,

Tree of Life | Made by Piné Lorraine Hawkes Eisfeller (1894–1990), New York | 1939 | 92 × 98 inches | Cotton; hand-appliquéd and hand-quilted, inscribed *PLE 1939*. Honoree Joyce Gross collected many outstanding twentieth-century quilts, including other quilts by Piné Eisfeller, *White Magic* and *The Garden*, similar to Rose Kretsinger's *Paradise Garden*. A photograph of a seventeenth-century quilted linen Persian bath carpet in Marie Webster's *Quilts: Their Story and How to Make Them* inspired Piné to create this stunning masterpiece. It won top prizes in the 1942 *Woman's Day* National Needlework contest, appeared on the cover of *American Quilter* (Summer 1997), and was selected as one of *America's 100 Best Quilts of the 20th Century* in 1999. *Courtesy of the Dolph Briscoe Center for American History, University of Texas at Austin, Joyce Gross Collection (W2h001.005.2008)*

Michael James, Nancy Halpern, and Jinny Beyer, to lecture and teach in California. She also organized the first quilt study tours to other parts of the country and developed quilt history study centers at major quilt conferences throughout the United States.

Seeking to learn all she could about quilts, Joyce looked for books and magazines on the subject and soon had acquired *The Romance of the Patchwork Quilt in America* by Carrie A. Hall and Rose G. Kretsinger. From this book, she discovered that Rose Kretsinger's quilts had been given to the Thayer Museum of Art (now the Spencer Museum of Art) at the University of Kansas. When she learned about an upcoming exhibition of the museum's collection, she was on her way.

At the museum in Lawrence, Kansas, she saw quilts hung for the first time. Joyce's own words say it all: "As I rounded the corner, my eyes fell upon a quilt unlike any that I had ever seen. It was Rose Kretsinger's *Paradise Garden* (see page 130) in clear, bright

Yellow Hawaiian Quilt made by Joyce Gross for her grandson, Dylan. *Photo Vicki Chase Photography, courtesy of Joyce Gross*

colors. It was beautifully designed and executed. I had never seen stuffed work and as you may know, it is used most effectively in that quilt. Beside *Paradise Garden* was Kretsinger's *Calendula*. To this day, they are two of my favorite quilts."

From Kansas, Joyce went on to see the quilt collections at the Art Institute of Chicago and the Denver Art Museum. She became intrigued with these wonderful quilts and decided she had to share them with her quilt friends. Joyce asked to have some of the quilts she had viewed sent to California for two exhibitions she was organizing. Both the Denver Art Museum and the University of Kansas agreed to send quilts. They were displayed from June 4 through July 13, 1973, at *The American Quilt* exhibit at the Bank of America World Headquarters building in San Francisco. The curator of art for the corporation wrote in a letter to Joyce, "We estimate that nearly 10,000 people per day passed through our grand plaza to look and marvel at the quilts on exhibit."

Much to Joyce's dismay, when she asked for information about the women who had created these masterpieces, the museums had little information. It seemed unbelievable to her that even such basic facts as their birth dates and birthplaces were unknown. Thus was launched Joyce's fascinating and fruitful search for information about quilts and quiltmakers that continues to this day.

Joyce has often said the telephone is a "favorite friend," and she used it to advantage while searching for information about the quiltmakers. She contacted relatives, friends, and, when possible, the quiltmakers themselves. She interviewed everyone she could identify as being connected with the quiltmaker, and they often shared with her their scrapbooks and correspondence as well as their recollections. Had it not been for her interest at a time when these items were still available, although not always considered meaningful or valuable, this important history might have been lost to researchers forever.

In September 1977, Joyce founded *Quilters' Journal* to provide a vehicle for dissemination of the growing body of research about quilts and quiltmakers. For ten years she served as publisher and editor of the *Journal*, which became an often-quoted source of scholarly quilt research and a standard entry in the bibliographies of other quilt-related articles and books. Through its pages, the histories as well as the quilts of such notable women as Jinny Beyer, Rose Kretsinger, Jean Ray Laury, Florence Peto, Bertha Stenge, Electra Havermeyer Webb, and many others were brought to life.

In November 1980, Sally Garoutte made history by organizing the first quilt research seminar, which launched the American Quilt Study Group (AQSG). Joyce was a founding member with Sally Garoutte and presented a research paper entitled "Four Twentieth Century Quiltmakers" at that first seminar.

Penny Tree | Unknown quiltmaker, Connecticut | Circa 1840–1875 | 69 × 86 inches | Cotton. This is one of sixteen quilts in the Briscoe Center's Joyce Gross Quilt History Collection that Joyce acquired from the family of noted quilt collector and historian Florence Peto (1884–1970). This quilt pattern is often called Foundation Rose and Pine Tree. In all, there are 990 small circles appliquéd in the blocks and border—careful planning and expert needlework are evident in these perfect circles. *Courtesy of the Dolph Briscoe Center for American History at the University of Texas at Austin, Joyce Gross Collection (W2h001.028.2008)*

Joyce is devoted to an event she started in 1981, a quilters' retreat that has come to be known simply and affectionately as Point Bonita. Beginning in about 1985, Joyce started bringing her research files to provide a research room connected to the event. Michael James (the Quilters Hall of Fame 1993 honoree) was one of the early artists in residence. Point Bonita continued under the direction of Joyce Gross until 2001, when Kathlyn Ronsheimer took over. Thirty years after its inception, Point Bonita's popularity within the quilt community remains high, as is evidenced by its long waiting list. Every January, a group of quilters and quilt historians immerse themselves in a weeklong "camp" overlooking beautiful San Francisco Bay. Prizewinning quilts have developed from this experience, as well as quilting careers, research projects, and lifelong friendships. A list of the attendees and artists in residence would create an interesting list of who's who among quiltmakers of the end of the twentieth century and beginning of the twenty-first century. Point Bonita is a true manifestation of Joyce's love for sharing her knowledge and her research collection.

Beginning with the first quilt top she purchased—for three dollars at a flea market—Joyce has been a collector of virtually all things related to quilts. In 1993, she exhibited her collection of quilts and ephemera at the American Museum of Quilts and Textiles in San Jose, California, in the exhibit *A Passion to*

Know: Portrait of a Quilt Scholar, Archivist, Author—Joyce Gross. In 1997, Joyce and her longtime friend and fellow Quilters Hall of Fame honoree Cuesta Benberry organized an exhibit and seminar, *20th Century Quilts 1900–1970: Women Make Their Mark*, at the Museum of the American Quilter's Society, Paducah, Kentucky.

Joyce Gross was on the leading edge of the late twentieth century's quilt revival. Her pioneering work in primary research, writing, and publishing was recognized in 1996, when she was inducted into the Quilters Hall of Fame. When introducing Joyce's keynote speech at the AQSG seminar in 1995, Cuesta Benberry stated, "I have recited some of Joyce's accomplishments in order to answer one question: How did Joyce Gross come to be termed a legendary quilt figure? In short, she did it the old-fashioned way. She earned it!"

Since her induction, Joyce has continued to add to her collection, most notably acquiring some quilts from the estate of Florence Peto. Gross was designated a "Quilt Treasure" by the Alliance for American Quilts. Her quilts were exhibited in 2005 at the International Quilt Festival's *America Collects Quilts: The Joyce Gross Collection* exhibit. In 2008, another group of her quilts was exhibited at the Long Beach location for the International

The Garden | Made by Piné Eisfeller, New York | 1938 | 84 × 93 inches | Cotton. Piné Eisfeller's inspiration for *The Garden* came from the photograph and description of an 1857 quilt in Ruth E. Finley's *Old Patchwork Quilts and the Women Who Made Them* (1929). In 1999, the Ultimate Quilt Search named Piné Eisfeller's *The Garden* and *Tree of Life* two of *America's 100 Best Quilts of the 20th Century*. Eisfeller's two masterworks combine elaborate design, hundreds of delicate motifs, and expert appliqué and quilting. *Courtesy of the Dolph Briscoe Center for American History at the University of Texas at Austin, Joyce Gross Collection (W2h001.003.2008)*

Joyce Gross discusses Bertha Stenge's quilt, *Tiger Lily* (c. 1940), shown in the exhibit *Legendary Quilts from the Joyce Gross Collection* at the Marion Public Library, Marion, Indiana, July 19, 1996. *Courtesy of Karen B. Alexander*

Selected Reading

Gross, Joyce R. "Four Twentieth Century Quiltmakers." *Uncoverings 1980*. Edited by Sally Garoutte. Mill Valley, CA: American Quilt Study Group, 1981. Reprinted in *Quiltmaking in America: Beyond the Myths*. Edited by Laurel Horton. Nashville, TN: Rutledge Hill Press, 1994.

————. *A Patch in Time: A Catalog of Antique, Traditional and Contemporary Quilts*. Exhibit sponsored by the Mill Valley Quilt Authority, 1973.

————. *Quilts of the West*. Catalog of the exhibit produced and organized by Joyce Gross, Bank of America World Headquarters, San Francisco, CA, 1976.

Gross, Joyce R. ed. and publisher. *Quilters' Journal*. Thirty-one issues from Fall 1977 to 1987.

Gross, Joyce, and Cuesta Benberry. *20th Century Quilts 1900–1970: Women Make Their Mark*. Catalog for the exhibit at the Museum of the American Quilter's Society, Paducah, KY, 1997.

Quilt Festival and that fall at the International Quilt Festival in Houston.

The Joyce Gross Quilt History Collection was acquired in spring 2008 by the Center for American History, later renamed the Dolph Briscoe Center for American History, and the Winedale Center for the Quilt (WCQ) at the University of Texas at Austin. The collection included more than 170 quilts by such noted American quiltmakers as Bertha Stenge, Florence Peto, and Piné Hawkes Eisfeller. There are 1,500 books in the collection, including important early quilt history texts, plus a large number of quilting magazines. The collection is 150 linear feet of archival material, including extensive files of original and photocopied correspondence from quiltmakers such as Florence Peto, Emma Andres, and Maxine Teele; biographical and subject research files; printed exhibition catalogs, pattern booklets, and exhibition posters; vintage textiles; photographs; and quilt-related ephemera. The acquisition was made possible in part by a generous gift from Karey Bresenhan (the Quilters Hall of Fame 1995 honoree) and Nancy O'Bryant Puentes, founders of Quilts, Inc. and producers of the International Quilt Market and Festival. Although it comprises such a large collection of items that it would be difficult for any institution to process completely, it is open for research through inquires and by appointment.

An exhibition from the Joyce Gross collection, *The World According to Joyce Gross: Quilts from the Dolph Briscoe Center*, opened at the San Jose Museum of Quilts & Textiles in August 2009, and later that fall some of those quilts joined others in an exhibition at the Bob Bullock Museum in Austin, Texas. Nancy Bavor, curatorial intern for the San Jose exhibition, said, "The quilts in this exhibition are tangible evidence of Joyce Gross's lifelong fascination with quilting. Joyce's impact on the quilt world, however, reaches far beyond her extensive quilt collection. Early on, she realized the importance of preserving not only the quilts themselves, but also the documentation about the women who made them."

Perhaps the longest and most widespread legacy of Joyce Gross will be the quilt historians, quilt artists, and quilt enthusiasts she brought together over many years at Point Bonita. Their work and knowledge of quilt history will be passed on to new generations in ways that are unpredictable.

Jeffrey Gutcheon

> *"I am an architect by training,*
> *and some of my best work has been concerned*
> *with expressing light and depth in the surface of a quilt."*
>
> —Jeffrey Gutcheon, *Diamond Patchwork* (1982), p. 7

Jeffrey Gutcheon was inducted into the Quilters Hall of Fame at the Continental Quilting Congress in Falls Church, Virginia, on October 5, 1990. *Courtesy of Beth Gutcheon Clements and David Gutcheon*

by Barbara Brackman,
updated by David Gutcheon

JEFFREY GUTCHEON'S COMPETING INTERESTS have always been diverse, and he has achieved distinction in music, architecture, and the visual arts. His induction into the Quilters Hall of Fame was one more honor for a musician who won a 1979 Tony Award for best musical. Trained in architecture, he has practiced informally since he graduated from the Massachusetts Institute of Technology, designing homes and commercial buildings. Jeffrey has taught a generation to view quilt design in a different way, through his books and classes.

In 1976, *The Quilt Design Workbook*, coauthored with his first wife, Beth Gutcheon, introduced ideas that quilters take for granted today. Before the age of computers and photocopiers, most quiltmakers designed a single block and multiplied that into a quilt top as they sewed. The Gutcheons advocated viewing the top as a design whole and coloring individual patches differently in each block. Looking back, Jeffrey says, "We gave the quilter the whole field of the quilt to look at. You could give a pattern to the color that was independent of the pattern in the quilt block. You might call that technique 'color patterning.'"

Another innovation adapted the visual artist's understanding of light to quilt design. "You assume a light source, a place from which the light comes. The color falls off as you get away from the light source. You can imitate a light effect with color and fabric, following the curve, the graph of light fall-off. You can also use transparency and other effects that rely on illumination."

Jeffrey also taught quilters a new way to view the four-sided grid so basic to quilt design. In his foreword to *Diamond Patchwork*, he wrote, "Even when I work in two dimensions I try to achieve a sense of space and spaciousness. So it was only natural to be thinking about patchwork that had a higher relief than quilting stitches alone usually offer. . . . It occurred to me that in the Baby Block tradition there was already a kind of quilt design that simulated three dimensions. . . . Since a diamond is the only geometric shape other than a square to have four equal sides, it became clear that I could draw any patchwork block pattern on a diamond. How exciting!"

Although Jeffrey credits other important designers, such as Michael James and Nancy Halpern, with guiding quilt design

Hamish to the Amish #1: Pretty Polly | Designed and made by Jeffrey Gutcheon | 1979 | 78 × 78 inches. This quilt was inspired by a Welsh "Strippie" quilt that Jeffrey saw in the American Museum in Britain. Jeffrey noted that the Welsh quilt "was the obvious antecedent to the Amish Stripe pattern so well known in the U.S.A. The only difference between the two lay in the coloring: the Strippie was bleached-out light tones and the Amish Stripe was made of rich Amish traditional colors. So I decided to make a few Amish Floating Diamonds in which one major element was changed—in this case, the Diamond, which is usually a solid color, has been changed to a large tropical print with a motif of parrots nesting in palm trees." *Courtesy of Beth Gutcheon Clements and David Gutcheon*

The Quilt Design Workbook was a collaboration of husband-and-wife team Beth and Jeffrey Gutcheon. Published in 1976, at the beginning of the quilt revival of the late twentieth century, this "how-to" book featured traditional quilt blocks reworked into contemporary settings, the individual work of both artists, and a glimpse into their design studio and work process.

beyond the grid, his innovations were the nudge people needed to forget their old ways of viewing.

Jeffrey was born in New York City in 1941 to Sylvia and Jack Gutcheon. Jack was in the textile business; he ran a small yarn company that manufactured skeins of viscose rayon. Both grandfathers were custom tailors. Sylvia's interest in textiles was in creating handcrafts. She influenced her son with the color she expressed through her needlework and with her piano playing.

Jeffrey earned a bachelor's degree in English literature at Amherst College in 1962 and a bachelor of architecture from the Massachusetts Institute of Technology in 1966. He taught architectural design at MIT and practiced in a firm. Jeffrey soon realized that although he loved design, he didn't have the temperament of a practicing architect or the patience for the long transition from concept to finished building.

Instead, he took a chance on his piano playing, something he never expected to use professionally. He moved back to New York City, living in the warehouse district that became known as SoHo. As a studio musician during the 1960s and 1970s, Jeffrey's piano and keyboard work appeared on numerous albums and hit records, such as Steve Goodman's and Gladys Knight's. With his own band, Hungry Chuck, he recorded an album that became popular in Europe and Japan, a mixture of American music—rock and roll, rhythm and blues, country, and jazz.

In his years in New York City, he continued to work informally as an architect and says he is proudest of the recording studios he designed, a case of mixing design and music. Among the studios

are Skyline and Hit Factory; he remembers well being at the Hit Factory when B. B. King recorded "The Thrill Is Gone."

Jeffrey and his wife, Beth, were married March 18, 1968. Their son, David, was born in 1970. As a young mother, Beth became fascinated by quilts and taught herself the techniques and traditional designs, which she immediately began to adapt with her own ideas. Quilts also captured Jeffrey's eye and he designed one for Beth to make. When he showed her his second idea, she encouraged him to sew it himself, so he learned to stitch, enjoying the technical challenges as he designed more complex patterns. "Complication is what I like," he says. "I like things that have layers and a certain ambiguity that's never resolved in the surface. You can have a longer-term relationship with the piece, always discovering new things."

Beth wrote the *Perfect Patchwork Primer*, one of the first of the new generation of quilt books, published in 1973. Illustrated by Jeffrey, the book featured traditional blocks with some of the Gutcheons' designs. Jeffrey's block *Card Trick* has become a modern classic. In 1973, the Gutcheons started their own company, Gutcheon Patchworks, Inc.

Jeffrey was one of several musicians who collaborated on the musical *Ain't Misbehavin'*, a tribute to Fats Waller's music. When it became a Broadway hit and a Tony-award winner, he and other musicians spent three years in court fighting for their rights and

Jeffrey Gutcheon standing next to his *Hamish to the Amish #1: Pretty Polly*.

Gridlock (Rubik's Flower Garden) | Jeffrey Gutcheon with Teresa McLaughlin | 1981 | 95 × 120 inches | Cotton. Here the traditional Tumbling Blocks pattern has served as the starting point, with the edges of the block constructed from variations on a sixteen-patch block composed primarily of printed floral fabrics that contrast with the grid of solid-colored fabrics. *Courtesy of David Gutcheon*

Gutcheon Patchworks also led a trend with its "documents," as contemporary copies of antique prints are called in the textile trade.

Jeffrey shared his information about the fabric business in a column for *Quilter's Newsletter Magazine* called "Not for Shopkeepers Only." The column, which began in 1981 and continued until 1993, was subtitled "A look at the marketplace—its products, its trends, and its effect on the individual quiltmaker." For more than a decade, he explained how to pick a good-quality cloth, why costs and thus prices go up, and how color trends are forecast—information quiltmakers could not find anyplace else. In 1990, he published a small book, *A Quilter's Guide to Printed Fabric*, which he subtitled *Probably More Than You Ever Wanted to Know about Making Cotton Prints for Quilters in the 1990s.*

Jeffrey Gutcheon's influence and his many creative innovations were recognized by his induction into the Quilters Hall of Fame in 1990. His subsequent quilt designs have reflected his continuing interest in altering traditional quilt blocks, looking for inspiration in the rich sources to be found in antique quilts.

As the new millennium dawned, Jeffrey reconnected with Jim Colegrove, his musical partner from the Hungry Chuck days, and together they formed a new group called Lost Country, which quickly garnered critical acclaim and local radio play. During this period, Jeffrey also designed a series of stunning homes for friends and clients, including one for himself in Deer Isle, Maine, near the Haystack Mountain School of Crafts, where he was a trustee in the 1980s.

Jeffrey retired to his home state of New York in 2008 and currently resides in Westchester. The fabrics he designed for the American Classics line are still avidly traded on eBay.

royalties. Jeffrey says he learned in the music business that you must protect what you own, so when quilters began appropriating his *Card Trick* pattern, assuming it was in the public domain, he called quiltmakers' attention to copyright law.

As he designed quilts, Jeffrey began looking closely at the available fabrics. It was difficult to find cottons with a good weave, loose enough to quilt through, but tight enough to prevent the batting from bearding through the top. Colors and prints were limited. His desire to give quilters more choices led another generation of Gutcheons into the textile business. In 1983, Gutcheon Patchworks, Inc. introduced the American Classic Line, cotton fabrics in prints and plain colors for quiltmakers. According to Jeffrey, "The idea of this line was to maintain a classical palette of quality images in quilting fabrics."

Selected Reading

Gutcheon, Beth. *Perfect Patchwork Primer*. Illustrated by Barbara Stockwell and Jeffrey Gutcheon. New York: McKay, 1973.

Gutcheon, Beth, and Jeffrey Gutcheon. *The Quilt Design Workbook*, New York: Rawson, 1976.

Gutcheon, Jeffrey. *Diamond Patchwork*. New York: Alchemy Press, 1982.

———. "Not for Shopkeepers Only." Column in *Quilter's Newsletter Magazine*, from no. 134 (July/August 1981) through no. 243 (June 1992).

———. *A Quilter's Guide to Printed Fabric*. Tacoma, WA: Gutcheon Patchworks, 1990.

Carrie Hall

1866–1955

"Rare old quilt of faded hue—
Your patches tell a wondrous story
Of treasured scraps and handicraft;
Of love and home, and dreams come true."

—Carrie A. Hall, "In a Museum,"
The Romance of the Patchwork Quilt in America (1935), p. 185

Carrie Hall was inducted into the Quilters Hall of Fame at the Continental Quilting Congress in Arlington, Virginia, on October 5, 1985.
Courtesy of the Kansas State Historical Society

by Diane Hammill

CARRIE ALMA HALL often declared, to anyone who would listen, that she was born with a needle in her hand, and thanks to the path of that needle in the hand of this independent pioneer woman, we have a rich record of America's early quilt heritage.

For Carrie Hall, the thread of life began in Caledonia, Wisconsin, on December 9, 1866. Her father, Dwight Hackett, an Illinois native having served in the Civil War, married her mother immediately after mustering out of the Union Army. Carrie's earliest memories of her father were tales he told of Abraham Lincoln's education and leadership, fostering in her a lifelong interest in all things Lincoln. Her intense desire for knowledge, love of books, and discriminating taste in fashion she attributed to her mother.

When Carrie was seven, her father was smitten with western fever and moved the family to a harsh pioneer existence on a 160-acre homestead in Smith County, Kansas. Through the grasshopper infestation and destruction of their first crop and many other hardships, this spirited family remained tenacious. "We braved it all," Carrie would write later, "and lived to be proud of Kansas."

Despite the family's poverty, quilts and books were necessary luxuries in their prairie home, where Carrie became an avid reader. Her mother often had to tell her to put down her book and help with household chores.

Carrie's skill as a needleworker also developed early. At seven, under the watchful eye of her mother, she pieced a Le Moyne Star quilt that proved to be a masterpiece, raising her status in the neighborhood. In 1881, it won first prize at the county fair. At ten she won a subscription to *Godey's Lady's Book*, the fashion bible of the time, as a reward for her excellent needlework.

In spite of her lack of a high school or college education, her thirst for knowledge qualified her to teach school and to become a county school superintendent for a time. In 1889, at age twenty-three, she moved to Leavenworth, Kansas, a thriving river port, railroad hub, and site of an important Army post.

George Washington Bicentennial | **Made by Carrie Hall, Leavenworth, Kansas** | **1932** | **86 × 92 inches.** "This quilt is an adaptation of a design by Mary Evangeline Walker in honor of the George Washington bicentennial. The silhouette of Washington with bunches of cherries in red and green, and the dates '1732' and '1932' in blue, form a framed medallion in the center of the quilt surrounded by a row of hatchets. The cherry trees are in red and green and the band of mosaics are in blue and white, representing the pavements of Washington, D.C.," according to the caption for plate CXIX in *The Romance of the Patchwork Quilt in America. Courtesy of the Spencer Museum of Art, University of Kansas, gift of Mrs. Carrie A. Hall (0000.0039)*

There she launched her career as a dressmaker at a time when the well-to-do entertained lavishly and dressed in fashions copied from New York and Paris. Catering to the tastes of local society, Carrie's dressmaking business prospered, and she employed many assistants. As a designer, Carrie chose styles from the latest Paris fashion magazines and used fabric imported from France. Examples of her gowns are available for study at the Leavenworth County Historical Museum.

During this time, Carrie married a young University of Kansas student named Patterson, who shortly after their marriage contracted tuberculosis and died. She remained a widow for several years, until 1906, when she married John Hall, a handsome young construction worker with the Missouri Valley Bridge Company. Maplehurst, where *The Romance of the Patchwork Quilt in America* was written, was their Leavenworth home. There is no record of children from either marriage.

Known in the business world as "Madam Hall," Carrie became a prominent club woman, quilt authority, lecturer, collector, and friend to many.

After World War I, following months of volunteer work knitting sweaters and socks for soldiers, she began making quilts. As the quilt revival grew in the 1920s, Carrie created sixteen quilts, including an original design she named Cross-Patch. Captivated by the plethora of beautiful patterns but realizing she could never make a quilt in each pattern, she conceived the idea of making a sample block of every known quilt pattern at the time. Little realizing the magnitude of this undertaking, she embarked

Carrie Alma Hackett. *Courtesy of the Kansas State Historical Society*

on a project that grew and grew until she had created well over 800 blocks, along with dozens of scrapbooks filled with quilt-related clippings.

In the late 1920s, the availability of ready-made clothing caused her dressmaking business to decline. Carrie again saw the need to redirect her life and embarked on a new career as a quilt lecturer. Dressed in a colonial costume of red moiré trimmed with frilled net fichu and cuffs, she presented more than eighty quilt history lectures, illustrated with her extensive quilt block collection, to women's groups and at department stores. Enthusiastic friends and fans encouraged Carrie to compile this material into an illustrated book.

So, in 1935, Carrie Hall coauthored *The Romance of the Patchwork Quilt in America* with Rose Kretsinger. The book contained quilt history drawn from personal accounts, women's magazines, and the scrapbooks in Carrie's collection. The photographs of Carrie Hall's quilt blocks made it the first comprehensive index to quilt patterns, their names, and their history. The book has remained popular to this day, due to its well-organized illustrations of more than eight hundred numbered blocks in traditional and early twentieth-century designs.

Elevating pattern identification to a logical plane, the book continued the work of Ruth Finley's 1929 volume *Old Patchwork Quilts and the Women Who Made Them*. Several patterns in the book came from Marie Webster's *Quilts: Their Story and How to Make Them*, Carlie Sexton's *Old Fashioned Quilts*, antique quilts in the collection of the Thayer Museum of Art (now the Spencer Museum of Art) at the University of Kansas, and periodicals of the day.

Carrie Hall probably met appliqué artist and fellow Kansan Rose Kretsinger while on the lecture circuit and asked her to write

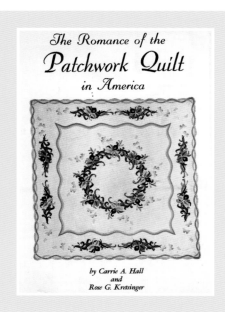

The Romance of the Patchwork Quilt in America by Carrie Hall and Rose Kretsinger was published in 1935. The photographs of Carrie Hall's quilt blocks made it the first comprehensive index to quilt patterns, their names, and their history.

Carrie Hall in the colonial costume she made to wear at her quilt lectures, Leavenworth, Kansas, about 1930. *Photo by Mary Ellen Everhard, courtesy of Barbara Brackman*

Carrie Alma Hall was inducted into the Quilters Hall of Fame at the Continental Quilting Congress in Arlington, Virginia, on October 5, 1985, for her significant contributions to the quilting world through collecting, lecturing, quiltmaking, and writing.

She would have been amazed that in 1998, her *George Washington Bicentennial Quilt* and part of her collection of quilt blocks were exhibited in Japan, with quilts made by honorees Rose Kretsinger and Marie Webster, in the *American Quilt Renaissance* exhibit.

the section of the book on "The Art of Quilting and Quilting Designs." In 1938, three years after the publication of their book, Carrie donated her block collection, research materials, scrapbooks, and a quilt she made in honor of the 200th anniversary of George Washington's birth to the Thayer Museum.

Carrie's enthusiastic collecting spirit spilled into other areas of her life as well. She amassed more than 3,000 books for her private library, which included Lincoln books and memorabilia, Theodore Roosevelt biographies, "Shakespeareana," and design and travel books. Her delightful second book, published in 1938, *From Hoopskirts to Nudity*, reviewed the fashion follies from 1866 to 1936, a world that Carrie Hall knew well.

World War II found Carrie making quilts for benevolent purposes as a Red Cross volunteer, but she also found herself dealing with serious legal and financial difficulties. A rumor persists that she absconded with money belonging to a club for which she served as treasurer.

Always resourceful, however, she quietly moved to North Platte, Nebraska, in 1941, where at the age of seventy-five she began to manufacture and sell playtime and character dolls of historical figures. She prided herself on the detail and craftsmanship of these dolls. With abundant sales, as well as loans and moral support from friends—including Emma Andres, her longtime Arizona correspondent, and Quilters Hall of Fame honorees Florence Peto, Grace Snyder, and Bertha Stenge—Carrie's talent and courage again enabled her to become financially stable.

In January 1955, she machine-pieced a Delectable Mountains quilt top for a special friend and a Nine Patch for a new baby. These would be Carrie's last quilts. At the age of eighty-eight, on July 8, 1955, her needle was stilled forever.

This book of historical patterns from Carrie Hall's blocks was written by Bettina Havig and published in 1999. More than eight hundred blocks are pictured in this book in full color, accompanied by the name or names by which Carrie Hall knew them.

Selected Reading

Brackman, Barbara. "Madam Carrie Hall." *Quilter's Newsletter Magazine*, no. 133 (June 1981).

———. "The Hall/Szabronski Collection at the University of Kansas." *Uncoverings 1982*. Edited by Sally Garoutte. Mill Valley, CA: American Quilt Study Group, 1983.

Hall, Carrie A., and Rose G. Kretsinger. *From Hoopskirts to Nudity: A Review of the Follies and Foibles of Fashion 1866–1936*. Caldwell, ID: The Caxton Printers, Ltd., 1938.

———. *The Romance of the Patchwork Quilt in America*. Caldwell, ID: The Caxton Printers, Ltd., 1935.

Havig, Bettina. *Carrie Hall Blocks: Over 800 Historical Patterns from the Collection of the Spencer Museum of Art, University of Kansas*. Paducah, KY: American Quilter's Society, 1999.

Jonathan Holstein

"*This is an exhibition of American pieced quilts, chosen in a particular way: all elements of craft expertise, all consideration of age, condition, historical or regional significance have been disregarded, and we have concentrated only on how each quilt works as a 'painting.' That is, does it form a cohesive, strong and important visual statement?*"

—Jonathan Holstein, *American Pieced Quilts*, Smithsonian Institution exhibit catalog (1972), p. 7

Jonathan Holstein was inducted into the Quilters Hall of Fame at the Continental Quilting Congress in Arlington, Virginia, on October 27, 1979. *Courtesy of Jonathan Holstein*

by Dr. Julia A. Berg

JONATHAN HOLSTEIN AND GAIL VAN DER HOOF sparked renewed interest in quilts as an art form through their 1971 exhibit, *Abstract Design in American Quilts*, at New York City's Whitney Museum of American Art. For Jonathan, this exhibit was the culmination of a lifelong interest in the arts and Americana that began when he was growing up in antiques-rich central New York State. Although no one in his family made quilts, he saw them in many homes; they were a part of the American folklore that fascinated him then, and they still do.

Jonathan maintained a strong interest in early American life and its artifacts through his years at Harvard College, where he was an English major. He attended law school after college and later worked as an editor on a trade magazine and as an art photographer, eventually becoming professionally interested in Native American art.

When he met Gail van der Hoof in Aspen, Colorado, in 1967, they discovered their mutual interest in modern art. Gail joined him in New York City in 1968, where their circle of friends included many artists. On weekends, they would escape to Pennsylvania and spend time looking at American antiques. They soon discovered troves of quilts in which there was little interest, and pieced quilts became an obsession for them.

They found the quilts astonishingly similar to many modern abstract paintings. In color, form, line, sense of composition, and scale, they could see obvious visual parallels to the modern art they loved. The quilts, however, had not been made by formally trained artists, and it seemed that the two worlds had never touched.

In the early 1970s, they discovered Amish quilts, and these quickly became of prime interest. They bought a little house in Lancaster, Pennsylvania, that Gail restored, and they searched that area of the state for Amish quilts, eventually amassing a large collection of examples from the classic period of Amish quiltmaking. They added examples of Midwestern Amish quilts as those became available on the market.

What started as a weekend amusement very quickly became a passion. They studied dated quilts to learn the fabrics and designs of the time, and they began to collect. Jonathan remembered, "They were affordable, they were everywhere, they were wonderful!"

Amish Center Diamond Quilt | Made in Lancaster County, Pennsylvania | Circa 1925 | 76½ × 78 inches | Wool and cotton. This quilt shows all of the features of the extraordinary and unique Amish achievement in pieced quilts: the perfect scale of the large-patterned forms, the drama at the center of the design balanced by extremely powerful borders, the brilliant combinations of passionate and intense colors, the very fine quilting as an under note to the composition, the glowing quality of the wools. *Courtesy of the International Quilt Study Center, Jonathan Holstein Collection (2003.003.0097)*

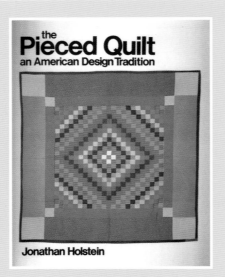

The Pieced Quilt: An American Design Tradition, written by Jonathan Holstein and published in 1973, provides a comprehensive history of pieced American quilts. The quilts selected for inclusion were those Holstein felt were the most visually interesting and made a distinct visual statement.

Jon and Gail during the installation of their exhibition of pieced quilts at the Everson Museum of Art in Syracuse, New York, 1971. The Everson was the first museum after the Whitney to mount an exhibition drawn from their collection. *Courtesy of Jonathan Holstein*

They talked with anyone who could give them information and read extensively in the limited sources on quilts that existed at that time. It all seemed to Jonathan like a mixture of fact and folklore. He used the rigorous analysis of art history disciplines that had seldom been applied to quilts. Jonathan and Gail shared their discoveries with artist friends who helped reinforce their feelings that this was an extraordinary body of indigenous American design.

They tested their thesis by exploring quilts from other regions. In New England, they found that quilts had different characteristics from those in Pennsylvania, but they were of comparable visual interest. This encouraged them to believe that the visual invention of quiltmaking was in fact a national phenomenon, and they set off on cross-country collecting trips. Their collection grew to the point that "in some rooms we could only walk between the rows."

Jonathan and Gail began to consider mounting an exhibition of their quilt collection. Art historians in the early 1970s barely took notice of quilts, and people usually thought of quilts in a bedding context. To change this image, Gail and Jonathan wanted their quilts displayed on the walls of a major art museum, like paintings. Their proposal to the Whitney Museum of American Art came at just the right time to expand the scope of the museum's exhibits from fine art to the decorative arts. The groundbreaking exhibit *Abstract Design in American Quilts* opened in June 1971 with sixty-two pieced quilts. The planned exhibition was extended until mid-September because of the favorable response from leading art critics. As Jonathan said, "By moving them from beds to walls, we changed their meaning; people interested in art but not necessarily in American art, folk or otherwise, could begin to assess quilts in terms of color, form, and line."

In October 1972, a second exhibition, entitled *American Pieced Quilts*, opened at the Renwick Gallery of the National Collection of Fine Arts in Washington, D.C. Later, the gallery added a number of quilts and divided them into two groups, which traveled to twenty-one American museums and two English venues under the auspices of the Smithsonian Institution Traveling Exhibition Service (SITES).

Jonathan Holstein's book, *The Pieced Quilt: An American Design Tradition*, a combination of historical study and aesthetic analysis of American quilts, was published in 1973. In 1975, he assembled an exhibition for the Shiseido Corporation in Tokyo and the American Cultural Center in Kyoto. The next year Jonathan and Gail sent an exhibition to the Kyoto Museum of Modern Art. These exhibits of American quilts were the first to be held in Japan and created widespread interest in quilting there.

In 1980, Jonathan and Gail assembled the first exhibition of Amish quilts, a group of thirty from Pennsylvania and the Midwest. Called simply *Amish Quilts*, it was seen in ten museums in the United States.

Jonathan wrote the introduction and quilt commentaries for the first state quilt survey, the Kentucky Quilt Project's *Kentucky Quilts 1800–1900*, published in 1982. In 1983, he helped select quilts from the Texas State Quilt Project for the exhibition *Lone Stars: A Legacy of Texas Quilts 1836–1936* and wrote the foreword to the catalog, published in 1986.

In 1983, his article "Collecting Quilt Data: History from Statistics" investigated the possibility of computerizing the data from all the state quilt projects. But this idea would have to wait until the late 1990s, when the Internet would provide opportunities for such broad-ranging projects.

Amish Bars Quilt | Quiltmaker unknown, probably made in Lancaster County, Pennsylvania | Circa 1890–1910 | 84 × 71 inches, 213 × 180 centimeters | Pieced, machine, wool, suiting serge, gabardine (wool). This was the first Amish quilt Holstein found (1969), and it was included in the 1971 exhibition *Abstract Design in American Quilts* at the Whitney Museum of American Art in New York. This and another Amish quilt in that exhibition were the first Amish quilts publicly displayed. *Courtesy of the International Quilt Study Center, Jonathan Holstein Collection (2003.003.0013)*

On the occasion of the twentieth anniversary of the Whitney Museum exhibit, Shelly Zegart and Jonathan Holstein organized *Louisville Celebrates the American Quilt*, a symposium accompanied by five exhibitions. *Abstract Design in American Quilts* was a reinstallation of the original 1971 Whitney exhibition, and *A Plain Aesthetic: Lancaster Amish Quilts* featured quilts from the earlier Amish quilt exhibit. An outgrowth of this symposium was the movement to create an international, comprehensive quilt information source whose establishment became one of the primary goals of the Alliance for American Quilts.

From 1992 to 1995, together with Shelly Zegart and Eleanor Bingham Miller, Jonathan coedited *The Quilt Journal: An International Review*, for which he wrote a number of articles. In 1995, he joined the planning committee of the Alliance for American Quilts. Since 1996, he has served as an adviser to the International Quilt Study Center at the University of Nebraska Lincoln.

In 2003, Jonathan announced that his historic collection of quilts and archival materials would be donated to the International Quilt Study Center, in a joint venture with its founders, Ardis and Robert James. Included in this extensive collection of more than four hundred quilts are the sixty-two quilts from the original Whitney Museum show and more than one hundred Lancaster County, Pennsylvania, and Midwestern Amish quilts.

Jonathan Holstein served as a driving force in the revival of quilts in the 1970s and initiated many "firsts" in the quilt arena. His work continues today, as he writes, lectures, plans exhibits, juries quilt exhibitions, and advocates for the scholarly study of quilts on an international level.

Selected Reading

Holstein, Jonathan. *Abstract Design in American Quilts.* Exhibit catalog. New York: Whitney Museum of American Art, 1971.

———. *Abstract Design in American Quilts: A Biography of an Exhibition.* Louisville, KY: The Kentucky Quilt Project, Inc., 1991.

———. *American Pieced Quilts.* Catalog for the Smithsonian Institution traveling exhibit, 1972–1974. New York: Viking Press, 1972.

Holstein, Jonathan, and John Finley. *Kentucky Quilts 1800–1900.* Louisville, KY: Kentucky Quilt Project, Inc., 1982.

Holstein, Jonathan, Eleanor Bingham Miller, and Shelly Zegart, eds. *The Quilt Journal: An International Review.* Louisville, KY: Kentucky Quilt Project, Inc., 1992–1995.

Carter Houck

"The renaissance of needlework now sweeping the country is just in time to pick up the thread of knowledge and expertise which winds its way down from the first settlers. . . . A whole new generation of quilters is gathering for lessons and for quilting bees."

—Carter Houck, *American Quilts and How to Make Them* (1975), p. 15

Carter Greene Houck was inducted into the Quilters Hall of Fame at the Continental Quilting Congress in Falls Church, Virginia, on October 5, 1990. *Photo by Myron Miller*

by Linda Wilson

CARTER HOUCK is a woman with a lifelong passion for "women's work"—needlework, fashion, quilting, sewing—who has used the threads of her experience to create a life that touches all who love textiles.

Carter Greene was born in Washington, D.C., because there were no hospitals near her family farm in what she calls the "absolute boondocks" of Fauquier County in northern Virginia. As a child, she was tutored at home and learned needlework from embroiderers in her family. Carter later inherited one of the family's Victorian crazy quilts, which showcased their skills.

Carter attended St. Margaret's School, an Episcopal girls' boarding school, in Tappahanock, Virginia, graduating at the age of seventeen. Interested in learning more about fashion, but knowing that her family would not allow her to live in New York City at such a young age, she wrote to *Vogue* magazine inquiring about fashion schools in the South. Carter accepted their recommendation and studied at the Richmond Professional Institute of the College of William and Mary in Richmond, Virginia.

Two years later, Carter fulfilled her dream of moving to New York City to get a "real fashion job." In the middle of World War II, very little was happening in the fashion world, so she worked for two pattern companies instead. These jobs provided valuable training for her later work as a needlework teacher, fabric store owner, and author of articles and books about sewing.

Carter married and moved to Oklahoma, where she had two children, then moved again, this time to Texas. Believing that the local newspapers needed a sewing column and that writing was a job she could do while caring for her small children, she approached the *Fort Worth Star Telegram* "with the brashness of a twenty-four-year-old" and got a job. She wrote and illustrated sewing columns three times a week for the *Telegram* from 1950 to 1952, when she moved back East.

Carter's other passions are mountain hiking and sailboat racing. She joined the Appalachian Mountain Club, which coordinates hiking and backpacking activities and helps maintain the Appalachian Trail. She has hiked trails far and wide, as well as

Zoo Animals | **Made by Carter Houck** | **36 × 36 inches** | **Cottons.** According to Carter Houck in her 1991 book, *The Quilt Encyclopedia Illustrated*, "Even the most serious quilters like to work in amusing styles and with designs taken from everyday life. One of the best outlets for such a happy form of quilting is a quilt for a child. . . . Sometimes a child's quilt is made as a wall decoration, and the child can take it through life" (pp. 41–42). *Courtesy of Carter Houck*

Pillows made by Carter Houck. *Courtesy of Carter Houck*

leading groups of hikers. Hiking, she says, "is sort of the opposite end of the world to quilting, except it goes back to the mountain heritage, the mountain women." Living on Long Island Sound for years gave her the opportunity to race sailboats. Carter believes that hiking and sailing imposed a discipline on her life, and thus a balance to her freelance writing.

From 1961 to 1968, she again wrote a sewing column, this time for *Parents* magazine. In the 1960s and early 1970s, she owned a fabric shop in Darien, Connecticut, and taught needlework. In 1973, she began to edit a monthly magazine, *Lady's Circle Needlework*. In 1974, she also became editor of *Lady's Circle Patchwork Quilts*, a position she held for almost twenty years. Her work on both magazines broke new ground in both the style of photography and the concept of traveling to see quilts from all over the United States.

The May 1988 issue of *Lady's Circle Patchwork Quilts* focused on quiltmakers and patterns from Missouri.

The influence of *Lady's Circle Patchwork Quilts* on the blossoming quilting movement is immeasurable. For the first time, people were able to see color photos of antique quilts in a monthly magazine and to read about quilters and quilt collections across the country. Carter's colleague, professional photographer Myron Miller, developed a unique style of quilt photography. By showing quilts on beds, Myron Miller imbued the quilts with warmth and life. As Carter wrote in her introduction to *American Quilts and How to Make Them*, "The quilts are a bit like very fragile spring flowers in that they look best in their natural setting and fade some if they are just seen hanging flat."

Carter had the innovative idea of devoting each issue of the magazine to a different state. By the time the state quilt documentation projects were being organized in the 1980s, Carter had already unearthed some real quilt treasures in museums and private collections.

At the time she wrote them, her sewing columns for the *Fort Worth Star Telegram* and for *Parents* magazine may have seemed to be just a way to make a living, but they paved the path for her later career as an author and magazine editor. Carter remembers well the first assignment she and Myron Miller were given. She had arranged to tour a group of historic homes in Connecticut that housed small quilt collections. The year was 1974, the year of the energy crisis. Carter and Myron "drove between what few open gas stations there were, saying prayers all the way." The two were so enchanted and inspired by the results of that particular quilt foray that they proposed a book to Charles Scribner's Sons of New York. The rest is history. *American Quilts and How to Make Them* was published in 1975, serving as one of the catalysts for the new quilt revival.

In addition to this major book, Carter has authored many others on needlework, sewing, and quilting. Her knowledge can truly be said to be encyclopedic, for she is the author of *The Quilt Encyclopedia Illustrated*, published in 1991. She coauthored two

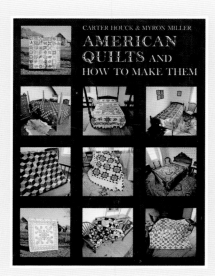

American Quilts and How to Make Them by Carter Houck and Myron Miller, published in 1975, illustrated forty-two old patchwork quilts that were based on traditional patterns but were unique because of some variation introduced by each maker. For this publication, Carter Houck contributed her knowledge of needlework and Myron Miller his skill as a professional photographer.

books with Robert Bishop for the Museum of American Folk Art: *All Flags Flying: American Patriotic Quilts as Expressions of Liberty* (1986) and *The Romance of Double Wedding Ring Quilts* (1989). Perhaps her most charming book is one written for children, *Warm as Wool, Cool as Cotton: Natural Fibers and Fabrics and How to Work with Them* (1975). And she collaborated with Quilters Hall of Fame honoree Donna Wilder on two books, *Creative Calendar Quilt: A Block for Each Month of the Year* (1996) and *Back to Basics: A Quilter's Guide* (1997).

After retiring from *Lady's Circle Patchwork Quilts* in 1993, Carter contributed a series of articles to *Quilter's Newsletter Magazine* called "Museums & Quilts." In these articles, she continued to share her discoveries of historic quilts from across the country, from New England and Virginia to Arizona and Hawaii, in museums both large and small.

Carter has also had a strong impact on the judging of major quilt contests, including the International Quilt Festival in Houston, the Vermont Quilt Festival, and quilt shows sponsored by the Museum of American Folk Art in New York City. With a wealth of knowledge about textiles, craftsmanship, and aesthetics, she possesses an eye for technical skill and artistic vision. Carter has found that the quality of both design and execution of quilts has improved considerably since she began judging in the 1970s, leading to the conclusion that quilt contests have great value in raising standards.

It is difficult to imagine the quilt renaissance without the constant presence, influence, and guidance of Carter Houck, and this is precisely the reason she was inducted into the Quilters Hall of Fame in 1990. Her sustained advocacy for quilts and other forms of needlework shines through in her lecturing, teaching, and writing. By highlighting quilts from all regions of the United States, she promoted networking among quilters, collectors, teachers, and quilt historians.

All movements need leaders who are able to recognize beauty and worth, and then are able to articulate these values to the public. The quilting revival of the late twentieth century has Carter Houck.

Carter Houck at her induction into the Quilters Hall of Fame during the Continental Quilting Congress at the Fairview Park Marriott, Falls Church, Virginia, October 5, 1990.

Selected Reading

Houck, Carter. *Nova Scotia Patchwork Patterns: Instructions and Full-size Templates for 12 Quilts*. New York: Dover, 1981.

————. *The Quilt Encyclopedia Illustrated*. New York: Harry N. Abrams and the Museum of American Folk Art, 1991.

————. Series on "Museums & Quilts." *Quilter's Newsletter Magazine*, nos. 261, 263, 265 (1994); 269, 271, 273, 275, 277 (1995); 279, 281, 283, 285 (1996); 289, 292, 294, 296 (1997); 301, 303, 305 (1998); 311, 313 (1999).

————. *White Work: Techniques and 188 Designs*. New York: Dover, 1978.

Houck, Carter, ed. 1973–1993). *Lady's Circle Needlework* and *Lady's Circle Patchwork Quilts* column, "Connections," 1989–1993.

Houck, Carter, and Myron Miller. *American Quilts and How to Make Them*. New York: Charles Scribner's Sons, 1975.

Nelson, Cyril I., and Carter Houck. *Treasury of American Quilts*. New York: Greenwich House, 1982.

Wilder, Donna, and Carter Houck. *Back to Basics: A Quilter's Guide*. Danbury, CT: Fairfield Processing, 1997.

Marguerite Ickis
1897–1980

"There is both meaning and memory in a fine quilt,
and there can be both history and heritage. . . .
The story of the quilt is the record
of the human family."

—Marguerite Ickis, *The Standard Book of Quilt Making and Collecting* (1949), p. 253

Marguerite Ickis was inducted into the Quilters Hall of Fame at the Continental Quilting Congress in Arlington, Virginia, on October 27, 1979. *Courtesy of the Friends of Dennis Senior Citizens, Inc., Dennis, Massachusetts*

by Stacie Seeger Matheson

"I'VE LIVED NINE LIVES," Marguerite Ickis once said, "and I've loved every one of them"—botanist, teacher, administrator, author, quiltmaker, editor, restaurant manager, researcher, and, finally, in retirement, artist. Like pieces of cloth and intricate stitches, her life resembles the elements of a patchwork quilt.

Marguerite Ickis was among the first group to be inducted into the Quilters Hall of Fame during the Continental Quilting Congress in October 1979. Author of *The Standard Book of Quilt Making and Collecting*, often called "the quilter's bible," Marguerite was honored for promoting quilting traditions and skills in the mid-twentieth century.

A fifth-generation member of a Scottish Presbyterian family, Marguerite was raised on a sheep farm in Adena, Ohio, not far from Steubenville, the county seat near the Ohio River. Taught to quilt by her mother and Quaker grandmother, she helped provide batting for quilts with wool produced on the family farm. She referred to her childhood in the early 1900s as "the golden age for this craft" and relished the social exchanges quilting brought into her life, with the quilting bees held on the farm and in neighboring communities.

In 1929, Marguerite received a B.S. degree in education from Ohio University in southeast Ohio. After graduation, she left her home state for New York City, where she obtained an M.A. degree in botany from Columbia University. Her career began as curator of botany at Massachusetts Agricultural College, a position she held for five years. In 1936, she joined the national staff of the Girl Scouts as Leader of Training in Nature and Arts and Crafts.

In 1940, she became assistant editor of *Recreation* magazine and dean of the Recreation Training School for the Works Projects Administration (WPA). While with the WPA, she constructed her *Art Deco Fans* quilt from scraps of costumes used in dramatic productions of the theater division of the Federal Art Project. She later returned to Columbia University to take a position as instructor in recreation and began a writing career.

Over the next twenty years, Marguerite authored an astonishing number of books on various arts and crafts topics, as well as the book that established her as an authority on quiltmaking—*The Standard Book of Quilt Making and Collecting*, which was published in 1949. A basic guide to the art of quiltmaking, it appealed to novice and experienced quilters alike. Reprinted in a paperback edition in 1959 by Dover Publishing Company, it has been one of

Art Deco Fans | Made by Marguerite Ickis, New York City | Circa 1940 | 62 × 72 inches | Satins, velvets, and velveteens. Marguerite Ickis made this eye-catching quilt while she was the arts and crafts consultant for the Works Projects Administration (WPA) Federal Art Project in New York City in the early 1940s. The quilt is made from fabric left over from costumes used in the theatrical projects of the WPA. *Courtesy of the American Quilter's Society, Collection of Holice Turnbow*

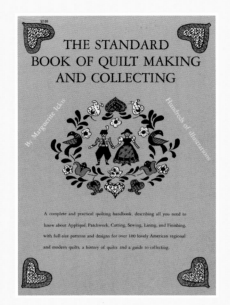

The Standard Book of Quilt Making and Collecting by Marguerite Ickis was published in 1949 and reprinted by Dover Publications in 1959. It is a basic guide to the art of quiltmaking and appeals to novice and experienced quilters alike.

quilt designs and techniques. Chapters on the elements of design, the selection of materials, design sources, pattern drafting, border treatments, and preparing the quilt frame take the quilter through the creative process with ease. The popular designs include pieced and appliquéd quilts, such as Tree of Life and Wild Rose Wreath patterns. Another chapter features quilts for special occasions, such as album, chintz, crazy, and yo-yo quilts. Also included are chapters on collecting quilts and the history and social importance of quiltmaking. The book clearly defines the utilitarian roles quilts play in our lives, but emphasizes the importance of quiltmaking as a creative and social resource.

Marguerite felt that the custom of passing quiltmaking skills from one generation to the next was lost with the onset of World War I. "The period of time from 1870 to World War I was the most popular time for quiltmaking. With the war there was a grand movement away from the farm to the city, and quilting was lost in the process. Quilting fell by the wayside along with many other ideas and values connected with the rural lifestyle." Her book made a significant contribution to the revival of quiltmaking in the second half of the twentieth century.

Although not credited as coauthor, Marguerite assisted her friend Dorothy Brightbill with her book, *Quilting As a Hobby*, published in 1963. The research on old quilts and textiles that Marguerite conducted for this book heightened her interest in collecting quilts and in making quilts from vintage fabrics found in thrift shops.

Retiring from the fast-paced life of New York City in 1975, Marguerite moved permanently to Dennis, Massachusetts, on

the publisher's best-selling books in the United States and Europe for more than forty years. Illustrated with more than one hundred traditional and unusual quilts and patterns, *The Standard Book of Quilt Making and Collecting* includes forty full-size patterns with complete instructions for planning and constructing the quilts.

The book was designed to provide an "understandable guide for the beginner" and to give the experienced quilter a resource for

Posters created for the WPA Federal Art Project. Marguerite Ickis worked as the WPA's arts and crafts consultant, assistant editor of Recreation magazine, and dean of the Recreation Training School during the early 1940s. *Courtesy of the Works Projects Administration Poster Collection (Library of Congress), artist Shari Weisberg*

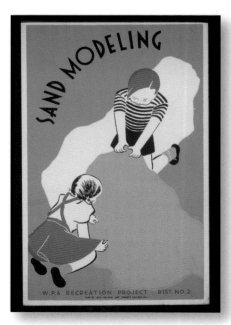

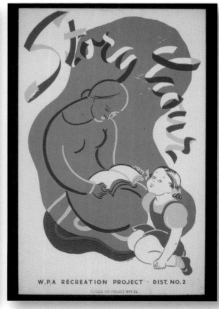

Interior by Marguerite Ickis, from a reproduction of one of her "naive" paintings (c. 1975) depicting children's games of her childhood.
Collection of the Quilters Hall of Fame

Cape Cod, at the age of eighty. She had summered there for many years and had even run a small inn and restaurant. In retirement, while continuing to make quilts, she took up yet another hobby, which she referred to as her "ninth life"—painting. She modeled her work after the "naives," the school of self-taught artists whose pictures convey stories. Using her own childhood memories of the Ohio farm, family, and friends, she painted scenes of quilting bees, young girls piecing quilt tops, and social gatherings.

In 1979, she received the news from Hazel Carter that she would be one of the first to be inducted into the Quilters Hall of Fame. The others honored that first year were Lenice Bacon, Dr. William Rush Dunton Jr., Ruth Finley, Jonathan Holstein, and Gail van der Hoof.

Marguerite and her friend, Louise Vaughn, traveled to the Continental Quilting Congress in Arlington, Virginia, to be present at the induction ceremony. As Marguerite was introduced to the crowd, she was welcomed with a standing ovation. She later expressed her delight at this honor, saying she felt like a celebrity in the spotlight, as Hazel presented her with a handcrafted pewter box with the Quilters Hall of Fame "Q" logo on it. A Cape Cod newspaper reported the award in an article: "At long last, national homage had been paid to the First Lady of Quilting."

Marguerite Ickis passed away in August 1980, less than a year after her induction. A memorial fund was established in her name for a recreation room at the Senior Citizens' Center in Dennis, Massachusetts, an appropriate dedication to an individual whose life was devoted to teaching others the enjoyment and importance of pursuing traditional arts and crafts. A display case in the Senior Center contains her Quilters Hall of Fame award and her "naive school" paintings.

Selected Reading

Brightbill, Dorothy, assisted by Marguerite Ickis. *Quilting As a Hobby*. New York: Sterling Publishing Co., 1963.

Garoutte, Sally. "Marguerite Ickis." *Quilters' Journal* 2, no. 1 (Spring 1979).

Ickis, Marguerite. *Folk Arts and Crafts*. New York: Association Press, 1958.

———. *The Standard Book of Quilt Making and Collecting*. Greystone Press, 1949. Reprinted by Dover Publications, Inc., 1959.

Ickis, Marguerite, and Reba Selden Esh. *The Book of Arts and Crafts*. New York: Dover Publications, 1954. Reprinted 1965.

Ardis and Robert James

"Of course there are always favorites,

but these . . . are frequently chosen for reasons

other than beauty or color or workmanship."

—Ardis and Robert James, interview with Jonathan Holstein

Ardis and Robert James were inducted into the Quilters Hall of Fame in Marion, Indiana, on July 16, 2011. *Photo by Geoff Johnson, courtesy of the Nebraska University Foundation*

by Jonathan Holstein

ARDIS AND ROBERT JAMES entered the burgeoning quilt world the same year the Quilters Hall of Fame was established—1979, when, at a quilt festival in Michigan, they bought their first quilt, simply because it appealed to Ardis visually. In *Masterpiece Quilts from the James Collection*, the catalog of an exhibition of eighty-eight of their quilts shown in Japan in 1998, Ardis is quoted as saying that first quilt "was a Mariner's Compass, with a sizable hole in the middle and had . . . the most interesting border I had ever seen." Bob encouraged Ardis's collecting and then, becoming intrigued by the quilts' aesthetic qualities, went on the hunt with her. Said Ardis: "He didn't want to be left out of the fun." On their first joint outing looking for quilts, they bought thirty-two.

From the beginning, the Jameses were collectors whose interest began with a single object, which led to another and another as their knowledge expanded. When I asked them if they had a favorite quilt or quilts in their collection, their response was: "Of course there are always favorites, but these . . . are frequently chosen for reasons other than beauty or color or workmanship. . . .

For example, an Iowa Amish quilt was Bob's favorite for a long time. Why? We had known Amish existed around Cedar Rapids, Iowa, but we had never actually looked closely at an Iowa Amish quilt and had to be taught why these were different from Ohio or Pennsylvania or Canadian Amish examples. So this quilt was a learning experience and therefore a favorite." Thus do wonderful obsessions begin and flourish.

Once started, however, the Jameses did something other early quilt collectors did not: They acquired contemporary quilts as well as earlier American quilts. As they recently noted, "In the earlier years, probably 10 or 20 percent of the collection was 'art' or contemporary quilts." Bob continues, "Both of us saw family quilts in the 1920s and 1930s, so we never really felt the contemporary or art quilt movement was a cataclysmic change in quilting—a significant change, but there had always been changes in quilts and quilting. Look at the difference in quilts from the years between the 1880s and the 1930s."

Additional impetus at the beginning of their collecting came when Ardis spotted a quilt at a show that was not for sale,

Elaborated Tangram | Michael James, Somerset, Massachusetts | 1976 | 91½ × 89½ inches | Cotton; hand-pieced and hand-quilted. Ardis James took a quiltmaking workshop with Michael James, admired his quilts, and was surprised by Bob at Christmas with a group of quilts by Michael James that included *Elaborated Tangram*. They feel this early example of Michael's work is important in illustrating the development of his art. *Courtesy of the International Quilt Study Center and Museum, Ardis and Robert James Collection (1997.007.1012)*

Ardis and Robert James at a program on March 28, 2008, dedicating the International Quilt Study Center and Museum. *Courtesy of the International Quilt Study Center and Museum*

determined to make it, and so was introduced to the craft of quiltmaking. In 1983, she went to a workshop by the contemporary quilt artist Michael James, and Bob noted it was a shame they had not purchased one of his works. That Christmas she was given slides of six of them so she could pick one, and when she couldn't decide, Bob bought all of them. They went on from there to collect the work of many other significant contemporary quilt artists from both the United States and abroad.

Ardis James christens the Quilt House, home of the International Quilt Study Center and Museum, as Robert James looks on, March 28, 2008. *Courtesy of the International Quilt Study Center and Museum*

As their collection grew and began to fill up their house (said Bob: After a certain point, "We had a house but no longer a livable house."), they did another thing that was unique at the time: They created a gallery for quilts at their home with broad platforms on which quilts were stacked where they could be seen. And there they graciously greeted visitors from all over the world who had heard about the collection and traveled to see it.

The Jameses' collection was also different from those of other seminal collectors because of the couple's interest in quilts from other countries, and with good reason. Bob's several careers had required him to travel broadly, including significant stints in Japan.

We collected foreign quilts very early on—just not a lot of them. When we started collecting, we always looked for quilts in Canada, Holland, England, France, and wondered about the influences to and from Central Asia, Turkey, Europe, the Hawaiian Islands, and so on. We always intended that the collection would sometime be truly international, like the Metropolitan Museum of Art or MOMA—but for quilts.

Bob and Ardis were both born in Nebraska in 1925, he in Ord, whose population was then, and is now, about two thousand. He lived both in the town and on a farm, where they still used horse-drawn equipment. Ardis was born in Lincoln. While just in high school, she worked for the *Omaha Stockman's Journal*, a once-significant publication in the field that became more and more her project as men left for World War II.

Before the decade of the 1940s had ended, Bob had achieved a B.S. in economics from Northwestern University, an M.B.A. from Harvard Business School, and a Ph.D. from Harvard's Graduate School of Arts and Sciences. Ardis had become secretary to a dean of the University of Nebraska in Lincoln. The Jameses met in 1948 when Bob visited his sister in Lincoln, and they were married the next year.

In the 1950s, Bob taught at MIT then decided to try government service, becoming the CIA's branch chief concerned with the communist bloc's trade, finance, and machinery industry. After four years there, he joined the oil industry, eventually becoming president of Mobil's Marine Transportation Company, with worldwide responsibilities. Finally he joined a New York commercial real estate development company, Enterprise Asset Management, with whom he has been associated for almost three decades.

All the while, he and Ardis were raising a family, which eventually included three children, and enjoying their house in Chappaqua, New York, where Bob maintained a large vegetable

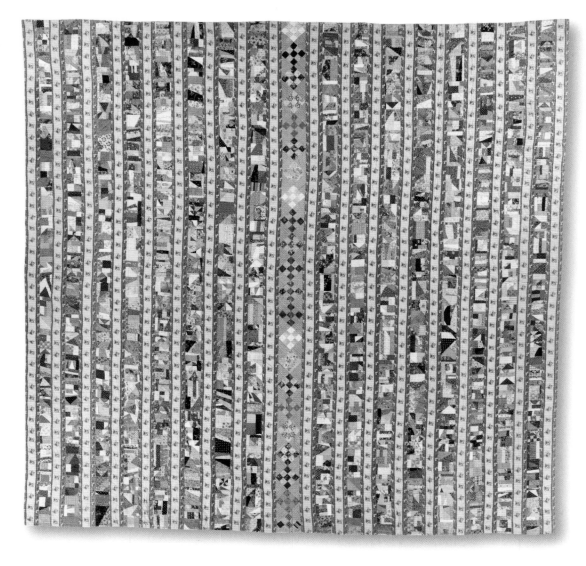

Crazy Strip | Quiltmaker unknown, probably made in Pennsylvania | Circa 1840 | 98 × 104 inches | Cotton; hand-pieced and hand-quilted. This early strip quilt uses materials that date from the late eighteenth to the mid-nineteenth centuries. While the pieced strips composed of little pieces of fabric are put together in a random mosaic fashion, it is not in the consciously random style later to be seen in so-called Crazy quilts. Rather, it was a frugal use of small pieces of fabric no doubt left over from other sewing tasks. The Jameses are especially fond of this rare early quilt for its visual impact, and they admire the verve with which the maker combined its unusual elements.
Courtesy of the International Quilt Study Center and Museum, Ardis and Robert James Collection (2009.039.0063)

garden, taking special pride in his tomatoes, a particular summer concern we have shared since we met. Ever interested in the world, Bob has had many other responsibilities, including his current involvement with a number of national and international organizations whose concerns range from strategic and military matters to human rights. To most, this might seem like an exhausting, lifelong round of obligations for Bob and, of course, Ardis. But those who know the Jameses have witnessed the intellectual curiosity that has marked their lives, and what has been accomplished in Nebraska seems to me a natural extension of their interest in the world, a desire to take part in its workings, and the energy to pursue those predilections. Fortunately for those who love quilts, it also indicates a significant degree of comfort with assuming major risks and the willingness to commit the resources necessary to accomplish significant goals. Bob

has noted that, aside from their mutual aesthetic choices, it was a combination of their distinctive talents that made their quilt venture successful: "I couldn't have done Ardis's part, and she couldn't have done mine."

I first met the Jameses in 1996 when I gave a lecture at the University of Nebraska–Lincoln (UNL) as part of a celebration of the first public display of the university's contemporary art quilts. For me, it was admiration at first sight: not just the quilts, which had been carefully and successfully chosen with aesthetics as a central consideration, but their clear-sighted planning and their absolute determination to make something significant happen in Lincoln. It was also clear, once I had met those at the university who would be involved in the venture, that it had every likelihood of being a resounding success and of the greatest importance to the future of quilt study and appreciation.

The Jameses had been discussing a quilt center with UNL for several years, and their negotiations culminated in 1997 with an agreement that established the International Quilt Study Center, its name indicating the couple's intention to spread a wide net. Its first base was in the Home Economics Building of the University. Patricia Crews, a professor whose doctorate was in textile science, became the center's able director and began to assemble staff.

I recently asked Ardis and Bob why, aside from their roots in the state, they had picked Nebraska for their endeavor.

We had worked on the . . . collection for some twenty-plus years, so had outlined pretty much what we expected . . . [for] whomever we could persuade to carry out our aims. We had approached several museums and discussed our aims with them. It became clear that most would probably do a good job of caring for and preserving quilts, but would not do an adequate job of showing quilts, would probably not care much for the contemporary or art quilts, had inadequate staff, were not prepared to do much research and writing or teaching, had no idea about how to build a memorable collection and no idea of how to get the money to do so, and so on. . . . But UNL had an open mind and was willing to listen to our aims [and dreams].

As it turned out, it was a perfect match. The university was supportive of both the idea and the actuality from the beginning, and the successful results of this collaboration were soon evident.

The center quickly outgrew its first facility, and just over a decade later, the following had been accomplished: A distinguished group of quilt collections had been added to the Jameses' initial gift of approximately one thousand quilts; a beautiful new museum, devoted entirely to the collection, exhibition, study, and preservation of quilts, had opened; university courses of study related to quilts had been established; and a distinguished staff had been assembled. Additionally, it was recognized from the beginning that an archive for quilt-related material needed to be an integral part of any international quilt center, and the university library system made space and the services of an archivist available for such a collection. Several important archives have already been received and more are promised—a growing resource for quilt scholars. The Jameses recently explained their name for the new building:

We named it "Quilt House" because it is intended to be much more than a museum. The number of publications, the leadership without overt competition with other quilt museums, the ability to work with quilters, collectors, and museums around the world, and, of course, the broad expanse of the exhibitions are examples. One of the best was the recent exhibition and publication on preservation: important for museums as well as for someone keeping grandmother's quilts. Important also for teaching, much of the work on the exhibitions was done with [and for] students. Just what we all had in mind: exhibition, publication, collection, preservation, history, and so on.

And so the vision Ardis and Bob had at the beginning of their serious collecting, of an inclusive collection embracing the best of what the entire world had to offer in quilts, past and present, and their desire to share it with that world, has been realized in an amazingly short time. For those who have been lucky enough to be on the bus, it has been a great ride, one that could not have happened without the Jameses' dedication and continuing generous support, and the willingness of the University of Nebraska to embrace their dream. Their gift is to the world and is unique among the efforts of those who have made the most significant contributions to the evolution of the understanding and appreciation of our common interest.

Twelve years ago, when the actualization of their dream of a quilt center in Nebraska had just begun, they said, "We never felt that we owned the quilts, but we were careful custodians and are pleased beyond description at the way they have come home." Their selection as the 2011 inductees into the Quilters Hall of Fame could not be more deserved, or more fitting. All who know them, or know of their contributions, will celebrate this moment.

Selected Reading

Ducey, C., and M. Hanson. *Quilts in Common*. Lincoln, NE: International Quilt Study Center & Museum, 2008.

Hanson, M., and P. Crews, eds. *American Quilts in the Modern Age: 1870–1940*. Lincoln: University of Nebraska Press, 2009.

Holstein, J., and C. Ducey. *Masterpiece Quilts from the James Collection*, Tokyo: Nihon Vogue, 1998, 8–9.

James, Ardis. *Contemporary Quilts from the James Collection*. Paducah, KY: American Quilter's Society, 1995.

———. *Quilts: The James Collection*. Tokyo: Kokusai Art, 1990.

Amur River | Patrick Dorman | 1984 | 89½ × 67½ inches | Cotton; hand-appliquéd, machine-pieced, and hand quilted. Patrick Dorman of Seattle, a freelance set designer, designed and made this quilt in 1984. His work has been influenced by the art of non-industrial peoples, those of the Native American tribes of the Northwest Coast, the Ainu of Japan, and, particularly in this quilt, the people who live along the Amur River in Siberia. *Courtesy of the International Quilt Study Center and Museum, Ardis and Robert James Collection (1997.007.1078)*

Michael James

*"In each of my quilts I attempt to chart some dimension
of my own conscious and subconscious being.
They are as much about me
as they are about formal phenomenon."*

—Michael James, artist's statement, 1993

Michael James was inducted into the
Quilters Hall of Fame in Marion, Indiana,
on July 17, 1993. *Photo by Larry Gawel,*
© *Michael James*

by Nancy J. Shamy

MICHAEL JAMES was born in 1949 in New Bedford, Massachusetts, the oldest of seven children born to Claire Savoie James and Robert A. James Jr., who were of English and French Canadian heritage. As a young child, Michael attended a French/English bilingual parish school, St. Anthony's in New Bedford. He studied painting and printmaking at Southeastern Massachusetts University, and later moved to Rochester, New York, for graduate studies in painting and printmaking at the Rochester Institute of Technology. In 1972, he married Judith Dionne; they have one son, Trevor.

In 1973, Michael completed his M.F.A. but ceased painting a few months after graduation. He had begun studying quilt history and techniques, and by late summer he exchanged paintbrush for needle and thread. His first exposure to Amish quilts was at a lecture by Jonathan Holstein at the Memorial Art Gallery of the University of Rochester in January 1974.

With his young family, Michael moved back to his boyhood home and began substitute teaching for his former high school art teacher. He also began to teach quiltmaking at adult education workshops throughout southeastern New England. By 1974, Michael had completed his first hand-pieced and hand-quilted full-size quilt, *Meadow Lily*. But he spent relatively little time with traditional quilt patterns before exploring and successfully producing what are known today as art quilts.

Michael James quickly mastered the techniques necessary for precision in quiltmaking, which became a hallmark of his work. These skills have been carefully articulated in the books he has written, *The Quiltmaker's Handbook: A Guide to Design and Construction* (1978) and *The Second Quiltmaker's Handbook: Creative Approaches to Contemporary Quilt Design* (1981).

In 1975, while teaching at the DeCordova Museum School in Lincoln, Massachusetts, he participated in the museum's exhibition *Bed and Board: Quilts and Woodwork*, one of the first nontraditional quilt exhibitions in the country. In 1976, his quilts were also part of the exhibition *Quilts for '76* in the Cyclorama Building of the Boston Center for the Arts. In 1976, Michael attended a quilt conference held in Ithaca, New York, where he met Beth Gutcheon, Jeffrey Gutcheon, Bonnie Leman, Jean Ray Laury, and Myron and Patsy Orlofsky.

In 1977, Michael began to teach quiltmaking throughout the United States and Canada, and trips to England (in 1980) and France and Switzerland (in 1983) soon followed. His first solo exhibition of quilts, organized by Bridgewater (Massachusetts) State College, included *Night Sky 1*, *Razzle Dazzle*, and *Tossed Salad*, among other works. He was awarded a Visual Artist Fellowship in Crafts by the National Endowment for the Arts (NEA) in 1978 and soon after moved into his new home studio in Somerset Village, Massachusetts, which more than tripled his workspace. He also received his first

Home Economics | Designed, machine-pieced, and machine-quilted by Michael James | 2005 | 126½ × 84½ inches | **Cotton and dyes.** Collection of the Racine Art Museum, Racine, Wisconsin. *Photo by Larry Gawel, © 2005 Michael James*

corporate commission and created *The Seasons* for the Waltham Federal Savings and Loan Association in the late 1970s.

Although Michael had always liked quilts and was fascinated by the history of quiltmaking, only his very early quilts were in a traditional style. When Michael began his series quilts, he also began to explore color gradations, primarily with strip piecing. With this new method, the sewing machine was used to create fabric from strips of many different colors. By cutting the resulting pieced cloth into curved shapes, he created a sense of movement as he explored the color and value transitions made possible by this technique. These strip-pieced quilts came to represent the Michael James style. Strip piecing also allowed for exploration of color interaction with linear designs, which was his primary focus at the time. He received numerous prestigious awards as well as a second NEA fellowship in 1988.

In the mid-1980s, he made a series of quilts based on musical and dance motifs (the Rhythm/Color series). He then began working with radical angles and more color/light exploration, advancing far from the earlier grid patterns. Swirls and waves with a strong sense of movement dominated his work. His style was further enhanced by experiences gathered in his travels, and he also drew inspiration from the natural world.

At the invitation of Nihon Vogue, Michael visited Japan for the first time in 1990, giving lectures and workshops in both Tokyo and Osaka. Later that year, as a beneficiary of an NEA U.S.A./France Exchange fellowship, he traveled to La Napoule, France, to join five Europeans and ten Americans as artists in residence at the La Napoule Art Foundation. During his residency, he worked exclusively on paper, completing a series of oil pastel drawings that eventually led him to a major breakthrough in his quilt work.

The University of Massachusetts (Dartmouth, formerly Southeastern Massachusetts University), Michael James's alma mater, awarded him an honorary doctor of fine arts degree in 1992. His induction into the Quilters Hall of Fame followed

Rhythm/Color: Improvisation 2 | Designed, machine-pieced, and machine-quilted by Michael James | 1986 | 79 × 79 inches | Cotton and silk. Michael James's work has always been concerned with formal elements of the quilt surface. Here, diagonal stripes and curved shapes break free from the underlying grid of blocks, seeming to dance across the surface. Checkerboards punctuate the complex abstract rhythms. A palette using many shades of brilliant color is a trademark of his work. *Photo by David Caras, © 1986 Michael James*

Lush Life | Designed, machine-pieced, and machine-quilted by Michael James | 1992 | 73 × 73 inches | Cotton and silk; machine-sewn. Private collection. *Photo by David Caras, © 1992 Michael James*

in 1993, along with more international travel, including trips to Florence, Italy, and Barcelona, Spain. The Smithsonian Institution acquired *Quilt No. 150: Rehoboth Meander* in 1994. This was also the year he received the first biennial Society of Arts and Crafts Award in Boston.

The early 1990s was a very prolific period for the artist, who introduced curved forms with angles into his work. *Lush Life* is regarded as a turning point for Michael, with a look back to his interest in biomorphic forms and ahead to the expressiveness of his more recent work.

While in Oslo, Norway, Michael was inspired by a sixteenth-century Russian icon with a simple but intriguing black-and-white geometric pattern, and not long after, *Ikon* was completed and exhibited in Quilt National 1997.

Two of Michael's quilts, *Aurora* (1978) and *Rhythm/Color: Improvisation* (1985), were selected for the exhibit *America's 100 Best Quilts of the 20th Century*. In the catalog entry for *Rhythm/ Color: Improvisation*, Alyson B. Stanfield states, "His mature work . . . is completely abstract and is characterized by exhaustive study of color relationships. Minute differences in tone and value appear to be the subject."

Michael James was honored in 1999 with a twenty-five-year retrospective of his work at the Museum of the American Quilter's Society in Paducah, Kentucky, and his quilts have been included in six Quilt National exhibits as well as in invitational shows at the Museum of Arts and Design (formerly the American Craft Museum) in New York City. Michael delivered the keynote address at the American Quilt Study Group Seminar in 2000. In 2001, he was named a fellow of the American Craft Council.

Since the organization's founding in 1997, Michael has worked closely with the International Quilt Study Center, beginning as an adviser. In 2000, Michael left his longtime home in Massachusetts

Digitally developed image surfaces printed with reactive dyes on cotton substrates. This self-portrait is a digital manipulation of a photograph that James printed on fabric but, as of the printing of this book, hasn't yet used in any work. He uses this image on his Facebook page because it refers to the nature of his current studio practice. *Photo by Judith James, © Michael James*

basics of the CAD programs are mastered, experimentation will open endless avenues for creative exploration. The danger is that this work can easily become facile, leading to vapid or predictable photo montages with little meaning or emotional resonance. This is a problem not unique to digital quilts, of course. It's a concern in any medium and with any materials or processes.

In 2005 and 2006, Michael spent time preparing for two major exhibits, including creating some of his most ambitious work to date, made for his solo show at the Racine Art Museum in the winter of 2006. Working with studio assistant Leah Sorensen-Hayes, he continued to develop new concepts using digital development and print media, and in 2008 showed a large group of new works, including the *Daybook* series, in *The Life in a Day* at Modern Arts Midwest in Lincoln, Nebraska. In order for a piece to qualify as a *Daybook* quilt, in addition to following a prescribed geometric format that he configured, James determined that once he began working on a top, he would not leave the studio until it was completed. Some went together effortlessly in as little as one hour; some took the better part of a studio day. Each of these pieces is approximately thirty-eight inches by twenty-four inches.

In a statement from 2007 about the *Daybook* series, Michael wrote: "In any case, the individual results can be taken as reflections of my mood or my emotional/intellectual impulses as I composed the surface arrangement. In this sense each of these works is an entry in a 'Daybook'—tied to a specific date and serving as a record of my relationship to my sources and my medium on the given day. . . . I refuse to insist on a singular meaning in any of these pieces as I know there are meanings lying within them that even I often fail to recognize."

To be sure, advances in technology have had an enormous influence on Michael's work in the first decade of the twenty-first century. Many of these more recently completed quilts were exhibited at the following venues: Fuller Craft Museum (Massachusetts, 2005), Racine Art Museum (Wisconsin, 2006), La Linguella (Elba, Italy, 2006), Festival of Quilts (United Kingdom, 2006), Seoul National University Museum of Arts (Republic of Korea, 2007), Modern Arts Midwest (Nebraska, 2008), and 15ème Carrefour International du Patchwork (Alsace, France, 2009).

Michael James, current chair of the Department of Textiles, Clothing and Design at the University of Nebraska–Lincoln, acknowledges the university for its strong support. In his own words: "If I had to try to satisfy the tastes of the small number of collectors in the area of the nontraditional quilt, my work would not have been able to evolve as it has. I have access to advanced technology that has allowed me to create a very different

to assume a position as senior lecturer at the University of Nebraska–Lincoln, in its Department of Textiles, Clothing and Design, the parent department of the International Quilt Study Center and Museum. He was granted tenure as the Ardis James Professor of Textiles, Clothing and Design in the College of Education and Human Sciences in 2003. Two years later, he assumed the position of department chair and currently continues to hold an administrative appointment.

He co-chaired the International Quilt Study Center's first symposium, "Wild By Design," in 2003. The year 2003 also brought a tremendous change in Michael's quilts, a change largely due to his increasing ability to successfully use sophisticated design software like Adobe Photoshop and Adobe Illustrator. In a feature article he wrote titled "The Digital Quilt" for *Fiberarts* contemporary textile art and craft magazine (November/December 2003), he further explained:

The capacity to place imagery on fabric is virtually unlimited. Almost anything that the imagination can conceive, combined with the facility offered by layering, transparency, tiling, color reduction, filtering, and other digital options, as well as photography and all that this medium brings to visual expression, is doable. This aforementioned facility doesn't come easily, but once the

type of quilt, one whose allegiances are cross-disciplinary and whose tendencies are progressive rather than conservative. By definition, art is inventive and forward looking, and embraces experimentation and change. I've always worked with this belief as an article of faith." While at the university he has also taught in the Visual Literacy Program, the foundation curriculum for all art, architecture, and design majors, and he regularly teaches courses for the graduate concentration in quilt studies, part of the textile history major.

Not only has Michael James created a distinctive and exceptional body of work in fiber art, he has also been a leader in fostering wider acceptance of nontraditional quilts. His induction into the Quilters Hall of Fame in 1993 honored his many contributions to contemporary quiltmaking. Without doubt, Michael continues to be a leader in the art-quilt movement, once expected to be short lived. Michael James has proved this underestimation wrong time after time.

Selected Reading

James, Michael. "Getting Our Bearings: Quilt Art at Century's End." *American Quilter*, Fall 1992, 52–54, 74.

———. "In the Beginning: Musings on the Birth of the Studio Art Quilt Movement." Keynote address, American Quilt Study Group seminar 2000. *Blanket Statements*, no. 64 (Spring 2001).

———. *The Quiltmaker's Handbook: A Guide to Design and Construction*. New York: Prentice-Hall, 1978. Reprint, Mountain View, CA: Leone Publications, 1993.

———. *The Second Quiltmaker's Handbook: Creative Approaches to Contemporary Quilt Design*. New York: Prentice-Hall, 1981. Reprint, Mountain View, CA: Leone Publications, 1993.

Lyon, David, Patricia Harris, and Patricia Malarcher. *Michael James: Studio Quilts*. Swansea, MA: Whetstone Hill Publications, 1995. Copublished by Editions Victor Attinger, Switzerland.

Daybook: 10 | Designed, machine-pieced, and machine-quilted by Michael James | June 2007 | 37 × 23 inches. Digitally developed image surfaces printed with reactive dyes on cotton substrates, machine-pieced and machine-quilted | Collection of the University of Nebraska Medical Center, Omaha.

Daybook: 17 | Designed, machine-pieced, and machine-quilted by Michael James | June 2007 | 36½ × 22½ inches | Digitally developed image surfaces printed with reactive dyes on cotton substrates, machine-pieced and machine-quilted | Collection of the artist.

Daybook: 15 | Designed, machine-pieced, and machine-quilted by Michael James | July 2007 | 36¾ × 22¼ inches | Digitally developed image surfaces printed with reactive dyes on cotton substrates, machine-pieced and machine-quilted | Private collection.

In addition to following a prescribed geometric format that he configured, James determined that for the pieces of his *Daybook* series, once he began working on a top, he would not leave the studio until it was completed. *Photo by Larry Gawel, © 2007 Michael James*

Helen Kelley

1927–2008

"There's nothing that beats the pleasure we feel

when we have clipped off the last thread end,

and our very own quilt,

child of our heart,

is finished."

—Helen Kelley, Patchworks website, May 2008

Helen Kelley was inducted into the Quilters Hall of Fame in Marion, Indiana, on July 19, 2008. *Photo by Bill Kelley, courtesy of the Estate of Helen Kelley*

by Georgia Bonesteel

WORDS AND STITCHES define Helen Kelley. Through her "Loose Threads" column in *Quilter's Newsletter Magazine* and her many creative quilts, she established herself in the quilt world. Beginning in 1946, when Helen started to quilt, she was on a forward path that has used her education and inquisitive skills to the utmost. Her columns were full of honest, practical experiences that relate to quilters' lives. They were comforting and corresponded to people's everyday joys and problems. Many readers kept her articles right on their bed stands, just like a good novel.

A prolific quilter, Helen made more than 150 quilts, including *Renaissance*, which was recognized among the one hundred best quilts of the twentieth century. Every stitch holds a story and is backed by hours of study.

Helen Longfield was born April 28, 1927, in Englewood, New Jersey, of English and German heritage. Her early years were spent on the East Coast, from New York to Georgia, where her father was a consulting engineer for textile mills. It was in her high school years in New Haven, Connecticut, that she developed a love of the theater. She attended Stephens College in Missouri, and graduated in 1947 with a degree in theater from

the School of Speech at Northwestern University in Illinois, where she joined the Delta Zeta sorority. At the University of Minnesota, she did graduate studies in speech pathology. Of course, this explained her knack for humor and style in both her writings and lectures.

Helen experienced all the difficulties of the Depression and World War II. In 1945, when she was home from school, her brother, Rennie, was released from the German POW camp Stalag VIIA where he had been taken prisoner in November 1944 while his military unit was pushing north from eastern France. She spent hours with him recording his experiences and wrote it out in a forty-page double-spaced manuscript that they called "Kriege." This early foray into writing began a career in which Helen would use the experiences of ordinary people to encourage others, which was the basis of her "Loose Threads" column.

In the 1940s, with Helen's fiancé in the Marine Corps, a quilt seemed essential. Not knowing another quilter, Helen studied the character and style of old quilts and was able to figure it all out. After marriage, she and her husband, Bill, lived for many years in Schenectady, New York, then moved to Erie, Pennsylvania, and Johnson City, New York, before Bill led them back to Minnesota,

Mother Goose | Made by Helen Kelley | 1978 | 45 × 60 inches. This delightful child's quilt was made by Helen Kelley for a granddaughter. An assemblage of colorful one-inch fabric squares, it depicts the cover of the classic *Real Mother Goose* book, illustrated in 1916 by Blanche Fisher Wright. *Photo by Bill Kelley, courtesy of the Estate of Helen Kelley*

his native state, in 1962. Amid all these moves, including those associated with his service in the Marine Corps, Helen toted her trusty Singer featherweight sewing machine with her to make clothing and costumes for herself and their children.

In time, their family grew to five children, and raising them became a challenge and a full-time endeavor for Helen. Their son, Billy, was born developmentally disabled, so his life required flexibility and creativity from everyone. Their daughter, Connie, is blind. Both Connie and Billy were diagnosed with type 1 diabetes when the family arrived in Minnesota, and Helen had to manage their insulin and diets among all her other duties. Their four daughters have grown into remarkably flexible and creative women. They all sew beautifully. Even their daughter Connie sews, although she is blind; the walls of her California condo are hung with quilts, both hers and Helen's.

While most people give gifts to family, Helen made special quilts in recognition of each family member. By the end of her life, Helen had five grandchildren and seven great-grandchildren, and her quilt role had evolved into "Grandma Kelley's" quilts.

One of Helen's most famous quilts is *The Unicorn* (1987), which began with traditional designs but changed once her research started. She was inspired by the symbolism in Renaissance paintings and the *mille fleur* tapestries in the Cluny Museum in Paris. On the back of the quilt, Helen listed the symbols used, such as the strawberry plant at the feet of Mary, representing righteousness.

Loose Threads is a compilation of many of the "Loose Threads" columns Helen Kelley wrote for *Quilters Newsletter Magazine.*

Another noteworthy quilt, *Renaissance*, seven years in the making, was finished in 1983. In this quilt, she set out to blend the art and traditions of Norway with American quilts, resulting in a stunning tribute to her husband's maternal grandmother, who came to America from Norway at eighteen and was known as "Granny" by the family. Each motif is a double appliqué with black applied first, under a second image inspired by Norwegian woven tapestry. Helen considers this a strong, groundbreaking quilt, especially since it was made during the bicentennial time when most quilters were still using traditional patterns. This quilt received recognition in many venues, including Marion Nelson's Norwegian American handicraft exhibit, which opened in St. Paul, Minnesota, and traveled to Seattle, Washington, and Oslo, Norway. It was later acquired by the Minnesota Historical Society.

At the end of her life, Helen still found creative inspiration by using old patterns in her exciting contemporary quilts. On her website, she stated that "ethnic needlework from around the globe has fascinated me. . . . The origins of American Indian ribbonwork and of Indian Star quilts have been of particular interest to me."

Helen's Postcard Quilts evoke precious memories of places she has visited. Finally numbering twenty-four quilts, all in a thirty-five-inch by fifty-inch format, they include images of Norway, Jamaica, Canada, New Zealand, England, Scotland, Wales, France, Austria, Switzerland, and many states and cities in the United States.

A nonpostcard quilt that Helen made to commemorate a family vacation in Jamaica was stolen from a quilt show in Chicago. She called this *Come Back to Jamaica* and gave a framed photographic copy to each of her daughters. Another of her quilts, *Crazy Jubilee*, or as her family knows it, *Victoria*, was acquired for the quilt collection at the International Center for Quilt Study in Lincoln, Nebraska.

Helen's writings have appeared in several books and countless magazine articles, and her own library reflected her ambitious research abilities. Her popular column, "Loose Threads," was published in *Quilter's Newsletter Magazine* from 1983 through 2008, with her last column appearing posthumously in the December/January 2009 issue. As a result of all of this research and writing, Helen's work as a writer, consultant, and historian continues to inspire and entertain readers.

Early on, Helen recognized the importance of putting a time period to quilts in her 1985 self-published book *Guidelines for Dating Quilts*. Her book *Scarlet Ribbons* was a twenty-five-year study of the Native American Indians' use of French silk ribbons for reverse appliqué floral designs. In 2003,

Helen Kelley with yellow roses at her induction into the Quilters Hall of Fame. *Photo by Bill Kelley, courtesy of the Estate of Helen Kelley*

Helen Kelley quilting one of several postcard quilts she made. *Photo by Bill Kelley, courtesy of the Estate of Helen Kelley*

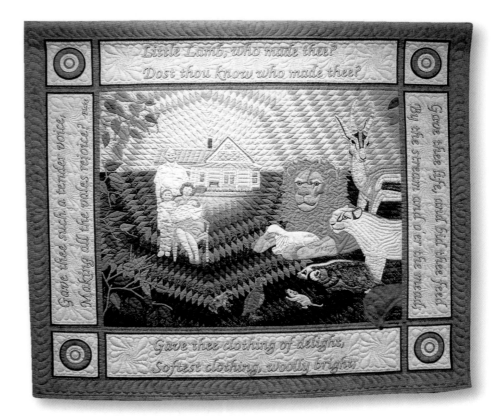

Little Lamb | Made by Helen Kelley | Completed in 1993 | 52 × 60 inches. This quilt was made for great-grandson Jonathan Reynolds Rolfsen. A Prairie Star design frames a small house in Pawnee City, Nebraska. Using the style of painter Edward Hicks, who was known for his Peaceable Kingdom paintings, Helen added some Nebraska animals to her picture and used a Victorian doorpost design for the border. The border is part of the "Little Lamb" poem by William Blake. *Photo by Bill Kelley, courtesy of the Estate of Helen Kelley*

Every Quilt Tells A Story: A Quilter's Stash of Wit and Wisdom was the first of three collections of favorite "Loose Threads" articles. *Helen Kelley's Joy of Quilting* won the Midwest Book Award for the best craft/hobby book in 2004. The title of this book was chosen to reflect Helen's pride that her mother had learned to cook under Irma Rombauer, author of *The Joy of Cooking*. A third collection of her writings, *Loose Threads: Stories to Keep Quilters in Stitches*, was published in 2008.

Nothing pleased Helen more than her family, her church involvement, and her meaningful Minnesota quilt guild, and she found a way to balance these three loves gracefully. As the first president of the Minnesota Quilters in 1978, she was very proud of the role they have played in sustaining the growth of the American quilt today. She helped with the Minnesota Quilt History Project by driving throughout Minnesota and the Dakotas to pick up and return quilts for documentation. At Minnesota Quilters meetings, Helen's nametag would show her as "Member Number 3," and she was always comfortable staying in the background, enjoying the work of others.

In 1998 she was named "Minnesota Quilter of the Year." Other awards included 1995 Artist of Distinction, Fiber/Metal Arts of Minnesota, and the 2000 Minnesota Textile Center's Spun Gold Award.

Helen enjoyed talking to other quilters. At the same time that Minnesota Quilters was forming, Helen found four other ladies whom she respected as quilters and who liked to get together frequently. They called themselves the Idiots and shared humor, coffee, and treats as well as serious thoughts about quilting. Her family has two small, unique friendship quilts that came from the group.

Helen designed four large biblical wall quilts for her church, North Como Presbyterian Church. She, and a great group of quilters from the church, pieced and quilted the four hangings. On permanent display in the church great room, they are *Women of the Bible*, *Jesus and the Children*, *I Am the Vine*, and *The Good Samaritan*.

Helen shared her quilt knowledge as a teacher, with more than 300 engagements in thirty-five states and nine foreign countries, where her teaching was well received due to her engaging style and meticulous research. Sharing quilt knowledge "across the pond" led to many opportunities for Helen. She gave a number of talks and workshops in England, at the American Museum in Bath and the Victoria and Albert Museum in London.

With her inquisitive mind, Helen was able to form wonderful friendships, especially with noted quilters. Her technique was just to write and request an audience. This worked with two English honorees of the Quilters Hall of Fame, Shiela Betterton and Amy Emms M.B.E., the North Country quilter who was decorated by the Queen.

Other honoree friendships for Helen included Mary Barton and Bonnie Leman. Helen recalled a wintry Iowa drive on ice with Bill to visit Mary. In her sweet and delicate manner, Mary shared her quilt expertise. Bonnie Leman was always very good to Helen also, so it was easy for her to respond to this trust.

In her understated and humorous way, Helen summed up her life in these words: "What have I done with my life? I am a pretty good sewer. I have a family who tolerates me. I am a pretty poor businesswoman since I give things away. Being the daughter of a Victorian woman meant that a well-bred woman never discussed money. However, I married a man who makes enough money to buy groceries, and I have made enough to buy fabric."

In a more serious vein, Helen stated that she had "a total commitment to inspiring and educating others about the history of quilts and their beauty." Her mission was to enable everyone she touched to grow by giving them an understanding of their own potential so they could experience the satisfaction and creative joy of making something beautiful. Helen's wonderful life of making quilts and encouraging others through her writing and friendship came to a close on September 1, 2008, when she suffered a heart attack at her home in Minneapolis, Minnesota. A line from her obituary summed up her work: "She was a colorful person, and her quilts all had a colorful story behind them. Just every stitch, every bit of her workmanship had great needlework."

Selected Reading

Kelley, Helen. *Dating Quilts from 1600 to the Present.* Lafayette, CA: C&T Publishing, 1995.

———. *Every Quilt Tells a Story: A Quilter's Stash of Wit and Wisdom.* Stillwater, MN: Voyageur Press, 2003.

———. *Helen Kelley's Joy of Quilting.* Stillwater, MN: Voyageur Press, 2004.

———. "Loose Threads." Column in *Quilter's Newsletter Magazine* from no. 149 (February 1983) to no. 407 (December 2008).

———. *Loose Threads: Stories to Keep Quilters in Stitches.* Stillwater, MN: Voyageur Press, 2008.

Helen Kelley signs a copy of her 2003 book, *Every Quilt Tells a Story: A Quilter's Stash of Wit and Wisdom*, a collection of her popular "Loose Threads" columns. *Photo by Bill Kelley, courtesy of the Estate of Helen Kelley*

Rose Kretsinger

1886–1963

*"Beautiful things appeal to the emotions and create
a sort of mental state of quiet and spiritual goodness. . . .
We might even liken the quilt to musical composition. It has its high
and low color tones, and its swelling and diminishing line rhythm;
all carrying the eye through a design composition."*

—Rose G. Kretsinger, *The Romance of the Patchwork Quilt
in America* (1935), pp. 261–262

Rose Good Kretsinger was inducted into
the Quilters Hall of Fame at the Continental
Quilting Congress in Arlington, Virginia, on
October 5, 1985. *Courtesy of Mary Kretsinger
and Barbara Brackman*

by Barbara Brackman

ROSE FRANCIS GOOD was born in the small town of
Hope, Kansas, on November 29, 1886, and lived most of her
adult life in the larger town of Emporia, Kansas. Rose's father
was a partner in Good & Eisenhower, a Hope dry goods store.
Shortly before Rose's birth, Milton Good sold his share to David
Eisenhower, and when the new baby was a few weeks old, Rose's
family returned to Abilene. David Eisenhower, who could not
make the Hope store profitable, moved two years later to Texas,
where he and his wife added a son, Dwight David, a future
president of the United States, to their family.

When Rose was in her teens, the family moved again, to
Kansas City, Missouri. Rose went to Chicago, where she received
a degree in design from the Art Institute of Chicago in 1908. After
spending a year studying in Europe, she returned to Chicago,
where she designed jewelry during her twenties.

In 1914, Rose Good retired from professional design and
moved to Emporia, Kansas, when she married a well-to-do
widower, William Kretsinger, who was an attorney and rancher
in his early forties. They raised two children, William and Mary

Amelia. Rose became an important figure in the clubs and
committees that formed the world of the women in her set.

Emporia considered itself more than a mere cow town or
railroad junction. It was the "Athens of Kansas," a nickname
bestowed by William Allen White, Emporia's resident sage. White
created a national image of his hometown as the small town, the
antithesis of urban, industrial New York City. The town became a
national symbol of front porch, Main Street values. White liked to
describe the town as egalitarian, but there was an upper class for
whom he edited his newspaper—"the best people of the city," he
called them.

In 1926, during the Colonial Revival, Rose took up quilting
at the age of forty. She had inherited an antique bed and decided
to follow the magazines' advice to cover it with a copy of an
authentic old quilt. Quiltmaking was also a form of therapy at
first. She found handwork consoling after losing her mother in
an automobile accident. Because her friends made such a fuss
over her quilt, she entered it in a fair, where, to her surprise, she
won the blue ribbon. Pleased with the success of her first effort,

Paradise Garden | Designed and appliquéd by Rose Frances Good Kretsinger, Emporia, Kansas | Quilted by an unknown quilter | 1946 |
94 × 94 inches | Cotton; appliquéd, stuffed, quilted. Rose Kretsinger designed and appliquéd this masterpiece, inspired by a quilt made in 1857 by Arsinoe Kelsey
Bowen, which was illustrated in Ruth Finley's book, *Old Patchwork Quilts and the Women Who Made Them*. This was Rose's last quilt. *Courtesy of the Spencer Museum of Art,
University of Kansas, gift of Mary Kretsinger (1971.0104)*

she began a second, and over the next two decades produced a remarkable group of quilts.

For her inspiration, Rose ignored commercial trends, focusing instead on quilts of the past. The patterns and kits of the day resulted in a predictable product, a quality Rose criticized. "Women are depending more upon the printed pattern sheet to save time and labor. These having been used time and again often become very tiresome." Rather than buying her patterns from magazines, she found most of her ideas in old quilts, borrowing family heirlooms from friends and sketching museum quilts. Instead of using the new multicolored dress prints, she preferred nostalgic calicoes and antique fabrics to give the old-fashioned look she wanted.

The extraordinary success of Rose's quilts lies in her reworking of the old designs. With her design background, she knew how to add drama with vivid colors and black accents, to add line with an overlay of quilting and a scalloped edge, and to add sophistication by reorganizing compositions, tightening up a wandering vine here and filling in a blank space there. She finished her works of art with bold borders. Rose's unique combination of traditional standards and modern design earned her local and national fame, as she won prizes in contests from the Lyon County Fair to New York City.

The Kansas City Art Institute mounted an exhibit of her quilts in the early 1930s, and her national reputation grew with the publication in 1935 of the book she coauthored with Carrie Hall, *The Romance of the Patchwork Quilt in America*. Rose's contribution was the section on the history of quilting, with photographs and diagrams of antique and contemporary designs.

The *Orchid Wreath*, made in 1929, is her only truly original design. When her daughter, Mary, asked for an orchid quilt to match her bedroom décor, Rose found inspiration in an advertising card she had seen at a soda fountain. Her other quilts, antique or commercial patterns redrawn, proved to be showstoppers in the national quilt shows of the 1930s and 1940s.

In the 1942 National Needlework Contest sponsored by *Woman's Day* magazine, her quilt *Calendula* won a second prize. The first prize was won by Piné Hawkes Eisfeller of Schenectedy, New York, for her variation of the heirloom medallion wreath quilt called *The Garden* (see page 90), made in 1857 by Arsinoe Kelsey Bowen and published in Ruth Finley's *Old Patchwork Quilts and the Women Who Made Them*. Second prize must have

Pride of Iowa | Rose Frances Good Kretsinger, Emporia, Kansas | 1927 | 84¾ × 87½ inches | Cotton; appliquéd, pieced, embroidered, trapuntoed, and quilted. This beautifully appliquéd quilt with graceful leaf border boasts fine quilting and trapunto work of a lyre harp and feather motifs. The red, green, and yellow reflect the color of the fabrics at the time Rose made this, but it is a good early-twentieth-century reproduction of the red and green quilts, with four large appliqué blocks made most often in Ohio but also elsewhere in the middle of the nineteenth century. *Courtesy of the Spencer Museum of Art Gift of Mary Kretsinger (1971.0097)*

American Quilt Renaissance: Three Women Who Influenced Quiltmaking in the Early Twentieth Century featured the work of Quilters Hall of Fame honorees Rose Kretsinger, Carrie Hall, and Marie Webster. The catalog was published in 1997 and served as the catalogue for an exhibition organized by the Indianapolis Museum of Art and the Spencer Museum of Art, which traveled to Japan.

Orchid Wreath | Rose Frances Good Kretsinger, Emporia, Kansas | 1928 | 91¾ × 91¾ inches | Cotton; pieced, embroidered, appliquéd, and quilted. When her daughter, Mary, asked for an orchid quilt to match her bedroom décor, Rose found inspiration in an advertising card she saw at a soda fountain. This quilt, Rose's only truly original design, was selected for inclusion in *The Twentieth Century's Best American Quilts. Courtesy of the Spencer Museum of Art, Gift of Mary Kretsinger (1971.0094)*

Selected Reading

Carter, Hazel. "Evolution and New Revelation: The Garden Quilt Design." *Blanket Statements*, American Quilt Study Group, no. 71 (Winter 2003).

Hall, Carrie A., and Rose G. Kretsinger. *The Romance of the Patchwork Quilt in America.* Caldwell, ID: The Caxton Printers, Ltd., 1935.

Leman, Bonnie. "Two Masters: Kretsinger & Stenge." *Quilter's Newsletter Magazine*, no. 128 (January 1981).

"Rose Kretsinger, Appliqué Artist." *Quilter's Newsletter Magazine*, no. 97 (December 1977): 24. (Interview with daughter Mary Kretsinger of Emporia, Kansas.)

Shankel, Carol, ed. *American Quilt Renaissance: Three Women Who Influenced Quiltmaking in the Early 20th Century.* Tokyo: Kokusai Art, 1997.

vexed Rose, for she wrote the terse criticism "Poor Design" under the magazine photo of Eisfeller's prizewinning *Cottage Garden*. Rose then designed her own version, which she finished in 1946 and called *Paradise Garden*, the quilt many consider to be her masterpiece. This quilt and her *Orchid Wreath* were selected by a panel of experts for the exhibit *America's 100 Best Quilts of the 20th Century* at the International Quilt Festival in 1999.

Emporia was an unusual place, where quiltmakers developed a community aesthetic with high standards for design, craftsmanship, and originality. Rose often displayed her quilts in contests and exhibits, inspiring others to attempt their own designs or to request her patterns. She communicated her design ideas and craftsmanship by example, sharing patterns and assisting other quiltmakers. With her talent, training, generosity, and competitive nature, she was at the heart of Emporia's exceptional quiltmaking community.

Rose did not do the quilting on her work. Many women before World War II hired professional quilters, a traditional division of labor. The Kretsinger children remember their mother sending her tops out to be quilted, although the quilters' names have been forgotten. It also seems apparent that Rose designed her own quilting patterns and worked closely with the quilters.

Rose appliquéd most of her quilts between 1926 and 1932. In 1940, she was widowed at the age of fifty-four, when William Kretsinger died of heart failure. She began her last quilt, *Paradise Garden*, shortly after his death. Rose died in Emporia in 1963 at the age of seventy-six.

In 1949, *Farm Journal* magazine sold two of her designs, *Oriental Poppy* and *Old Spice*, the only full-size patterns she published. In 1971, her daughter, Mary Kretsinger, donated twelve quilts made by Rose and two made by Rose's mother to the Spencer Museum of Art at the University of Kansas. Rose Kretsinger was inducted into the Quilters Hall of Fame in 1985, with her coauthor, Carrie Hall.

Rose Kretsinger's quilts continue to inspire quiltmakers to the present day. In 1992, the Wichita Art Museum and the Kansas Quilt Project organized the exhibit *Midcentury Masterpieces: Quilts in Emporia, Kansas*, which featured the appliqué work of Rose Kretsinger and her Emporia friends. In 1998, her quilts toured Japan and were featured in the publication *American Quilt Renaissance: Three Women Who Influenced Quiltmaking in the Early 20th Century*, along with the work of honorees Carrie Hall and Marie Webster.

Jean Ray Laury

1928–2011

Jean Ray Laury was inducted into the Quilters Hall of Fame at the Continental Quilting Congress in Arlington, Virginia, on November 6, 1982. Courtesy of Lizabeth Laury

"If you are asking me to offer any advice, it would be to risk everything all the time and to quit trying to be safe. Once you're willing to risk your whole reputation on something, then you can leap forward."

—Jean Ray Laury, *Keeping It All Together* (1983), p. 15

by Elizabeth Palmer-Spilker

IF THE CREATIVE WORK OF JEAN RAY LAURY was gathered in one place, it would take a small army to move it. Not only is her work extensive—quilts, books, and articles—but it also transcends the artist, something that pleases Jean greatly. Beyond the physical manifestation of her art are the countless workshops and lectures she has presented and the numerous women who have benefited from her encouragement and support.

Jean's quilts are known for their coloration and geometry, and most notably for the use of printing and cartooning—using text and storytelling blocks in surface design. Her contemporary and meticulous techniques have earned her pioneer status in the late twentieth century's quilting revival. The subject matter is unconventional, often humorous or political, and very personal.

Jean's sense of humor emerges in her quilts as she pokes fun at herself and life in general. She finds that the humility of cloth and the simplicity of quilting itself allow a quilt to convey a message, which may even jar the viewer's senses, without being confrontational.

Jean Ray was born March 22, 1928, in Doon, Iowa, second of the four daughters of Alice Kloek and Ralph Robert Ray. During her high school years, her family moved to Oak Ridge, Tennessee, where she graduated from high school in 1945. Her childhood love of drawing and painting led her to pursue a degree in art and education at Iowa State Teachers College, Cedar Falls.

After college, she moved to California, where she plotted weather maps in the geology department at UCLA while her fiancé, Frank Laury, was in Navy flight training. After he received his wings, they married and moved to San Diego, where he was stationed and where their son, Tom, was born. The young couple next entered graduate school at Stanford University, where they both studied art and design. Their daughter, Lizabeth, was born while they were living in student housing.

The quilt Jean made for a class project at Stanford in 1956 launched her career. She retained a vivid memory of a quilt she had seen years earlier in a Nebraska museum. The quiltmaker had recorded his own life by piecing bits of old Civil War uniforms into

Tom's Quilt | Designed and made by Jean Ray Laury, California | 1956 | 50 × 74 inches. This quilt, made for a design class at Stanford University, was exhibited at the de Young Museum in San Francisco and then went on tour. In 1960, the quilt was featured in *House Beautiful*, sparking a revolution in quilt design with its use of contemporary images of children's toys, games, food, and everyday objects. *Courtesy of Lizabeth Laury*

his quilt. This inspired Jean to express her own life in her quilt, setting a precedent for much of her future work.

This quilt, which she named *Tom's Quilt* for her four-year-old son, featured bold colors and graphic images that would appeal to any child: an ice cream cone, a train, a birthday cake, the sun, flowers, children playing, and a host of other visions. Included in a Stanford student exhibit at the de Young Art Museum in San Francisco, the quilt was chosen for a world tour sponsored by the United States Information Service.

Jean's career was off and running. In 1958, she entered her quilt in the highly esteemed Eastern States Exposition at Storrowton Village in Springfield, Massachusetts. Her work captured the attention of contest judge Roxa Wright, needlework editor for *House Beautiful*. Roxa encouraged Jean, calling her work "the first attempt she had seen to modernize the art of quiltmaking that combined good design and contemporary color with inherent simple and structural integrity that should be the basis of any quilt."

Jean's successful writing career developed in tandem with her quiltmaking. Roxa Wright invited her to write for *House Beautiful*, where her first article was published in the January 1960 issue. Jean's work has also appeared in *Woman's Day*, *Better Homes and Gardens*, *Family Circle*, *Cosmopolitan*, *Needle and Craft*, and many other publications.

Week at a Glance | Designed and made by Jean Ray Laury, California | 25 × 60 inches (two panels) | All-wool felt; appliquéd, with silk-screen printed lettering, hand painting, and embroidery. This piece offers a glance into every homemaker's week. We all make plans and have visions for the coming days. Then reality sets in. *Courtesy of Lizabeth Laury*

Ho for California! Pioneer Women and Their Quilts, authored by Jean Ray Laury and the California Heritage Quilt Project, discusses the history of quiltmaking in California, shows the routes many of the quilts took to get to California, and documents the quilts of California women. Published in 1990, it was among the earliest of the statewide documentation quilt books.

In 1982, Jean began writing her column, "Keeping It All Together," for *Quilter's Newsletter Magazine*, followed by her "Talking It Over" series in 1984, which delivered her supportive advice with a sense of humor.

Jean Ray Laury was widely acknowledged as a leader of the quilt revival that started in the 1960s. Through her writing, teaching, and lecturing, she encouraged quilters to experiment with ideas and techniques, and to express their own lives in their work. She wrote the first contemporary quilting books, *Applique Stitchery* (1966) and *Quilts and Coverlets: A Contemporary Approach* (1970).

Jean enjoyed a special rapport with young mothers, who face difficulties allowing their creativity to flourish while caring for their families. Her book, the highly regarded *The Creative Woman's Getting-It-All-Together at Home Handbook*, published in 1977, was directed at this group of women.

Jean was an original and prolific writer in a variety of styles on a wide range of topics. She also illustrated her humorous Sunbonnet Sue series and the children's storybook, *No Dragons on My Quilt*. Her recent titles, *Imagery on Fabric*, *The Photo Transfer Handbook*, and *The Fabric Stamping Handbook*, focus on surface design.

She drew inspiration from children and their fresh approach, and she tried to keep a similar lack of barriers in her own work. Other sources of inspiration were the serene setting of her home in the foothills of California's Sierra Nevada Mountains, as well as current events.

The *Senator Van Dalsem Quilt*, also known as *Barefoot and Pregnant*, was inspired by an insensitive comment made by an Arkansas senator. It uses cartooning effectively to satirize the senator's remarks. This quilt was selected as one of *America's 100 Best Quilts of the 20th Century* during the Ultimate Quilt Search by panelists representing the Alliance for American Quilts, the American Quilt Study Group, the International Quilt Association, and the National Quilting Association.

Jean's first major exhibit was held at the Museum of Contemporary Crafts (now the Museum of Arts and Design) in New York City in 1960. She also exhibited at the American Crayon Company, the de Young Art Museum in San Francisco, and in a series of one-woman shows at the California State University Fresno Art Museum. Numerous group shows include the Smithsonian's *Full Deck Art Quilts*.

Old quilts also inspired this thoroughly modern quiltmaker. Jean Ray Laury worked on the California State Quilt Project and authored the book about the project's findings, *Ho for California: Pioneer Women and Their Quilts* (1990). She remembered when a particularly unusual quilt from the nineteenth century was being unfolded, she could feel the power of the quiltmaker's message across the many decades.

A pioneer herself, Jean Ray Laury was inducted into the Quilters Hall of Fame in 1982. She was honored by the San Francisco Women's Foundation and received a California State Arts Commission grant and the Fresno Women Making History Award. In 1997, Jean received the Silver Star Award, presented by Quilts, Inc. at Houston's International Quilt Festival.

After retiring (her husband laughs at the use of that term) she took commissions and wrote fiction, including work on a quilter's

Selected Reading

Laury, Jean Ray. *Applique Stitchery*. New York: Reinhold Publishing, 1966.

———. *Imagery on Fabric: A Complete Surface Design Handbook*. Revised edition. Lafayette, CA: C&T Publishing, 1997.

———. *Quilts and Coverlets: A Contemporary Approach*. New York: Van Nostrand Reinhold Co., 1970.

———. "Talking It Over." Column in *Quilter's Newsletter Magazine*, from no. 161 (April 1984) through no. 216 (October 1989).

Laury, Jean Ray, and the California Heritage Quilt Project. *Ho for California: Pioneer Women and Their Quilts*. New York: E. P. Dutton, 1990.

Imagery on Fabric: A Complete Surface Design Handbook by Jean Ray Laury was so popular that it went into a second updated and expanded edition by 1997. Laury offered a comprehensive array of transfer processes that continue to be employed by contemporary quilt artists.

memoir, called *Growing Up in Doon: The 1930s*. Before it could be published she died of respiratory complications on March 2, 2011. Through her quilts, her writing, and her teaching, Jean Ray Laury truly inspired thousands of women to express their own creativity.

Bonnie Leman

1926–2010

*"Geography prevents us from having
a real old-fashioned quilting bee,
but we can all get together through this magazine, chat,
and exchange our ideas and news in a modern quilting bee."*

—Bonnie Leman, "The Needle's Eye," first issue of *Quilter's Newsletter* (1969), p. 2

Bonnie Leman was inducted into the Quilters Hall of Fame at the Continental Quilting Congress in Arlington, Virginia, on November 6, 1982. *Courtesy of Mary Leman Austin*

by Debra Bissantz

BONNIE LEMAN'S LEGACY TO THE QUILT WORLD is enormous. For her twenty-seven years at the helm of *Quilter's Newsletter Magazine*, she was at the forefront of the late twentieth century's quilt revival. What started with a five-dollar ad in a midwestern newspaper mushroomed into a mail-order business, two quilting magazines, a publishing company, and worldwide quilting competitions and shows.

Bonnie Hale was born in Purdin, Missouri, where she excelled in both academics and sports. She was the valedictorian of her class, as well as a basketball player and table tennis champion. Throughout her life she was a formidable table tennis player until she fell and broke her wrist while playing the game.

She entered Park College, near Kansas City, Missouri, at the age of sixteen and graduated three years later with a degree in home economics and a minor in English. After moving to Colorado in 1953, she obtained her teaching credential from the University of Denver, where she met her husband, George, a fellow graduate student.

Bonnie's quilting story began in 1968, when she and George realized that they needed additional income for their family of six children. They decided to start a mail-order business that Bonnie could run from the kitchen table, allowing her to stay home with the children. Experienced in sewing and needlecrafts, and inspired by her mother's collection of old *Kansas City Star* quilt patterns, Bonnie researched quiltmaking. When she realized there were very few published quilt patterns and no pattern templates available, she decided to develop plastic templates for traditional patterns.

Soon George and Bonnie Leman were running a fledgling mail-order quilting template business, which they named Heirloom Plastics. Their entire advertising budget of five dollars was spent on a classified ad in *Capper's Weekly*, a newspaper popular in small towns in middle America, where Bonnie hoped quiltmaking was still being practiced.

Included in one of the template orders she received was a suggestion from a customer that Bonnie start a newsletter about quilts. She said, "By this time, I had fallen in love with quilts,

Quilter's Newsletter Magazine 25th Anniversary Quilt | Assembled by Linda Holst, quilted by Jonna Castle | 1994 | 98 × 98 inches. Forty-nine center blocks made by quilters and friends of Bonnie Leman; sixty border blocks made by associates, friends, and family. Quilters Hall of Fame founder Hazel Carter contributed a block, as did honorees Cuesta Benberry, Jinny Beyer, Georgia Bonesteel, Karey Bresenhan, Nancy Crow, Carter Houck, Michael James, and Jean Ray Laury. Each of the seven Leman children made one of the border blocks. The quilt was presented to Bonnie at the International Quilt Market and Festival in Houston in November 1994. *Photo by Mellisa Karlin Mahoney, courtesy of the* Quilter's Newsletter Magazine, *collection of Bonnie Leman*

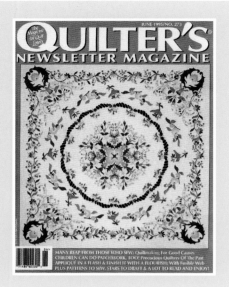

June 1995 issue of *Quilters Newsletter Magazine*, edited by Bonnie Leman.

their history and designs, and I was captivated by the idea of a publication called *Quilter's Newsletter*. I thought it might be the perfect way for me to use my teaching background in home economics and English." Because she knew from her research that there was very little material about quilts currently in print, she was enthusiastic about the idea of a newsletter that included quiltmaking information, history, and patterns, as well as advertising space for their plastic templates.

Even though she was then expecting their seventh child, she told George, "I have to start this newsletter! It offers so many exciting possibilities, and it would be such fun to do." He encouraged her, and within several weeks she had put together a sixteen-page issue on her portable typewriter. That first issue appeared on September 21, 1969, the same day their baby boy, Matthew, was born.

The response to this first issue was so great that Bonnie optimistically subtitled the second issue "The Magazine for Quilt Lovers." She made it her goal to improve every issue and decided to publish monthly. *Quilter's Newsletter* soon became a leading force in the late twentieth century's quilt revival. The magazine gradually evolved from what Bonnie described as "a novice publisher's homemade newsletter" of sixteen black-and-white pages to a handsome full-color magazine with eighty or more pages.

As editor in chief, Bonnie was responsible for all aspects of the publication. At first, she wrote all the copy and designed

many of the patterns. The magazine's first employee was Bonnie's daughter Mary, who drew some of the illustrations as an after-school job. In the early 1970s, Bonnie began to expand the scope of the magazine's content as well as the staff, and in July 1974, with issue number 57, she changed its name from *Quilter's Newsletter* to *Quilter's Newsletter Magazine* (QNM). Over time, the number of Leman Publications' employees increased from one to more than sixty, and the number of subscribers to *QNM* grew from 5,000 to more than 220,000 in more than 110 countries around the world.

As the interest in quilting grew, there were still very few quilt shops. In 1972, Bonnie and her husband opened a quilt shop called Quilts and Other Comforts and gave the same name to their mail-order business. Five years later, the Lemans sold the retail shop, but retained the mail-order business.

The Lemans were particularly busy during the U.S. bicentennial, which sparked a revival of the art of quilting, with quilt shops, quilt guilds, and exhibitions proliferating all across the country. George had given up his teaching career and was now devoting all his time to the quilting business. He developed a traveling quilt show in a custom-made vehicle he called "the Quilt-mobile." During 1975 and 1976, George traveled to quilt shows and events around the nation, with the children taking turns to accompany him.

In the early 1980s, Leman Publications joined the computer age and began to grow in new directions. George learned about more sophisticated mailing equipment, and Bonnie learned desktop publishing. The company also expanded by starting a book publishing company, Moon Over the Mountain, by adding a wholesale division, and by entering the international market. Many years later, Bonnie would reminisce, "The kitchen-table publishing I enjoyed so much in the early 1970s became just a happy memory."

In response to requests of *QNM* readers for more quilt patterns, she started a second magazine in 1982 entitled *Quiltmaker*. Because quiltmakers were asking for more colors to work with, Bonnie produced a line of solid-colored fabrics named Columbine Cottons, and later tried her hand at printed fabric design.

In 1986, *QNM* sponsored the first worldwide quilt competition and exhibit, *Quilts: Visions of the World*, in conjunction with the debut of Quilt Expo Europa in Salzburg, Austria. This biennial competition has been a force for uniting quilters around the world.

Home Sweet Home | 1989 | 78 × 78 inches. This quilt is made of some of the winning blocks from the Home Sweet Home contest *Quilter's Newsletter Magazine* held to celebrate twenty years of publication. Hundreds and hundreds of blocks were submitted by an international readership. The quilt features work from quilters in the United States as well as Canada, England, Germany, Holland, Japan, Korea, Scotland, United Arab Emirates, and Zimbabwe. *Photo by Melissa Karlin Mahoney, courtesy of Mary Leman Austin*

Bonnie's editorials, "The Needle's Eye," frequently aired significant and controversial issues in the quilt world. Questions about the status of quilts as art, the conservation of old quilts, and the importation of reproduction quilts by the Smithsonian generated intense interest. Her columns have had a profound influence on quiltmakers worldwide.

Leman Publications became a subsidiary of Rodale Press in 1991, and in December 1994, Mary Leman Austin, who had been working in the family business since she was a teenager, became executive director. Bonnie remained as editor in chief until September 1996, when she retired after twenty-seven years of leadership and innovation. Amazingly, Bonnie had also found time to author or coauthor seven books about quilting, and to edit or publish another seventeen books.

Bonnie received numerous awards, including induction into the Quilters Hall of Fame in 1982. She also was honored with the first Silver Star Award in 1994, presented by Quilts, Inc., the parent company of the International Quilt Festival and Quilt Market.

Bonnie herself credited many people for her success. When interviewed, she stated: "I have been inspired by many people along the way, among them the talented people who have worked with me to give quilt lovers the best that we could, and certainly by the quiltmakers of long ago who left us such a beautiful legacy. But I have to say my main inspiration has always been the 'ordinary, everyday' home quilters who simply make quilts for beds, or to give to someone, or just to have because they are beautiful and they love them. It has been the quilters out there who are making quilts because it is a part of what they do to make a home. Perhaps they make a quilt for a person to love or remember them by or to

During the U.S. Bicentennial, Bonnie's husband, George, traveled to quilt shows and events around the nation in this Quiltmobile, a custom-made vehicle that carried a traveling quilt show they had developed. *Courtesy of Mary Leman Austin*

express their creativity. Quiltmaking is a part of their lives that they tell their stories through."

Bonnie Leman enriched all of our lives by sharing these stories in the pages of *Quilter's Newsletter Magazine*. She was an inspiration for quilters worldwide by showcasing both heirloom and contemporary quilts and by challenging her readers to create their own personal artistic expressions.

After she retired, Bonnie Leman enjoyed putting together a family cookbook, cherished by her children. She did some painting, traveled with her family, was a devoted attendee at the annual Cherry Creek Arts Festival, and indulged her love of reading by reading hundreds of books.

She died on September 4, 2010, at the age of eighty-three. Her son, Andrew, said in her eulogy: "She was an inspiration and a role model not only to her family, not only to the people who knew her personally, but through her books and magazines to countless hundreds of thousands of women and men throughout the world. . . . She built a company that celebrated the humblest and most innocent of art forms, brought people together, unleashed their creativity, and expanded their horizons. She facilitated the growth of an entire industry that has brought joy and fulfillment to a generation and more, forever improving lives and livelihoods. She held herself, and everyone who worked with her, to the highest standards, and spared no effort to make everything she did as good as it could possibly be."

The pages of Bonnie Leman's magazine provided the stage on which many of the stars of the quilt world were introduced during the quilt revival of the late twentieth century. Many of the other honorees of the Quilters Hall of Fame appeared on the pages of *Quilter's Newsletter Magazine*, and many were encouraged by Bonnie Leman to accomplish great things.

Selected Reading

Bishop, Robert, Karey P. Bresenhan, and Bonnie Leman. *Hands All Around: Quilts from Many Nations*. E. P. Dutton, 1987.

Leman, Bonnie, *How to Make a Quilt: 25 Easy Lessons for Beginners*. Denver, CO: Leman Publications, 1971. Revised by Bonnie Leman and Louise Townsend. Denver, CO: Moon Over the Mountain, 1986.

———. *Modern Quilting: Quilt Patterns for Contemporary Quiltmakers*. Book 1. Denver, CO: Leman Publications, 1977.

———. (founder and editor in chief). *Quilter's Newsletter and Quilter's Newsletter Magazine*, from September 1969 through September 1996. Author, "The Needle's Eye" column and numerous articles and patterns.

———. *Quilts: Discovering a New World*. Exhibit catalog. Denver, CO: Leman Publications, 1992.

Amish Storm at Sea | Maker unknown | Circa early twentieth century | 70 × 80 inches | Hand-quilted and machine-pieced. Bonnie Leman's personal collection included several Amish quilts. She was particularly drawn to their bold graphic qualities and considered them fine art. This quilt was obtained during some of Bonnie's travels as she attended quilt shows around the Midwest in the early 1980s. *Photo by Melissa Karlin Mahoney, courtesy of Mary Leman Austin*

Ruby McKim
1891–1976

"Quilts—We never have too many. . . .
Something useful, something beautiful
or fittingly clever when finished
should of course be the aim of every woman
who enjoys doing handwork."

—Ruby Short McKim, *Better Homes and Gardens*, March 1930

Ruby Short McKim was inducted into the Quilters Hall of Fame in Marion, Indiana, on July 20, 2002. *Courtesy of Christina Fullerton Jones*

by Christina Fullerton Jones

RUBY IRENE SHORT was born July 27, 1891, in Millersburg, Illinois, to Morris Trimble Short, a frontier missionary for the Reorganized Church of Jesus Christ of Latter-day Saints (now Community of Christ), and Viola Vernon Short.

In 1899, the family moved to Independence, Missouri. Although Morris died two years later, Viola decided to stay in Independence, and Ruby graduated from Independence High School in 1910. While at school, Ruby won the coveted Art Award in her senior year. She served as art editor for the high school yearbook, which featured her whimsical pen-and-ink drawings— her first works to appear in print.

In an era when young girls were usually sheltered at home until marriage, in 1910, at the age of nineteen, Ruby set off for New York City to study design with Frank Alvah Parsons at the New York School of Fine and Applied Arts (today known as Parsons The New School for Design). Excited by everything in the big city, her letters home were filled with drawings of whatever she was creating: ceramics, jewelry, or portraits of studio models. This style of correspondence continued throughout her life.

Returning home a year later, Ruby began teaching in the fall of 1911 for the Independence public schools and by 1912 was supervisor for drawing, a position that covered grades one through twelve. In 1916, she began teaching at Kansas City Manual Training High School and sponsored a club for students interested in the fine arts. This was also the year her needlework designs were first published in the *Kansas City Star*. Her *Bedtime Quilt* was made up of twenty "Quaddie Quilties," embroidered squares illustrating Thornton Burgess's popular stories of woodland creatures.

Ruby married a former high school classmate, Arthur McKim, on July 16, 1917. As soon as their baby, Betty, born October 31, 1918, could be left with the grandparents, Ruby and Arthur took to the road to sell Ruby's patterns and design ideas to publication syndicates across the country. As Betty grew, the letters from Mama contained drawings of whatever she and Arthur saw that day:

Oriental Poppy Quilt | Designed by Ruby McKim, made by Rosie Werner | 2011 (pieces from an original kit, circa 1930) | 48 × 30 inches | Cottons; machine-pieced, hand-quilted and appliquéd, embroidered. The McKim Studios catalog description of this pattern (pictured at bottom right) emphasized the piecing over the appliqué work on the quilt: "The pieced poppy is all straight sewing, the sort that may be run up on the sewing machine, while the bottom half of the block has two leaves and a stem that whips down by hand." Originally it was offered in red, scarlet, and "boilproof" black and green for the appliqué. *Photo by Merrily McKim Tuohey*

145

A McKim block from her State Flower series that appeared in newspapers nationwide in 1931–1932. *Courtesy of Merikay Waldvogel*

children playing in the ocean, Daddy resting in a big chair after a hard day. Ruby's spelling was sometimes questionable, but her drawings made the letters like small storybooks to little Betty, waiting at home. When their second child, Marilyn, was born five years later, the grandmothers informed them that Ruby's traveling days were over.

After a short stint in St. Louis, the family returned to Independence and converted the first floor of Viola Short's home into offices and made the second floor into apartments for the two grandmothers. By 1925, McKim Studios had become a home-based mail-order business that oversaw the publication of Ruby Short McKim's designs in newspapers and magazines throughout the United States. The McKims also published catalogs of patterns and kits, under titles like *Patchwork Patterns* and *Designs Worth Doing*.

101 Patchwork Patterns, originally published by Ruby Short McKim in 1931, has been revised and reprinted with several different covers by Dover and remains a popular resource for quilters.

In January 1922, Ruby began a sixteen-year career with *Child Life* magazine with her Alice in Wonderland series. She was soon supplying designs to other magazines and syndicated features. The *Kansas City Star*, the *Omaha World-Herald*, the *Nebraska Farmer*, *Woman's World*, *Successful Farming*, and the *Indianapolis Star* were among the publications that featured McKim designs. Ruby also became the artcraft editor at *Better Homes and Gardens*, designing kits and patterns for quilts and other home decorating projects.

Many of Ruby's quilts reflected her interest in children and education. The *Jolly Circus*, *Nursery Rhymes*, *Colonial History*, *Bible History*, and *Bird Life* quilts were just a few of her series that appeared in the 1920s. *Farm Life*, *State Flowers*, *Flower Garden*, and *Patchwork Parade of States* were among her popular series in the 1930s. Each new pattern was eagerly awaited, clipped out, and saved by women who were determined to collect the entire series. The newspapers running her patterns often sponsored contests for the quilts made from these patterns, which attracted hundreds of entrants and thousands of enthusiastic viewers. Many of these collections have survived, have been reprinted, and are even offered on the Internet, proving that the popularity of the McKim designs persists to this day.

Ruby inspired others to think and act creatively. She found joy in teaching others to apply the principles of balance and proportion in art that would grace the home in an attractive but still useful manner. Ruby's creativity flowed into every aspect of her life, and she was fortunate to have a husband who recognized her talent and the need to express it. They thought of themselves as the "Two Ones"—each totally independent in what they did but totally dependent on the other for support and inspiration.

In 1931, Arthur oversaw the publication of Ruby's book, *One Hundred and One Patchwork Patterns*. The book served as a comprehensive pattern encyclopedia and how-to book for avid quiltmakers at a time when obtaining this information was a daunting task.

Shortly after the book was published, the family went to Europe to explore other publishing markets. They came home with a contract for a paper in Australia and a new idea for another business—imported, domestic, and antique dolls by mail order. During the mid-1930s, McKim Studios gradually evolved into Kimport Dolls, a business that continued for the rest of their lives and was later carried on by their son, Kim, who was born in 1933.

Throughout Ruby's life, art was her passion. She sketched with watercolors on vacations and family outings. She created homemade tags for presents that had limericks to match the small pictures she drew as clues as to what was inside. Even snack time with the family involved artistically cut little sandwiches (with very strange fillings made from leftovers) arranged with flair upon platters. But best of all, to me and to her other grandchildren, she would make each of us a sock doll with colored-pencil-drawn faces whenever we stayed overnight. (Being a very thrifty person, she would recycle the dolls back into socks the following morning.) The dolls were accompanied by a magical story with whatever three characters we requested, skillfully interwoven. Bedtime finished with her singing the old spiritual "Swing Low, Sweet Chariot" as a lullaby.

It was only at her funeral, when I heard the words to the spiritual being sung, that I realized the full impact she had on the members of my family. I knew why I had to write or draw whenever happy or sad. Creativity must be cultivated . . . and she was the gardener of our lives. She passed these lessons on to us and also to the thousands of women who used her designs to decorate their homes for their families.

Ruby was a wife and mother, an artist and businesswoman, and a charming person to know. She had two personal mottoes that I will always remember: "If you don't feel good, put on your company face and keep going," and "You only fail when you don't try." She always smiled and she never failed. Ruby's husband, Arthur, passed away in 1967. At his death, she penned a poem as a tribute to the part he played in her life, and it was sent to all their mail-order friends as a final memorial to their life together. Ruby died nine years later, on June 28, 1976.

Ruby Short McKim's induction into the Quilters Hall of Fame in 2002 recognized her important contributions to the quilt revival of the early twentieth century, through her widely distributed designs, her book, and her business.

Selected Reading

Filo, Jill Sutton. Articles on Ruby McKim patterns. *American Patchwork and Quilting.* February, April, August 1998; February 1999; February 2000; February 2001.

———. "Ruby Short McKim: The Formative Years." *Uncoverings 1996.* Edited by Virginia Gunn. San Francisco: American Quilt Study Group, 1997, 63–94.

McKim, Ruby Short. *One Hundred and One Patchwork Patterns.* Independence, MO: McKim Studios, 1931. Revised and reprinted, New York: Dover, 1962.

"Ruby Short McKim: A Memorial." *Quilter's Newsletter Magazine,* no. 86 (December 1976): 14–15.

Stehlik, Jan. "Quilt Patterns and Contests of the *Omaha World-Herald,* 1921–1941." *Uncoverings 1990.* Edited by Laurel Horton. San Francisco: American Quilt Study Group, 1991.

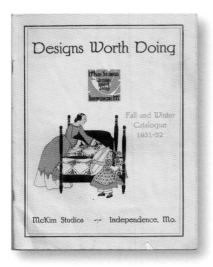

This Fall and Winter 1931–32 edition of *Designs Worth Doing* is one of several catalogs of quilt patterns printed by Ruby McKim's firm, McKim Studios of Independence, Missouri. The statement on the back of the catalog bore Ruby Short McKim's signature and outlined her firm's philosophy: "Adventures in Home Beautifying are always a thrill but [with our help] they need never be hazardous nor the results uncertain. In creating our new series of *Designs Worth Doing,* we have kept the most inexperienced needleworker in mind and have held to the ideal of practical homecrafts worthy the time and money of the busiest of women." *Courtesy of Merikay Waldvogel*

Patsy Orlofsky

Patsy Orlofsky was inducted into the Quilters Hall of Fame at the Continental Quilting Congress in Vienna, Virginia, on July 24, 1987. *Photo by Ken Gabrielsen*

"We do not believe that quilts must be in pristine condition in order to be appreciated. Many quilts will be worn, the fabrics deteriorated, the colors faded, but we believe this to be the life of the quilt."

—Patsy and Myron Orlofsky, *Quilts in America* (1974), p. 11

by Merikay Waldvogel

THE ORLOFSKY NAME will forever be linked to the late twentieth century's "bible of quilt history," *Quilts in America*. Patsy and Myron Orlofsky had a keen interest in American decorative arts but lamented the lowly place American quilts held in that field. To remedy the situation, the husband-and-wife team embarked on a three-year project to research quilts and quilt history. The result was *Quilts in America*, originally published by McGraw-Hill in 1974.

A review in *Quilter's Newsletter Magazine* lauded the book for being "considerably more comprehensive than similar books to date. Collectors will find most of the information they need here to establish the age of their quilts, and footnotes to help them if they want to look up more details about a given subject." The reviewer correctly predicted that the book, with 300 photographs of quilts, would become an extraordinarily valuable text for quilt collectors, dealers, and students of quilt history.

Patsy is the daughter of Shirley and Harry Kulp, and was born in 1943 in Chicago. She attended elementary and secondary

schools in Highland Park, Illinois. In 1965, she graduated from Skidmore College, Saratoga Springs, New York, with a B.S. degree. For the next three years, she traveled throughout Spain and studied art history and Spanish at the University of Barcelona. After returning to New York State in 1968, she taught crafts at the Storefront Arts Center in White Plains.

In 1968, Patsy married Myron Orlofsky, an early collector of postwar contemporary art who shared her fascination with "the dynamism of authentic objects of American folk art." Together they collected about 300 handmade American quilts, paying as little as twenty-five cents for some. Patsy recalls that "people thought of quilts then as 'Betsy Ross colonial kitsch.' We wanted quilts to take their rightful place in the field of American antiques. We had lots of coffee table antique books with only minor mention of quilts. We decided to produce a textbook on quilts and quilt history. We consulted every article and book printed about quilts, and included everything: tools, people, aesthetic ideas, ethnic variations."

Framed Center Quilt | Quiltmaker unknown | Circa 1800–1925 | 98 × 99½ inches. Patsy Orlofsky found this quilt at a flea market in Massachusetts in 1971. The center panel, with stylized urn, was block-printed by the renowned John Hewson (1745–1822), whose fabrics are regarded as the finest examples of American textile printing of the late eighteenth and early nineteenth centuries. *Photo by Arthur Vitols of Helga Photography, courtesy of Patsy Orlofsky*

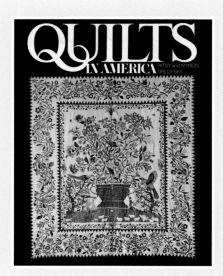

The first edition of *Quilts in America*, 1974. For many years, this book was the bible of quilt history scholarship. It was the most comprehensive and was, therefore, referred to often by the beginning generations of quilt scholars.

Patsy Orlofsky in the Textile Conservation Workshop she founded, where conservators work to preserve rare quilts and other textiles. As Patsy says, "We try to stop time for them so they will continue to last." *Photo by Ken Gabrielsen, courtesy of Patsy Orlofsky*

As soon as their landmark book was published, Myron and Patsy began lecturing at quilt events, including at the University of California and Yale University, and also served as consultants to quilt exhibits. In 1975, Patsy contributed to the exhibits *American Pictorial Quilts* at the Vassar College Art Gallery and *Quilts and Coverlets* at the Star of the Republic Museum in Texas.

In 1976, Myron and Patsy were invited to lecture on quilts at the American Folk Studies Seminar of Cornell University in Ithaca, New York, which was also attended by future Quilters Hall of Fame honorees Jonathan Holstein, Gail van der Hoof, Bonnie Leman, and Jean Ray Laury. Tragically, on the way home from this conference, Myron suffered a fatal heart attack, leaving Patsy pregnant with their only child, Sam, who was born in October 1976. Needless to say, Myron's death necessitated major changes in Patsy's life plans. In 1977, her interest in quilts and textiles led her to establish the Textile Conservation Workshop (TCW) in a historic nineteenth-century building in South Salem, New York.

Today, Patsy still serves as the executive director of this nonprofit organization, widely recognized as a leading conservation center, where Patsy and her staff of specialists and interns care for textiles ranging from the rare and fragile to the historic and artistic. Each year, they treat around 300 pieces, including archaeological and ethnographic textiles, quilts, woven coverlets, samplers, domestic and ecclesiastical textiles, historic flags, political memorabilia, rugs, and costumes. Each item receives a proposed-treatment report and before-and-after photographs for documentation. State-of-the-art equipment is used, including two specially designed suction tables—flat-plane porous structures providing a controlled airflow for use with liquid to gently draw the stains out of fragile textiles.

Patsy has played an active role in the conservation community, participating in seminars and writing articles. In the 1980s, she studied in the master's degree program for preservation administration in Columbia University's School of Library Service and served as program director for the New York State Conservation Consultancy. She also served on the board of directors for the National Institute for Conservation of Cultural Property and has been an adviser or consultant for numerous museums and organizations. She presently serves on the Ethics and Standards Committee and the Kress Conservation Publication Fellowship Committee of the American Institute for Conservation and is a member of the Collections Committee at the Cooper-Hewitt Museum.

After the Orlofskys' book *Quilts in America* went out of print, its price quickly escalated to hundreds of dollars per copy.

Realizing the great demand for the book, the most comprehensive quilt history to date, Patsy began to work on a new edition. This was published in 1992 by Abbeville Press, to the delight of quilt historians and collectors. In 2005, the book was again reissued in paperback.

Patsy still lives in a handsome Victorian house next door to the Textile Conservation Workshop. Her living space reflects another of her interests, that of contemporary art. "I have never made art," she says, "but I have always appreciated every facet of the arts. Textile conservation is an esoteric field. One needs a background in studio art, art history, organic chemistry, not to mention patience and a fine hand. The goal in bench conservation is to combine artistic ability and scientific knowledge while restoring and retaining the material and culturally significant qualities of an artifact."

Patsy Orlofsky relishes her role as "a facilitator of fine arts craftsmanship," helping her coworkers maintain an aesthetic perspective on their technical tasks. An outreach education and survey program for small museums and historical societies was established in 1985. With intervention on a preventive level for sizable collections, Patsy believes the need for individual laboratory treatments of specific objects will be reduced, thereby saving artifacts, time, and funds.

Because of its unusually diverse staff and its dedication to mentoring, the workshop has been uniquely qualified to provide an important service to the field, filling a gap not covered by formal conservation schooling. As a regional conservation lab, the workshop has been the major training center for textile conservation interns in the United States of America for the last twenty-five years.

Her appreciation of the beautiful objects she works with is expressed in her own lectures and publications, in TCW's educational program for small museums and historical societies, and in a number of pro bono services that the nonprofit center provides on behalf of textiles everywhere. Her staff gladly answers phone queries on how to cope with rust stains on an old quilt or the bleeding dyes on a sampler. In 1987, Patsy Orlofsky was inducted into the Quilters Hall of Fame in honor of the significant contributions she has made to the field of quilt study and textile preservation.

A photograph of Patsy Orlofsky taken in the summer of 2007. *Courtesy of Patsy Orlofsky*

Selected Reading

Orlofsky, Patsy. "The Collector's Guide for the Care of Quilts in the Home." *The Quilt Digest 2*. San Francisco: The Quilt Digest Press, 1984.

———. "Textile Conservation." *Conservation Concerns: A Guide for Collectors and Curators*. Edited by Konstanze Bachmann. Washington, DC: Smithsonian Institution, 1992, 79–84.

Orlofsky, Patsy, and Myron Orlofsky. "Dating Heirloom Quilts." *Quilter's Newsletter Magazine*, no. 65 (March 1975).

———. *Quilts in America*. New York: McGraw-Hill, 1974. Reprint, New York: Abbeville Press, 1992.

Orlofsky, Patsy, and Phyllis Dillon. "A Conservation Profile." *The Clarion*. New York: Museum of American Folk Art, Spring/Summer 1986, 75–79.

Anne Orr
1869–1946

"Do your best in workmanship, design, and careful selection of color, so that the finished article will justify any work and be an heirloom to hand down for generations."

—Anne Orr, "The Story of Storrowton and Its Quilt Contest," *Good Housekeeping Magazine*, Pamphlet No. A-5300 (no date)

Anne Champe Orr was inducted into the Quilters Hall of Fame at the Continental Quilting Congress in Arlington, Virginia, on October 15, 1980. *Courtesy of J. Scott Grigsby*

by Merikay Waldvogel

DESIGNER AND SUCCESSFUL BUSINESSWOMAN Anne Orr developed a worldwide reputation for sophisticated needlework patterns and accurate instructions. She sold patterns by mail order and served as the needlework editor for *Good Housekeeping* magazine for twenty years.

The epitome of the southern gentlewoman, Anne Champe was born on April 17, 1875, to Emma Claiborne and Benjamin Franklin Champe of Nashville, Tennessee, where she grew up and attended local schools. She studied art at a private finishing school for young ladies, and at the age of nineteen married John Hunter Orr, a handsome young man whose family owned a wholesale grocery supply business. Their wedding in her parents' mansion in 1894 was said to be one of the most brilliant gatherings ever assembled in the city of Nashville.

After her marriage, one of Anne Orr's first projects was raising funds for the construction of the Woman's Pavilion for the Tennessee Centennial Exposition held in Nashville in 1897. This group of fund-raising women formed the Centennial Club, which has spearheaded campaigns for civic pride, cultural enrichment, and social services for more than one hundred years.

The *Southern Woman's Magazine*, published by several prominent Nashville women, appeared in 1913. Anne Orr became its art editor, providing monthly columns on antique collecting and needlework. With this exposure, she set up a mail-order pattern service, and in 1915, she received her first copyright for a booklet, called *Centerpieces and Lunch Sets in Crochet Work*. In 1917, Coats Thread Company began publishing her pattern booklets, starting with *Crochet Book for Gown Yokes and Boudoir Caps*.

In 1917, the *Nashville Banner* described Anne Orr as "a pioneer in the application of art to everyday life. No longer does art consist of pictures and statuary for the privileged few. Many of the simplest and least expensive articles of household usage have been made artistic and attractive."

Anne's hometown needlework business, it was reported, had just received an advance order for 500,000 copies of one of her booklets. Anne Orr had made a name for herself on the world stage in a remarkably short period of time.

In 1921, Anne Orr became needlework editor of *Good Housekeeping* magazine, a position she held for the next twenty years. She contributed a monthly column about needlework, and readers ordered patterns from the magazine's New York offices.

Heirloom Basket | Designed by Anne Orr, pieced by Elizabeth Bates Greer (c. 1880–c. 1960), quilted by Dolly Mae Long (1872–1955), Lancaster, Kentucky | 1935 | 69 × 91½ inches | Cottons. This Anne Orr design, reminiscent of cross-stitch patterns, appeared in the January 1935 issue of *Good Housekeeping*. *Courtesy of Merikay Waldvogel, private collection*

In the 1920s, her needlework articles featured crochet, cross-stitch, embroidery, knitting, needlepoint, and tatting, reflecting her personal interests as well as the popular needle arts of the time. Only rarely did a quilt pattern appear.

Anne Orr was concerned about the accuracy of her directions and employed a number of Nashville women to produce handcrafted items using her patterns. One news article reported that she employed one hundred women.

The Orrs had three daughters, who made their debuts at Nashville society balls. Later, two of them, Anne and Mary, managed the Anne Orr Studio. In 1928, at the age of fifty-three, Anne Orr became a widow with a lavish house and lifestyle to maintain. Her thriving needlework business may have provided the financial stability the family needed as the economic depression widened.

At the end of the 1920s, Anne Orr took note of the revival of quiltmaking and added some traditional quilt patterns to her needlework offerings. By 1932, when she published a pattern booklet titled *Quilts and Quilting—Set No. 100*, she had introduced modern designs to tempt contemporary women who may not have considered quilting as a hobby. Her line of pieced patterns reminiscent of cross-stitch became her trademark in quilt design.

Because of her national reputation as a needlework designer and writer for *Good Housekeeping*, Anne Orr was chosen to judge the first national quilt contest held at the Eastern States Exposition at Storrowton Village in Springfield, Massachusetts, in 1932. The following year, she was a final round judge for the Sears National Quilt Contest at the 1933 Chicago World's Fair. In 1939, *Good Housekeeping* and Macy's Department Store sponsored a quilt

Plate 2, Set B of *Cross-Stitch Charts*, copyrighted by Anne Orr in 1915 showing the influence of her cross-stitch-style quilt designs. *Courtesy of Merikay Waldvogel*

contest in association with the New York World's Fair, and again Anne Orr was a judge.

In January 1940, Anne Orr's final needlework article appeared in *Good Housekeeping*. She later wrote briefly for *Better Homes and Gardens* in 1943 and entertained the idea of designing patterns for the Stearns & Foster Co. Mountain Mist patterns. She did design quilt patterns for their competitor, Lockport Batting Company, which brought out an edition of her last pattern book, *Anne Orr Quilts—Book 50*, originally published by Anne Orr Studios in 1944.

The book's introduction, which Anne wrote herself, summarized the success of her career:

> Anne Orr is no newcomer to the field of textile and pattern design. For more than two decades she has greeted American women through the pages of national magazines, and her name has become a by-word wherever women knit, tat, or do any kind of needlework. She has a following in three generations: mothers, daughters and grand-daughters. . . .

Quilting with Anne Orr, originally published in 1944, was reprinted by Dover publications for quilters during the late-twentieth-century quilt revival.

QUILTING
WITH
ANNE ORR

Anne Orr

Anne Orr's work has endured because she has never been a faddist. Her patterns and designs have always had the basic appeal of superior good taste that women everywhere are quick to recognize. Her ideas are young, fresh, alive and they are firmly grounded upon experience. Anne Orr knows the mechanics of her craft. She is a creative pioneer, who can interpret needlework for the novice as well as for the expert.

Although her life and accomplishments paralleled those of other quilt luminaries of the first half of the twentieth century, such as Ruth Finley, Florence Peto, Bertha Stenge, and Marie Webster, no evidence exists that she ever met them. Some of her sophisticated center medallion floral designs appear to have been inspired by Marie Webster's patterns.

Anne Orr died unexpectedly on October 29, 1946. The *Nashville Banner* obituary praised her ability to "capture beauty from everything around her and weave it into the tapestry of her life." Her daughter, Mary Grigsby, kept the Anne Orr Studio open until the mid-1950s, and one granddaughter maintained the Orr pattern copyrights after the business closed.

Selected Reading

Dubois, Jean. *Anne Orr Patchwork*. Durango, CO: La Plata Press, 1977.

Orr, Anne. *Anne Orr Quilts—Book 50*. Nashville, TN: Anne Orr Studios, 1944.

———. *Quilting with Anne Orr*. Nashville, TN: Anne Orr Studios, 1944. Revised, New York: Dover Publications, 1990.

———. *Quilts and Quilting—Set No.100*. Nashville, TN: Anne Orr Studios, 1932.

Waldvogel, Merikay. "The Marketing of Anne Orr's Quilts." *Uncoverings 1990*. Edited by Laurel Horton. San Francisco: American Quilt Study Group, 1991. ("Notes and references" section lists many *Good Housekeeping* articles by Anne Orr.)

———. *Soft Covers for Hard Times: Quilt-making & The Great Depression*. Nashville, TN: Rutledge Hill Press, 1990.

Anne Champe Orr in front of her home in Nashville, Tennessee, in 1930. *Courtesy of J. Scott Grigsby*

Plate 4, Set B of *Cross-Stitch Charts*. *Courtesy of Merikay Waldvogel*

In 1978, Dover Publications, in conjunction with the Center for History of American Needlework, issued *Crocheted Designs of Anne Orr*, a selection of her needlework patterns from eight instruction books, published from 1916 to 1923. Several others followed, including *Quilting with Anne Orr* in 1990, with updated instructions.

Anne Orr was inducted into the Quilters Hall of Fame in 1980, along with Averil Colby, Florence Peto, Grace Snyder, and Bertha Stenge.

Florence Peto

1881–1970

*"Now the quilt is finished and should it happily escape
the ignominy of being locked away in a chest
(use a quilt and love it!),
it will bring cheer to the best bedchamber
and perhaps acclaim for its creator."*

—Florence Peto, *American Quilts and Coverlets* (1949), p. 63

Florence Peto was inducted into the
Quilters Hall of Fame at the Continental
Quilting Congress in Arlington, Virginia, on
October 15, 1980. *Courtesy of Joyce Gross*

by Debora Clem

AN AUTHOR, HISTORIAN, collector, designer, lecturer, and quiltmaker, Florence Peto was a woman ahead of her time. She described her first book, *Historic Quilts*, published in 1939, as "not strictly a quilt book in the sense that it tells how to make a quilt. Rather, it is a history of quilts and their makers—a social history of early America." With this goal in mind, she anticipated the late twentieth century's interest in quilts as documents of women's history. *Historic Quilts* launched her career of quilt and textile collecting, curating, lecturing, and writing.

Florence Cowdin was born in Brooklyn, New York, in 1881, the oldest girl of Ella and Jasper Cowdin's four children. She married Joseph Peto in 1900 and had two children, John and Marjorie. They lived in Brooklyn until 1940, when they moved to northern New Jersey.

Florence was a prolific writer, beginning her career about 1919 by writing popular stories for magazines. After she became interested in antiques and began collecting quilts, she wrote numerous articles for *American Home, McCall's Needlework and Crafts, Hobbies,* and *Antiques*, from the 1930s to the 1960s. Photographs of quilts from her collection often appeared in these same magazines. Her articles began as mostly historical pieces, but later she also included patterns and quiltmaking tips.

Her second book, *American Quilts and Coverlets*, published in 1949, included a manual of instruction on how to make a quilt, together with more information and pictures of historic quilts and coverlets. She also wrote on other subjects of interest to her, such as glassware and Staffordshire pottery.

She started lecturing in the late 1920s and was much sought after by women's clubs and other organizations. A publicity flyer stated that her lecture "is especially adapted to historical societies, educational, civic, and church groups, and is an appropriate complement to a quilt exhibition or as the feature of a Colonial tea." She illustrated her lectures with a flip chart of more than fifty quilt cloth pattern blocks that she had meticulously drafted and stitched. After she stopped lecturing, she made some of the blocks into pillows to be sold, writing to a friend, "I feel as if I were betraying old friends."

Hearts and Flowers | **Made by Florence M. Cowden Peto, Tenafly, New Jersey** | **1954** | **83 × 98 inches.** Florence Peto designed and made this quilt using antique fabrics from her collection. The center medallion was cut from a pink toile with a charming romantic scene, in early-nineteenth-century style. Fourteen six-pointed stars surround the center, with corners made from the same cherub fabric that appears in the lower part of the quilt. The outer border is a chintz dating from about 1820–1840. The inscription *F. Peto 1954* is embroidered on the back. The quilt won a blue ribbon at the Storrowton Village show in 1958. *Photo by Peter Jacobs Fine Arts Photography, courtesy of the Peto Family Collection*

Florence even lectured on the radio. In the early 1940s, her broadcasts on WNYC in New York City were made in conjunction with the Index of American Design, an Arts Service project of the Works Progress Administration. She also lectured on stations WJZ and WAAT in New Jersey.

Florence Peto began to collect quilts and vintage fabrics when her children were grown and she needed a hobby. She exhibited at many quilt shows, women's exhibitions, and antique fairs, most notably the Women's International Expositions of Art and Industries held at the Grand Central Palace in New York City in the 1940s and early 1950s. In 1948, she curated an exhibit of her complete collection of fifty quilts for the New York Historical Society.

Many museums on the East Coast benefited from her collecting and research activities. She was instrumental in having the magnificent Mary Totten *Rising Sun* quilt donated to the Smithsonian Institution, a story told in her book *Historic Quilts*. The Shelburne Museum in Vermont, the Newark Museum in New Jersey, the Philadelphia Museum of Art, and the Henry Ford Museum in Michigan acquired pieces from her collection, including some quilts by her own hand.

In addition to writing for publication, Florence Peto was also a prolific letter writer. Today, these letters serve as valuable documents for understanding twentieth-century quilt history. Her correspondence with Emma Andres of Arizona was published in *Quilters' Journal*, edited by Joyce Gross, and her correspondence with Bertha Stenge was helpful in Cuesta Benberry's quilt kit

research. Letters to Elizabeth Richardson of Tennessee provide a record of Florence's own activities.

Florence knew several people who would also become Honorees of the Quilters Hall of Fame. She considered Dr. William Rush Dunton Jr. a friend who shared her enthusiasm for the history of quilt design, and she convinced Chicago quiltmaker Bertha Stenge to use antique fabrics in some of her own quilts. Lenice Bacon paid her a call in 1947, at first mistaking Florence for the maid before enjoying a long visit together.

Despite a hectic life with publishing deadlines and out-of-state travel, Florence found time to make her own quilts. She preferred early nineteenth-century patterns and styles and used her antique fabrics in her own designs. Florence was also an early lap quilter, since she discovered it was easier to work on smaller sections of a quilt.

After Bertha Stenge introduced her to contests, Florence won several prizes at state fairs with her antique quilts or with those she had made herself. In the 1950s, she also designed kits for Paragon. Her *Calico Garden* was selected in 1999 as one of *America's 100 Best Quilts of the 20th Century*, and its pattern was made available by the Shelburne Museum.

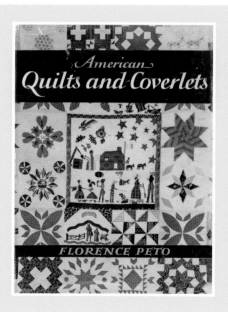

American Quilts and Coverlets by Florence Peto, published in 1949, was "a history of a charming native art together with a manual of instruction for beginners."

Florence Peto looking very happy surrounded by quilts. *Courtesy of Joyce Gross*

Florence Peto and her quilts. *Courtesy of Joyce Gross*

Selected Reading

Cochran, Rachel, Rita Erickson, Natalie Hart, and Barbara Schaffer. *New Jersey Quilts: 1777 to 1950: Contributions to an American Tradition.* The Heritage Quilt Project of New Jersey. Paducah, KY: American Quilter's Society, 1992.

Gross, Joyce. "Four Twentieth Century Quiltmakers." *Uncoverings 1980.* Edited by Sally Garoutte. Mill Valley, CA: American Quilt Study Group, 1981. Reprinted in *Quiltmaking in America: Beyond the Myths.* Edited by Laurel Horton. Nashville, TN: Rutledge Hill Press, 1994.

Peto, Florence. *American Quilts and Coverlets.* New York: Chanticleer Press, 1949.

———. Articles in *Antiques*: April 1938, May 1938, November 1939, January 1940, September 1941, July 1942, June 1944, March 1948, June 1949, August 1949, January 1950, August 1953.

———. "Hand-Made White Elegance." *Antiques*, March 1948. Reprinted in *Needlework: An Historical Survey.* Edited by Betty Ring. Pittstown, NJ: Main Street Press, 1984.

———. *Historic Quilts.* New York: The American Historical Company, Inc., 1939.

Florence's first quilt, named *Marjorie: A Personality Quilt*, was made up of appliqué blocks referring to her daughter's childhood and career. Mother and daughter were very close throughout their lives. As an Army nurse serving in Europe during World War II, Marjorie frequently wrote home to Florence, who compiled the letters for publication in 1947 as *Women Were Not Expected: An Informal Story of the Nurses of Second General Hospital in the ETO* (European Theater of Operations).

Florence Peto was obviously a lively woman with a wonderful sense of humor, as shown in her letters. She wrote to Emma Andres in March 1941 about her heavy schedule of lectures: "They keep me talking and talking. It is a wonder someone hasn't popped me into the U.S. Senate—the only place where there is more talking than I do! . . . So when you do not hear from me, picture me with my mouth open."

Florence Peto died in 1970 at the age of eighty-eight, just as the curtain was rising on the late twentieth-century quilt revival. Her meticulous collecting, researching, and writing have played a significant role in the history of quilts and quiltmaking in this country. Her documentation of quilts and quilters, textile history, and collecting customs is important to any researcher interested in quilt history. The quilts she designed have inspired others to make use of antique fabrics and to reproduce some of the magnificent heirloom quilts of the nineteenth century.

Florence Peto was a spirited lady with a passion for quilts. That passion has left a magnificent legacy to all quilters and lovers of quilts, a legacy recognized by her induction into the Quilters Hall of Fame in 1980.

Yvonne Porcella

*"In my career, I do not set goals, but rather just let things develop.
I will admit that there is a compelling need for me to be creative. . . .
Color and inspirations are what drive me;
anything I see, read, or hear can be the substance of my work."*

—Yvonne Porcella, "A Compelling Need to Create,"
Quilters Hall of Fame Newsletter, no. 14 (Fall 1998)

Yvonne Porcella was inducted into The
Quilters Hall of Fame in Marion, Indiana,
on July 18, 1998. *Courtesy of Yvonne Porcella*

by Alyson B. Stanfield

YVONNE PORCELLA laughs when she remembers her first quilt, which she made as a wedding gift in 1963. "I'm thankful there's no record of that quilt," she says, recalling it was made of two sheets and was tied rather than quilted. She has come a long way.

She grew up as Yvonne Bechis in Watsonville, California, south of San Francisco. Her memories do not include a family member who quilted; instead, she calls her family "inventive," adding, "It was common for us, if we wanted something, to make it . . . whatever [it was]." Her father had a wood-burning business, while her mother taught Yvonne and her sister to sew and knit. Upon graduation from high school, Yvonne entered the University of San Francisco, where she received her bachelor's degree in nursing in 1958. That same year, she married Robert S. Porcella, who practiced family medicine. She gave up nursing in 1979 but keeps her license current.

Yvonne is a workaholic—exceedingly devoted to whatever she is doing until its completion. While raising four children in the 1960s, she continued to sew and make clothes for her family. She grew tired of making clothes only to see the same fabric on someone else, so she decided to make her own fabric, teaching herself to weave on a child's loom. She grew increasingly serious about her creative endeavors and carried her spinning wheel and loom around to local fairs and craft shows. Yvonne also became deeply involved with the Northern California Handweavers and the wearable art movement that had its roots in the Haight-Ashbury district of San Francisco. Her woven textiles became garments, and when she realized the heavy fabrics were too hot to wear, she added patchwork to her repertoire and used the handwoven pieces as focal points in her "collage garments."

In 1972, Yvonne's first gallery exhibition highlighted her weavings and wearable art. The wearables were based on ethnic clothing brought home by returning Peace Corps volunteers. She mixed patterns and materials from Japan, Guatemala, Germany, and Afghanistan to create unique garments that appropriated geometric patterns in the deep indigos and reds of the cloth from those countries.

Yvonne's first book, *Five Ethnic Patterns*, was published in 1977, followed the next year by *Plus Five Ethnic Patterns*.

Gigantus Interruptus | Designed and made by Yvonne Porcella | 2009 | 48 × 36 inches. The theme of Yvonne's quilt is California's future potential for "The Big One." The artist states, "Off Highway 395 you can visit a very large fissure caused by movement of the earth. You cannot see the bottom . . . , but it could be filled with molten lava. Are we prepared for the next earthquake? The green represents the forest floor, which is seemingly peaceful without a hint of what lies beneath the surface."
© 2009 Yvonne Porcella

In the late 1970s, she brightened her palette and focused more on patchwork for garment construction. She also started experimenting with silk. Pure, lively colors replaced the deep, rich tones of the ethnic clothing tradition. A number of Yvonne's garments entered the collection of the Oakland Museum in 1995.

In 1971, Yvonne attended the West Coast Quilters' Conference in Portland, Oregon, where she met quilt artist Beth Gutcheon, and future Hall of Fame honorees Virginia Avery, Jinny Beyer, Jeffrey Gutcheon, and Michael James. Soon she was working on her first art quilt, *Takoage*, which is now in the collection of the Renwick Gallery of the National Museum of American Art, Smithsonian Institution. She remembers her feelings upon its completion: "There's no one in the world that's made a quilt like this! . . . I was so frightened that people would think I was over the top because it was so different."

Known primarily for her use of color, Yvonne has taken her art quilts in two seemingly separate directions. Vintage Porcella quilts, such as *Takoage*, contain vibrant colors and distinct patterns, mixed courageously. The piecework in these early art quilts is an extension of the way she had approached her wearables, in which colors, patterns, and cultures were mixed without regard for "rightness." Rhythm is an important element and is achieved through the careful selection of patterns and colors. Polka dots, stripes, florals, and solids are combined to create a surface energized by complex textures.

Yvonne's quilts soon evolved into strip-pieced, quilted kimonos that were inspired by a 1978 trip to the Asian Art

President Hazel Carter (right) presents an engraved box to Yvonne Porcella in recognition of her induction into the Quilters Hall of Fame, July 18, 1998, in Marion, Indiana. *Courtesy of Rosalind W. Perry*

Museum in San Francisco. Like her quilts, these kimonos were intended to be appreciated as art. She knew she wanted to avoid their practical use when she saw models wearing them incorrectly, so she began making oversized kimonos to be appreciated for their form rather than their function. She took the statement to its ultimate conclusion in 1986 with *Snow on Mt. Fuji*, an eleven-foot tall, six-layer kimono created for the traveling exhibition *The Art Quilt* and now in the collection of New York Citys' Museum of Arts and Design.

In 1986, the first book to include her art quilts was published, *Yvonne Porcella: A Colorful Book*—a book of pure color, pattern, and inspiration. Upon seeing six years of her work in print, Yvonne began to rethink her direction. To her trademark stripes and checkerboards she appliquéd popular imagery and personal references, and her narrative quilts were born.

Over the years, Yvonne's work has appropriated figures and objects taken from her daily life. Her titles for these bold and colorful quilts are every bit as playful as the quilts themselves: *It's About Beets & Perfume* and *Non Fat, Low Cholesterol, Chemically Enhanced Frozen Dairy Dessert*. In more recent pieces, the iconic images have broken from the confines of the smaller grids and dominate the entire surface. But they are still trademark Porcella: a fantasy world of checkerboards, stars, and polka dots with a healthy dose of humor.

The other side—the classical one—of Yvonne Porcella encompasses quilts created with lyrical, translucent colors inspired by the Japanese "floating world," *ukiyo-e*. *The Tale of Genji*, a tenth-century Japanese novel by Murasaki Shikibu, is the strongest source of inspiration for these quilts, which are

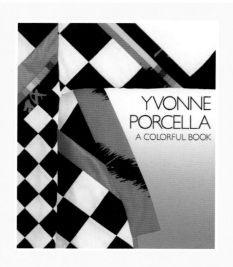

Yvonne Porcella: A Colorful Book, published in 1986, is a book of pure color, pattern, and inspiration and was the first to include Yvonne's art quilts. Upon seeing six years of her work in print, Yvonne began to rethink her direction.

magically transformed from hand-dyed and hand-painted silks that mimic the most beautiful formations of the earth, sky, and sea. Shapes float freely in the infinite space, reminiscent of the surrealist paintings of Joan Miró. For Yvonne, these quilts seem to fulfill a need to be painterly. Their creation has coexisted with her primary-colored quilts, which in some ways gives her a split personality. According to Yvonne, "the painted silks are the calm, peaceful, restful side and the bright contemporary colors, the more jarring, humorous, happy, uplifting side." Their lyrical titles include *In Autumn the Evening Shows Its Lavender* and *Enchanting Is the Plum*.

Lately, Yvonne has been motivated to experiment with new techniques that are less stressful on her hands. She prefers fused fabrics, which are looser and less defined than the shapes that were previously appliquéd, allowing her to combine cotton and silk fabrics into the same piece.

Selected Reading

Fox, Sandi. *Yvonne Porcella: Art Quilts and Kimonos, 1981 to 1995.* Exhibit catalog. Atlanta, GA: Connell Gallery, 1995.

Porcella, Yvonne. *A Colorful Book.* Modesto, CA: Porcella Studios, 1986.

———. *Colors Changing Hue.* Lafayette, CA: C&T Publishing, 1994.

———. "A Compelling Need to Create: Remarks by Yvonne Porcella at Her July 18th Induction." *Quilters Hall of Fame Newsletter,* no. 14 (Fall 1998).

———. *Magical Four Patch & Nine Patch Quilts.* Lafayette, CA: C&T Publishing, 2001.

———. *Pieced Clothing: Patterns for Simple Clothing.* Lafayette, CA: C&T Publishing, 1994.

———. *Six Color World: Color, Cloth, Quilts and Wearables.* Lafayette, CA: C&T Publishing, 1997.

———. *Yvonne Porcella: Art and Inspirations.* Lafayette, CA: C&T Publishing, 1998.

Answering the Riddle | Designed, hand appliquéd, machine-pieced, and hand-quilted by Yvonne Porcella | 102 × 110 inches | Cottons. When the invitation came to make a quilt for the Ninth International Triennial of Tapestry, held at the Central Museum of Textiles, Lódz, Poland, in 1998, Yvonne reflected upon the historical context of tapestry, where there has been a long tradition of portraying complicated pictures that serve as documents of the times. As the new millennium approached, Yvonne reflected upon the twentieth century, known as the "Century of Progress," and upon the new discoveries that will have the power to change lives in the next one hundred years. She wondered, "Will contemporary ideals also survive—global village, worldwide communication, peace?" *Photo by Sharon Risedorph, © 1997 Yvonne Porcella*

Yvonne is a tireless advocate for the art quilt movement through her teaching, writing, and curating, and is amazingly generous with her ideas and advice. In 1989, she founded Studio Art Quilt Associates (SAQA), a nonprofit organization dedicated to educating the public, documenting the art quilt movement, and advocating the recognition of the quilt as art. The organization sponsors annual educational conferences and consults on regional and national exhibitions, while encouraging critical writing. Yvonne proved her commitment to the mission of SAQA by continuing as president of the board of directors until 2000, at the request of its members. The cause isn't finished, since she remains troubled by the lack of serious attention given to fiber artists by collectors, galleries, and museums. She sees a great deal of work ahead for all involved.

Yvonne is a favorite speaker across the country and has shared her talents with students in Japan, France, Germany, Australia, and Switzerland. In 1998, she was selected as one of a handful of artists to represent the United States in the Ninth International Triennial of Tapestry in Lódz, Poland.

Her honors include the Silver Star Award presented by Quilts, Inc. at the International Quilt Festival in 1998, and selection of her quilt *Keep Both Feet on the Floor* as one of *America's 100 Best Quilts of the 20th Century*. In 1998, her many contributions to the art quilt movement were recognized by her induction into the Quilters Hall of Fame.

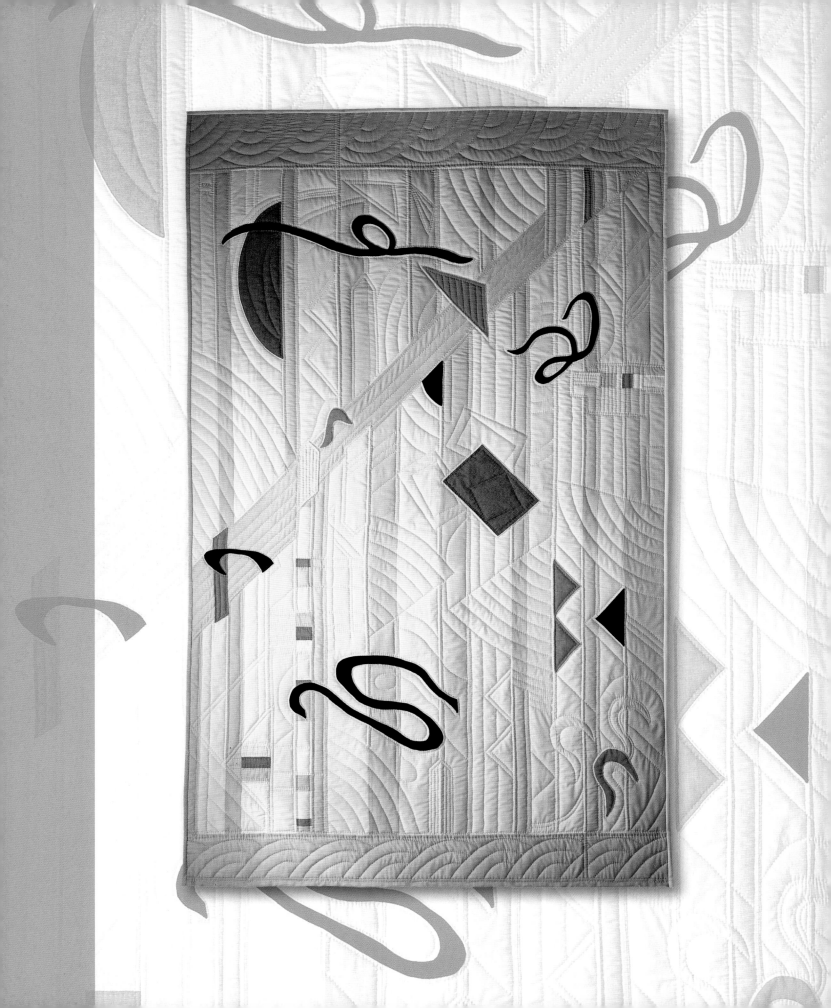

Bets Ramsey

"*When I touched the quilts, the past and the grandmother I had never known became very real. It was the beginning of a new career I would follow for the rest of my life: making quilts and wall hangings, writing, teaching, and lecturing about them, and curating quilt exhibitions.*"

—Bets Ramsey, "Naming a Life: An Autobiography,"
unpublished manuscript in author's collection

Bets Ramsey was inducted into the Quilters Hall of Fame in Marion, Indiana, on July 16, 2005. *Courtesy of Bets Ramsey*

by Laurel Horton

BETS RAMSEY'S DISTINGUISHED CAREER reflects her multiple roles as fabric artist, educator, writer, and exhibition curator over a period of more than fifty years. Her fabric art has appeared in 42 solo exhibitions in museums and galleries throughout the Southeast and beyond and has been represented in more than 160 other juried and invitational exhibitions of quilts, crafts, and art. In addition, she has curated 56 exhibitions of quilts and crafts for art galleries and museums. Her love of quilts is also evident in her written work, including four books, six research papers, five museum catalogs, and numerous articles and reviews.

Betty June Miller was born in Chattanooga in 1923 and lived in Tennessee until 1928, when her family moved to Oak Park, Illinois. While in the fifth grade, she received praise for her drawing and painting projects and decided to make art her career. Observing her mother's interest in crafts, Bets experimented with a variety of needlework skills. She started a Grandmother's Flower Garden quilt in 1938, put it aside for other interests, and finished it thirty-four years later. She graduated from Oak Park–River Forest Township High School in 1941, and that summer she and a friend, having taken classes in advanced tailoring and clothing design, set up a dressmaking business in the Millers' dining room.

Her family moved back to the Chattanooga area in the fall of 1941, and Bets enrolled at the University of Chattanooga. Her education was put on hold for several years by marriage, the birth of a daughter, and divorce. Bets returned to Chattanooga and graduated with a B.A. with honors in art in 1950. The following year she married Paul Ramsey, whose rising career as a poet and literary scholar resulted in a series of moves around the country. Between 1951 and 1964, the family lived in ten different houses in five states. During these years, while raising their four children, Bets also maintained an art studio at home, taught art classes, and exhibited her stitchery and fabric collages.

In 1966, the family returned to Chattanooga to stay, and Bets found additional opportunities to teach and to exhibit her work. She remembers the summer of 1967 in particular as her "coming of age" as an artist. While her husband did research in Washington, D.C., Bets and the children rented a cottage on Great Cranberry Island, off the coast of Maine. They all participated in the local crafts fair, and Bets exhibited her work alongside that of several recognized artists. "My artwork had achieved a certain amount of success on Cranberry, and I thought perhaps I, too, could become recognized as an artist."

Diverse Opinions | Designed and made by Bets Ramsey, Chattanooga, Tennessee | 1988 | 37¼ × 63 inches. After being invited to lecture at and provide a piece for the American Craft Council Southeast Conference in Tuscaloosa in 1988, Bets Ramsey made this hanging. It was the only contemporary quilt selected for the exhibition *The Art of Tennessee*, a historic overview organized in 2003 by the Frist Center for the Visual Arts in Nashville. *Photo © David B. Jenkins, courtesy of Bets Ramsey*

In 1968 George Cress, the chair of the art department at the University of Chattanooga, invited Bets to teach a class in design. Bets found this a satisfying experience and, at the age of forty-seven, decided to go back to school to get a master's degree in crafts from the University of Tennessee. For a seminar with Marian Heard, Bets selected quiltmaking from a list of research topics, never imagining where this would lead her. She studied all the quilt books in the library, and she interviewed relatives about her grandmother's quilts. "When I touched the quilts, the past and the grandmother I had never known became very real. It was the beginning of a new career I would follow for the rest of my life: making quilts and wall hangings; writing, teaching, and lecturing about them; and curating quilt exhibitions."

In 1974, Bets began teaching quiltmaking classes at the Hunter Museum. That year, the museum director asked her to plan public programs in conjunction with the local showing of Jonathan Holstein and Gail van der Hoof's landmark exhibition, *The Pieced Quilt*. The resulting Southern Quilt Symposium was the first public seminar devoted to quilts.

As an annual event through 1991, the symposium emphasized quilts as art in a museum setting. For each of these events, Bets was in charge of the exhibition, presentations, and registration, as well as refreshments. The local community assisted in housing those who traveled to attend the symposium. This was important because it was at the beginning of women traveling and staying overnight to pursue their study of quilt history. Annual thematic exhibitions featured the work of contemporary fabric artists and quilters of the era, including Michael James, Nancy Crow, Georgia Bonesteel, and Hazel Carter.

In 1980, Bets attended the inaugural meeting of the American Quilt Study Group and presented a paper, "Design Invention in Country Quilts of Tennessee and Georgia." She thus became one of the founding members of AQSG and served on the board of directors from 1983 to 1989.

Bets codirected (with Merikay Waldvogel) the Quilts of Tennessee documentation project, 1983 to 1987, which resulted in a traveling exhibition, a book, and many spin-off lectures, exhibitions, publications, and consultancies. Her articles for the annual AQSG publication *Uncoverings* were often written to provide depth and balance to subjects of topical interest.

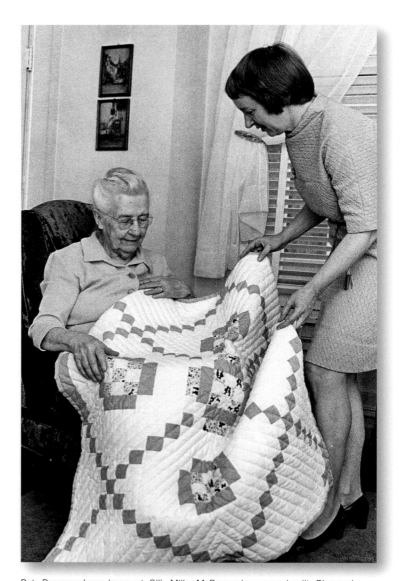

Bets Ramsey shows her aunt, Ollie Miller McBrayer, her second quilt, *Blue and White Crib Quilt*, which Bets made in 1972 and which was quilted by her mother, June Winter Miller. *Courtesy of Bets Ramsey*

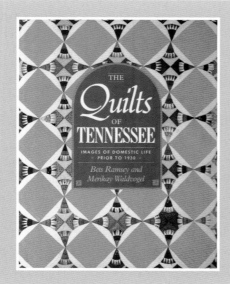

The Quilts of Tennessee: Images of Domestic Life Prior to 1930 was written by Quilters Hall of Fame honorees Bets Ramsey and Merikay Waldvogel and published in 1986. This book accompanied the exhibition of quilts discovered during the Tennessee state quilt documentation project, which surveyed 1,425 quilts.

Star of Hope in Time of War | Bets Ramsey, Nashville, Tennessee |
2007 | **46 × 45 inches.** *Star of Hope in Time of War* was selected to represent
artists of the twenty-first century in *Tennesseans: A People's Legacy*, an exhibition
at the Tennessee State Museum honoring the retiring governor. The legacy is
expressed through showing one work of art for each decade that has passed since
the chartering of the state in 1796. The choice of this quilt was unusual in that
it is a protest piece expressing the futility of war. Jennifer Core of the Tennessee
Sampler Project is on the left in this image with Bets Ramsey at the exhibition
opening. *Courtesy of the Tennessee State Museum*

Selected Reading

Ramsey, Bets. "Art and Quilts: 1950–1970." *Uncoverings 1993*. San
Francisco: American Quilt Study Group, 1994.

————. "The Land of Cotton: Quiltmaking by African-American Women
in Three Southern States." *Uncoverings 1988*. San Francisco:
American Quilt Study Group, 1989.

————. *Old and New Quilt Patterns in the Southern Tradition*.
Nashville: Rutledge Hill Press, 1987.

————. "The Quilter." Weekly column, *Chattanooga Times*, 1980–1998.

Ramsey, Bets, and Gail Trechsel. *Southern Quilts: A New View*. McLean,
VA: EPM, 1991.

Ramsey, Bets, and Merikay Waldvogel. *The Quilts of Tennessee:
Images of Domestic Life Prior to 1930*. Nashville: Rutledge Hill
Press, 1986.

————. *Southern Quilts: Surviving Relics of the Civil War*. Nashville:
Rutledge Hill Press, 1996.

From 1980 to 1998, Bets wrote a weekly column, "The Quilter," for the *Chattanooga Times*. Each column featured a quilt pattern, typically connected with a recent book, exhibition, or other event. The columns not only delighted local readers and quilt friends over the years, but the compilation of these approximately nine hundred items (now in the AQSG Special Collection at the University of Nebraska–Lincoln, Love Library) formed a weekly journal of quilt-related interests through much of the late twentieth century.

Throughout her career, Bets has maintained a presence in both the craft and the quilt worlds, negotiating a path between the extremes of these often mutually exclusive populations. She was a founding member of the Tennessee Association of Craft Artists in 1965 and is a member of the American Crafts Council and other art and craft organizations. In 2009, Bets received the Tennessee Governor's Award in the Arts for her achievements as an artist and her contributions to the practice of quiltmaking and its history.

Following the death of her husband in 1994, Bets sold her house in Chattanooga and moved to a roomy condominium in Nashville. Pondering how to direct her professional career, she decided to make her own artwork her first priority. "Finally I could see myself as an artist," she says. "I began to understand that in the past I had refused to claim the title and take the responsibility for living it. Now I know that I am an artist and that is my work. I will continue to curate exhibitions, to write articles, and give lectures because that is what I do, but my studio work comes first."

During the summer of 2003, a retrospective exhibition, *Stitched from the Heart: Fiber Art by Bets Ramsey*, featuring forty quilts and wall hangings spanning as many years, was shown at East Tennessee State University and Belmont University. Bets's work is characterized by a subdued yet exuberant elegance of color and pattern and a careful attention to refined technique, reflecting both her formal training in design and her love of historic textiles.

Beginning her career at a time when being a woman, an artist, and a quilter garnered little public honor, Bets Ramsey seems to have arrived at the heart of her life's work after years of meaningful preparation, all while maintaining close ties to family, friends, church, and community. She continues to add to an already impressive legacy of artistic creation, published research, and, perhaps most notable of all, the gift of her friendship and encouragement to a generation of quilters and scholars.

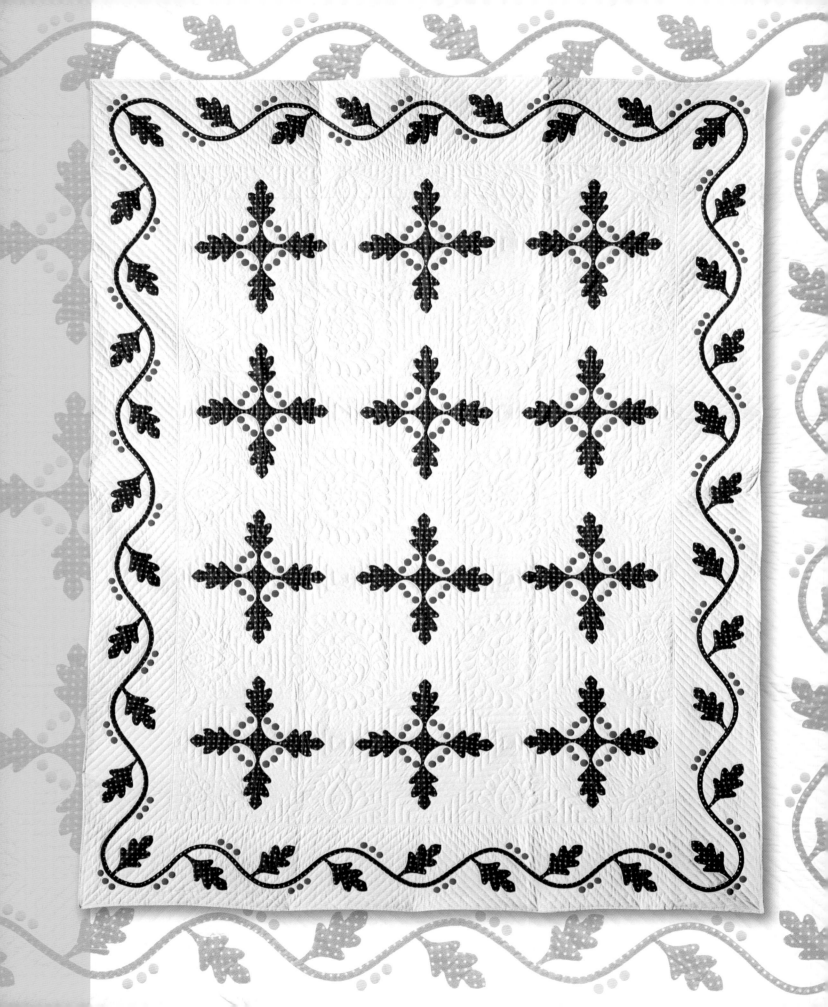

Mary Schafer

1910–2006

"Mary has great respect for those early quiltmakers.
Her aim in life is to upgrade the quality of quilts today.
Her own perfectionist approach to quiltmaking is an inspiration."

—Joyce Gross, "Mary Schafer," *Quilters' Journal*, vol. 1, no. 3 (Spring 1978)

Mary Schafer was inducted into the Quilters Hall of Fame, Marion, Indiana, on July 21, 2007. *Courtesy of Michigan State University Museum*

by Karen B. Alexander

MARY VIDA SCHAFER was born April 27, 1910, in Austria-Hungary, moving to the United States in 1915. Although her mother died soon after she arrived in America, Mary's interest in needlework was nurtured while she was still quite young by the women in her neighborhood, at the request of her father. However, she was not exposed to quiltmaking until she was in her forties.

In 1956, Mary rescued a wet, sandy quilt from the trunk of her son's car. She cleaned and repaired the sorry-looking quilt in an attempt to save it and then recreated the quilt, adding her own border and quilting designs.

This seminal experience changed Mary's life. Though she was able to reproduce the beautiful old quilt, she could not find the pattern in any book or magazine. Once ignited, her curiosity about traditional quilts knew no bounds, thus launching her study and collecting of historic quilt patterns, as well as her creation of exquisitely stitched new quilts to honor them.

Mary faithfully researched the history of each pattern at a time when very few were pursuing quilt history and modern technology was not there to help facilitate research. She soon subscribed to all the early quilt pattern magazines of the day—Glenna Boyd's *Aunt Kate's Quilting Bee*, Joy Carddock's *4J's*, and others—and

carried on a voluminous correspondence with many of the early pattern collectors and historians, reinforcing her intent to ground her quiltmaking in historical accuracy. Mary also corresponded with Florence Peto, Joyce Gross, Lenice Bacon, Patricia (Almy) Randolph, editor of *Nimble Needle Treasures*, and others.

Mary's quiltmaking and the focus of her research went through many phases. She deliberately brought her growing knowledge of quilt history to the reproduction of each pattern, thoroughly researching the origins of each quilt. Mary would put her own stamp upon each quilt without straying from the traditional look of the overall pattern, and she usually added her own border designs. She also drafted her own original quilting patterns and marked her tops for quilting. Then, like many quiltmakers of the time, Mary found other women to do the quilting.

In 1965, Mary was greatly inspired by the words of honoree Marie Webster in *Quilts: Their Story and How to Make Them* (1915): "To raise in popular esteem the most worthy products of home industry, to add to the appreciation of their history and traditions, to give added interest to the hours of labor which their construction involves, to present a few of the old masterpieces to the quilters of today."

Oak Leaf and Cherries | Mary Schafer, Flushing, Michigan | 1969 | 88 × 79 inches | **Cotton with polyester filling.** During Mary's self-named "Challenge Period," she attempted "to raise in popular esteem" the appreciation of quilts and to honor those who played key roles in quilting history. As part of this, Mary selected *Oak Leaf and Cherries*, one of the patterns featured in Rose Wilder Lane's book, *American Needlework*. Mary stuffed the cherries, created an original quilting design, and added a unique appliquéd border. *Photo by Fumio Ichikawa, courtesy of Michigan State University Museum (1998.53.67)*

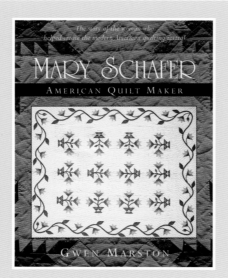

Mary Schafer: American Quilt Maker by Gwen Marston discusses Mary's role in helping to create the modern American quilting revival.

Mary Schafer in the Betsy Ross costume she wore when lecturing, with her Pennsylvania Dutch quilt. This photo appeared on the cover of honoree Joyce Gross's *Quilters' Journal*, Spring 1978 (vol. 1, no. 3). *Courtesy of the Joyce Gross Quilt History Collection, Dolph Briscoe Center for American History, University of Texas at Austin*

Thus began a self-imposed series of challenges, beginning with a tribute to honoree Ruth Finley in 1967 by reproducing her *Clamshell* quilt. In September 1970, this quilt won a blue ribbon for best pieced quilt as well as the "Popular Prize" at the first National Quilting Association exhibit in Greenbelt, Maryland. The exposure garnered as a result of winning these ribbons helped nudge Mary into a more public role that would only grow as opportunities to speak and teach began to come her way.

In 1971, Mary's very close friend Betty Harriman of Buneston, Missouri, died at age eighty-one. Although the two women had never met face to face, their friendship had been deeply cemented by correspondence and phone calls for over a decade. Mary acquired Betty's unfinished quilt tops, as well as quantities of blocks, patterns, fabric swatches, project notes, and sketches. As Mary pored through these boxes of Betty's treasures, she made the decision to finish a number of Betty's quilts.

In the space of ten years, Mary completed fourteen of Betty's quilts. Meanwhile, she also completed her own series of bicentennial quilts and continued her project of reproducing challenging quilt patterns from earlier quiltmakers. She began to explore the differences between old and new Amish-made quilts so that she could speak knowledgeably about them in her lectures. Since the price of authentic old Amish quilts was rising dramatically, Mary was once again faced with the prospect of making her own.

As quilt books, exhibits, and contests proliferated in the late 1970s, Mary continued to enter and win contests, as well as to research traditional patterns. The Fall 1972 issue of *Nimble Needle Treasures* featured numerous variations of the North Carolina Lily pattern from the Schafer collection, spanning more than one hundred years.

After she saw honoree Jinny Beyer's award-winning 1977 quilt, *Ray of Light*, Mary began to research and reproduce eighteenth- and nineteenth-century medallion quilts, anticipating another great revival that emerged as more and more reproduction antique fabrics were introduced. Never one to be content with only one or two examples, Mary fully explored this genre by making multiple medallion quilts.

In 1977, two paths seemed fated to converge when Mary contacted another quilter interested in traditional quiltmaking, Gwen Marston. With friend Joe Cunningham, Gwen quickly introduced Mary Schafer to a wider quilt audience, beginning with a series of exhibits of Mary's work in 1978 at the Robert E. Whaley historic house in Flint, Michigan. Thus began still another new chapter in Mary's quilting life. Within two years, Gwen and Joe had documented Mary's collection and published a catalog.

With the assistance of her friends to handle exhibit planning and promotion, Mary was free to continue exploring new directions in her quilting. Once the Whaley exhibits began, Mary planned her quiltmaking around the theme of their annual exhibit: 1980, heirloom quilts; 1981, whitework quilts; 1982, medallion quilts; and in 1983, her final Whaley House quilt exhibition, appliqué quilts.

Mary was inspired by *Crib Quilts & Other Small Wonders* by Thomas K. Woodard and Blanche Greenstein to begin making doll and crib quilts with all the dedication with which she had explored other historic genres. In 1983, twenty-five doll and crib quilts she had made were exhibited in Flint and Rochester, Michigan. She made at least another twenty in the ensuing years.

Another noted quilt collector from Michigan, Merry Silber, suggested that Mary reproduce quilts from Mary's own antique quilt collection and exhibit them side by side with the antiques. By 1986, Mary had reproduced twenty-six quilts and exhibited them alongside the originals at the Birmingham–Bloomfield Art Association in Birmingham, Michigan, along with thirty quilt blocks Mary had made and given to Cuesta Benberry (now in the collection of the Quilters Hall of Fame). At this event, the Michigan State Senate presented Mary with a proclamation honoring her for her contributions to the art and study of quiltmaking.

In 1987, four of Mary's quilts were included in the Michigan Quilt Project's book and exhibit. Mary's manuscript *Q Is for Quilt*, written in 1979, was donated to the project as a fundraiser and was subsequently published by the Michigan State University Museum.

In 1988, Mary was honored by the Michigan Women's Foundation for outstanding contributions to the arts. With the generous support of the Ruth Mott Fund and numerous individuals and quilt groups, the core of Mary Schafer's collection was purchased for the Michigan State University Museum, where it resides today for quilt lovers to study and enjoy for generations to come.

Sadly, not long after she was told of her selection for the Quilters Hall of Fame, Mary Schafer passed away, on December 21, 2006, just six months before her induction.

The quilting community owes Mary a great debt of gratitude for her dedication to the study and reproduction of historic quilts.

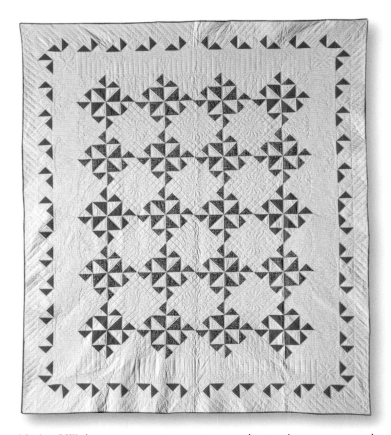

Linden Mill | Mary Schafer, Flushing, Michigan | 1956 | 80 × 94 inches | **Cotton.** After rescuing the original Linden Mill quilt, Mary took on the challenge of creating this reproduction. When it was finished, Mary had enough quilts to cover all of the beds in her household and turned back to other forms of sewing for a short time.
Photo by Keva, courtesy of Michigan State University Museum (1998.53.51)

Selected Reading

Cunningham, Joe. "Fourteen Quilts Begun by One Woman and Finished by Another." *Uncoverings 1986*. Mill Valley, CA: American Quilt Study Group, 1987.

Marston, Gwen. *Mary Schafer: American Quilt Maker*. Ann Arbor: University of Michigan Press, 2004.

———. *The Mary Schafer Quilt Collection*. Flint, MI: Gwen Marston, 1980.

Marston, Gwen, and Joe Cunningham. *Mary Schafer and Her Quilts*. East Lansing, MI: Michigan State University Museum, 1990. Foreword by Cuesta Benberry.

Worrall, Mary. "Mary Schafer: Quilter, Quilt Collector, and Quilt Historian." *Great Lakes, Great Quilts: From the Michigan State University Museum*. Edited by Marsha MacDowell. Lafayette, CA: C&T Publishing, 2001.

Grace McCance Snyder

1882–1982

"I wished that I might grow up to make the most beautiful quilts in the world, to marry a cowboy, and to look down on the top of a cloud."

—Grace Snyder, *No Time on My Hands*, 1963

Grace Snyder was inducted into the Quilters Hall of Fame at the Continental Quilting Congress in Arlington, Virginia, on October 15, 1980. *Courtesy of Tom Yost*

by Carol Bosshardt

MARRYING A COWBOY was a common dream for a young Nebraska girl in 1889. Making "the most beautiful quilts in the world" and "look[ing] down on the top of a cloud" are still challenging dreams. But piecing together those three dreams was unimaginable for most pioneers whose social network included more cattle than people and whose fabric source might be a yearly barrel of hand-me-downs from extended family who lived in more "civilized" parts of the country. Although the isolation and hardships of pioneer life challenged Grace McCance Snyder, they failed to stop her. Through the challenges, Grace pieced together diverse patches including those three unlikely dreams. Grace's inclusion among the quilters inducted into the Quilters Hall of Fame culminated a lifetime of practical perfection and recognized the fulfillment of her dream to "make the most beautiful quilts in the world."

Grace's autobiography, *No Time on My Hands*, coauthored with her daughter, Nellie Snyder Yost, details her birth in Missouri and move to Nebraska at the age of three, her courtship and marriage to Bert Snyder, the birth of their children,

routine daily activities, even the influence of the weather on cattle feeding, quilting, and visiting with neighbors. The book outlines her dreams and illustrates the difficulties she faced in reaching them.

Her dream to make beautiful quilts developed early, as Grace observed her mother's appreciation for "nice things" and her efforts to make her sod homes as comfortable as possible. Although Grace was always a bit of a tomboy, the refining influence of Margaret Blaine McCance and her "tiny, quick stitches" encouraged her daughter, from early childhood, to value the best quilt practices possible. Shortly after the six-year-old girl began herding the family cattle, she asked for scraps to piece into a little Four Patch quilt for her cornhusk doll.

Quilts appear throughout Grace's life story because of their importance in warming people, animals, and even family cars. During Grace's first job, as a teacher in 1901, she quilted while snowed in for months at a time. This quilt, the first she made from store-bought fabric rather than scraps, later graced the bed of Grace and Bert Snyder's first sod home.

Flower Basket Petit Point | Hand-pieced and hand-quilted by Grace McCance Snyder, near Sutherland, Lincoln County, Nebraska | 1942–1943 | 92 × 94 inches | Cotton. This masterpiece quilt contains over 85,000 tiny pieces. Grace corresponded both with the manufacturer of the china that inspired her quilt (the Salem China Company of Ohio, which gave her a set of the china) and with Wendelin Grossman, the German designer of the china pattern. In 1999, the quilt was chosen by a panel of experts as one of *America's 100 Best Quilts of the 20th Century*. Photo by R. Bruhn, courtesy of the Nebraska State Historical Society, Museum of Nebraska History, Lincoln

Grace's dream of marrying a cowboy came true when A. B. Snyder (also known as "Pinnacle Jake" or "Bert") claimed Grace's heart and hand in 1903. Their four children were born between 1904 and 1914. With the exception of a brief move to Oregon in 1927 so the youngest two daughters could attend high school, Grace and Bert spent most of their life together on the ranch near Tryon, Nebraska.

The ranch theme and images from farm life run through many of Grace's quilts, whether they were published patterns or original designs. When Grace appliquéd her *Covered Wagon States* quilt (an *Omaha World Herald* pattern), she customized the cowboy using Bert's cowboy nickname, Pinnacle Jake. Several original quilts with brand block designs exist, and one *Brand Raffle Quilt* found its way back to the Lincoln County Historical Museum in North Platte, Nebraska, many years after it was originally raffled off. The brand design is so finely detailed and executed that from a short distance, the brands appear to be embroidered, although they are actually appliquéd.

In addition to the cowboy images, Grace's love for nature also appears in many floral images in her quilts. Some flowers ramble across the quilts, such as the wild rose border on *Flower Basket Petit Point* and the overall designs of *Mrs. McGill's Cherries* and *Appliqué Grapes*. Others are confined to bouquets like the *Hexagon Flowers Quilt*.

Although they were physically isolated in the Nebraska Sandhills, Grace and her cowboy were always aware of opportunities and challenges that tied their family and community to a broader world. The U.S. mail helped Grace piece together a broad social network in spite of her physical isolation. In addition to maintaining family ties with siblings and parents who moved from Missouri to distant states, Grace ordered a sewing machine through the mail four years after she married Bert. By 1917, she became the postmistress for Lilac, Nebraska, where four families picked up their mail from a cracker box, and a telephone line finally reached the Snyder ranch.

A move to Salem, Oregon, in 1927 to find better schools for her two youngest children freed Grace from the daily chores of a busy ranch family and allowed her to spend more time making the finest quilts possible. Before and after her move to Oregon, Grace and her Tryon neighbors pieced and quilted for each other and neighbors in need. Daughter Billie treasured a Pinwheel quilt the neighbors made for the Snyder family before they left for Oregon. One patch included her mother's name and handiwork. During her five years in Oregon, Bert's sister, Alice, invited Grace to her neighborhood quilting club. Grace wrote to Nellie, who had returned to Nebraska, that she made Sawtooth, Double Wedding Ring, Log Cabin, and Necktie quilts.

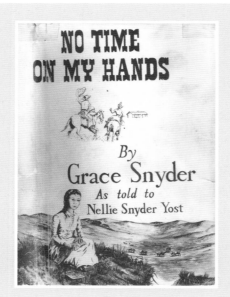

No Time on My Hands includes the reminiscences of Grace Snyder, the matriarch of a pioneer Nebraska family, which she wrote in her eightieth year. She felt she had been blessed "by having no time on my hands."

Grace and Bert Snyder.
Courtesy of Tom Yost

Although Grace made and used many everyday quilts, she was also aware of the distinction between everyday and show quilts. In a time when some newspapers ignored "women's news" and printed only the men's fair premiums, the *Tryon Graphic* newspaper documented women's work as well as livestock and crop reports. The September 28, 1939, *Graphic* named many of Grace's county fair prizes, from the first- and second-place ribbons Grace won for her quilts to the first-place ribbon she received for her pillowtop entry and the third-place ribbon awarded to her "Tea Towel Display."

The *Tryon Graphic*, like many other newspapers of its time, printed its news on preprinted paper that included needlework patterns and advertisements as well as national and world news. These patterns, along with letters to and from extended family members and friends, helped Grace connect with an early national network of quilters. According to her daughter Nellie, "She then began to envision a large collection of outstanding quilts . . . and, toward that end, began to study old quilts and quilt history."

Wind Blown Tulip (a Marie Webster design), *Mrs. McGill's Cherries*, and the *Lincoln Quilt* (an Anne Orr design) are well-known patterns Grace completed in the 1930s. In addition to making and modifying published patterns, Grace also began designing her own patterns. Granddaughter Josee Forell recalls

Grace sketching a tiger lily from her garden for the *Tiger Lily Quilt*, one of Grace's less-well-known quilts, which is still in family hands. In the 1940s, Grace's *Semi-Circle Saw* and *Return of the Swallows* quilt patterns appeared in the *Kansas City Star*.

Grace became interested in making quilts with thousands of tiny pieces when she saw a photo of Albert Small's *Mosaic Hexagon* quilt, with each piece the size of a dime. Grace's own version, *Flower Basket Petit Point*, made about 1941, won many prizes and was included in the list of *America's 100 Best Quilts of the 20th Century* and identified by some as one of the top ten quilts of the twentieth century.

Many quilters have seen or even own the same Salem China Company dishes that Grace used as inspiration for her *Flower Basket Petit Point*. To give the needlepoint effect, Grace translated a petit point flower basket from a plate into thousands of one-inch blocks made up of four to eight pieces. She spent sixteen months in 1942 and 1943 designing, cutting, and piecing the quilt, which contains more than 85,000 tiny pieces in thirteen basket blocks set on point and surrounded by an elaborate rose-vine border that may have been inspired by the wild roses found on the Snyder ranch.

The dish pattern for Grace's *Bird of Paradise* quilt is much less well known, although Nellie mentions it in her epilogue to *No Time on My Hands*. *Bird of Paradise* outlines a central petit

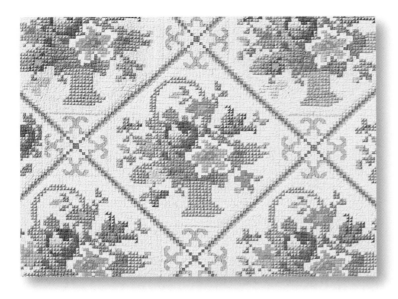

point patchwork design reminiscent of *Flower Basket Petit Point* and *Hexagon Mosaic*. Although Grace switched colors in her bird, the needlepoint design is very similar to a Leigh Ware dish. The scalloped ribbon border also features the purple and green colors Grace used in the sashing for *Flower Basket Petit Point*, although its border effect is more reminiscent of the border and scallop designs found in *Appliqué Grapes*, *Mrs. McGill's Cherries*, and the less-well-known *Morning Glory*.

After she began making the world's most beautiful quilts, Grace's dream of "looking down on the top of a cloud" was fulfilled in ways she could not have envisioned as a child. Airplane travel increased rapidly during the first half of the twentieth century. Grace and Bert's son Miles even owned a small plane for checking cattle and transporting supplies to their home near Tryon, Nebraska, where roads were few and very rough. After *Flower Basket Petit Point* won the sweepstakes award at the Nebraska State Fair and *Hexagon Mosaic* and *Covered Wagon States* won blue ribbons, Grace and her quilts flew above the clouds often and farther and farther from home. Grace and *Flower Basket Petit Point* traveled to the Eastern States Exposition at Storrowton in Massachusetts and won "a fistful of top ribbons" at the International Women's Exhibition in New York in 1950, judged by future Quilters Hall of Fame honoree Florence Peto.

Nellie wrote that her mother's quilts appeared "in huge quilt shows in Texas, Virginia, California, Washington, Tennessee, Louisiana, Michigan, Kansas, Colorado, Iowa, and Utah." Grace and her daughters, especially Nellie, continued to travel with the quilts. For many years, the family said that Nellie would reserve one seat for the quilts to fly beside her as the quilts traveled across the United States.

In 1973, the Stuhr Museum of the Prairie Pioneer in Grand Island, Nebraska, produced a slide presentation, "The Three Dreams of Grace McCance Snyder," to run with an exhibit of Grace's prized quilts. At the age of ninety-one, Grace beamed with pride as she answered the question "How could an isolated pioneer woman achieve these three impossible dreams?" Through all the challenges, Grace enjoyed the adventures life offered her and pieced together her love for her cowboy, the wonderful flora and sky of western Nebraska, and an appreciation for beautiful quilts.

Although Grace has been dead for almost three decades now, the members of her family continue to treasure her quilts and to share them with the larger quilt community on a regular basis. Daughter Billie Lee Thornton continued Nellie's writing legacy as she told personal and family stories in her books. When Andrea Warren's *Pioneer Girl* version of Grace's childhood story came out, members of the family brought their quilts to a preview of the book at the North Platte Library. In October 2001, a Snyder exhibition was held at the Kellogg Center in Lincoln, Nebraska. The first *Threads Across Nebraska* exhibition series in Grand

Grace Snyder is shown holding the engraved box commemorating her induction into the Quilters Hall of Fame in October 1980. Her daughter, Nellie Yost, wrote to President Hazel Carter: "Mother is so proud of her lovely box, and we are all proud of her and her award. It is, indeed, an honor. . . . She said to me, 'I'm so glad I lived to see this.'"

Hexagon Mosaic | Made by Grace Snyder | 1940 | 84 × 104½ inches | Cottons; hand-pieced and hand-quilted.

Inspired by a black-and-white photograph of a 1939 quilt by Albert Small, Grace Snyder used 58,640 fabric pieces in an incredible array of colors to create her *Mosaic* quilt. *Photo by Melissa Karlin Mahoney, courtesy of the International Quilt Study Center and Museum (2009.032.0002)*

Island, Nebraska, featured an extensive exhibition of Grace's show and family quilts.

From April 10 through June 14, 2009, the International Quilt Study Center (IQSC) in Lincoln, Nebraska, hosted a Snyder exhibition, *Grace Snyder: A Life in Extraordinary Stitches*, curated by Janet Price, the IQSC collections manager. Video clips as well as photographs and captions from the exhibit can be seen at the IQSC website.

Grace's dreams and her practical efforts to raise a family in the wide-open Sandhills of western Nebraska continue to challenge quilters and those who appreciate quilts to reach for impossible dreams. When we look at the clouds and the world around us we, too, can piece together a stronger quilt network and beautiful images, whether the fabric comes from a barrel of used clothing or an online fabric shop.

Selected Reading

Crews, Patricia Cox, and Ronald C. Naugle, eds. *Nebraska Quilts and Quiltmakers*. Lincoln, NE: University of Nebraska Press, 1991.

"The Meeting Place: Grace Snyder of North Platte, Nebraska." *Quilter's Newsletter Magazine*, no. 88 (February 1977): 24–25.

Price, Janet, IQSC Collections Manager, curator. "Grace Snyder: A Life in Extraordinary Stitches." www.quiltstudy.org/exhibitions/online_exhibitions/snyder.html.

Snyder, Grace. *No Time on My Hands*. As told to Nellie S. Yost. Caldwell, ID: Caxton Printers, 1963. Reprint, Lincoln, NE: University of Nebraska Press, 1986.

Wiebusch, Marguerite. "An Afternoon with Grace Snyder." *National Quilting Association Patchwork Patter*, February 1976.

Bertha Stenge
1891–1957

"An Artist with a Needle—
Meet Bertha Stenge,
Chicago's Quilting Queen,"

—*Chicago Daily News*, January 15, 1955

Bertha Stenge was inducted into the
Quilters Hall of Fame at the Continental
Quilting Congress in Arlington, Virginia, on
October 15, 1980. *Courtesy of Joyce Gross*

by Merikay Waldvogel

THE WOMAN who would become "Chicago's Quilting Queen" was born in 1891 to a tailor, Max Sheramsky, and his wife, Frances. Bertha grew up and attended school in Alameda, California, where friends and family remembered her love of arts and crafts. She attended the San Francisco School of Art and designed stained-glass windows. By 1910, she had her own studio adjacent to her parents' house and, although only nineteen, was listed in the census as an artist.

Two years later, Bertha moved to Chicago, where she married Bernhard Stenge, a young lawyer recently graduated from Northwestern University. Bertha and Bernhard lived on the Near North Side of Chicago for forty-five years and raised three daughters, Frances, Ruth, and Prudence.

Bertha Stenge made her first quilt in 1929, while recovering from an illness. She used the *Grandmother's Garden* quilt pattern series published in the newspaper's Nancy Page syndicated quilt column. She entered the local contest for the best quilt using this pattern and won the $25 second prize. Thus encouraged, Bertha began entering and winning more contests.

In 1933, she entered the Sears Roebuck & Co. national quilt contest for the Chicago World's Fair, which offered a $1,000 grand prize, with a bonus of $200 if the quilt expressed the theme of the fair. Bertha completed her original design based on Chicago's history in just four months and won an award of merit, but no cash prize. Bertha went on to make other album quilts, including *One Woman's Life* (1941), *The Quilt Show* (1943), *Map of Canada* (1947), *American Holidays* (1948), and *Ladies of Fashion* (1952).

The Sears contest affected Bertha Stenge's quiltmaking style in a significant way. It was at the 1933 Chicago World's Fair that she first saw a quilt with trapunto quilting, Margaret Rogers Caden's *Star of the Bluegrass*, which won the grand prize. The following year, using a pattern called Palm Leaf, she rearranged the usual layout to create a central diamond space and added elaborate trapunto designs. This quilt brought her a first-prize ribbon at the Women's Pageant of Progress in Chicago in 1936 and the grand prize at the 1940 New York World's Fair.

Bertha produced several more quilts with original trapunto designs, including three quilts that appeared in the November

The Quilting Party | Designed, hand-pieced, appliquéd, and quilted by Bertha Stenge, Chicago, Illinois | 1950 | 76 × 80 inches. Honoree Florence Peto inspired Bertha Stenge to make this prize-winning quilt in a traditional center medallion style, using vintage fabrics that Florence had given her. The quilting party shown in the center is a faithful rendition in fabric of a folk painting illustrated in Florence Peto's book, *American Quilts and Coverlets* (1949), plate 29. The quilt was selected as one of *America's 100 Best Quilts of the 20th Century*. Photo by Gary Andrashko, courtesy of the Illinois State Museum, gift of the Frank Mason family

1940 issue of *Ladies' Home Journal*: *Rachel's Wreath* (1935), *Iva's Pin Cushion* (1936), and *Ruth's Ring* (1937). The captions read, "New Quilt Designs: Modern-looking quilts in their restraint, the pattern of their quilting and the pastel shades of the appliqué motifs." For just ten cents, readers could buy a pattern for one of Bertha Stenge's "modern quilts."

In 1941, Eugene Neuhaus, her art teacher from her student days in San Francisco, took note of her prizewinning quilts and proposed a one-woman exhibit at the art gallery of the University of California at Berkeley. Bertha sent thirteen quilts, including her most recent pictorial, *One Woman's Life*, which Neuhaus praised for its "symbolic representation of the life of the artist."

In 1942, the staff at *Woman's Day* magazine announced its National Needlework Exhibition in New York City, in conjunction with the Nineteenth Annual Women's International Exposition of Arts and Industries. To qualify for the grand prize of one thousand

Bertha Stenge at her quilting frame, about 1950. *Courtesy of Joyce Gross*

Bertha Stenge's *The Quilt Show* appeared on the cover of *Quilter's Newsletter Magazine* in January 1980 (no. 118). Appliquéd ladies display thirteen miniature traditional quilts, each only six inches square. The quilt is now in the collection of the Art Institute of Chicago.

dollars, each entry must have won a prize at a county or state fair. Bertha Stenge entered her *Victory Quilt* and her *Peace Quilt*, which had won prizes at an Illinois county fair. The awards ceremony was held in Madison Square Garden in New York City, while an audience of thousands listened on the radio.

Bertha's *Victory Quilt*, with a theme appropriate to wartime and her signature trapunto quilting, won both the one-hundred-dollar prize for appliqué and the one-thousand-dollar grand prize for best of show. Her *Peace Quilt* won a third-place twenty-five-dollar award in the quilting category. When asked what she planned to do with her winnings, she patriotically responded that she would purchase war bonds.

Bertha Stenge was on hand to accept the prizes for her quilts. Photographs of the quiltmaker receiving the prize checks appeared in the February 1943 issue of *Woman's Day*, and the following month, a color photograph of her *Victory Quilt* was featured in the magazine.

The wire services sent the photos of Bertha and her winning quilts to newsrooms throughout the country. The hobby that started when she was ill and confined to bed made an interesting story. She was a mother, a Red Cross volunteer, and a prizewinning quilter, but also a trained artist who was astutely tuned in to the judges' standards.

With the national spotlight on a Chicago resident, the Art Institute of Chicago filled two galleries with an exhibition of her quilts in the summer of 1943.

Selected Reading

Barber, Rita Barrow. *Somewhere In Between: Quilts and Quilters of Illinois.* Paducah, KY: American Quilter's Society, 1986.

Gross, Joyce R. "Bertha Stenge." *Quilters' Journal* 2, no. 2 (Summer 1979): 1–5, 7.

———. "Four Twentieth-Century Quiltmakers." *Uncoverings 1980.* San Francisco: American Quilt Study Group, 1981. Reprinted in *Quiltmaking in America: Beyond the Myths.* Nashville, TN: Rutledge Hill Press, 1994.

Waldvogel, Merikay, and Barbara Brackman. *Patchwork Souvenirs of the 1933 Chicago World's Fair.* Nashville TN: Rutledge Hill Press, 1996.

Waldvogel, Merikay, and Jan Wass. "A Cut and Stitch Above: Quilts by Bertha Stenge." *The Living Museum/Illinois State Museum* 59, nos. 1 & 2 (Spring 1997): 10–13.

Florence Peto, a prominent collector and antiques writer, read about Bertha Stenge and decided to seek her out. The two women entered into a long friendship, opening new opportunities for each other. In September 1947, *American Home* magazine featured quilts by both Bertha Stenge and Florence Peto in the same article.

Bertha often sent quilts by mail to Florence for her to use in her exhibits, lectures, and publications. Florence included Bertha's *The Quilt Show* in her 1949 book *America's Quilts and Coverlets* as an example of a modern quilt.

Florence also proposed that modern quiltmakers should reflect the heritage of American antique quilts by using vintage fabrics and the center medallion format. Although Bertha was not easily persuaded, she eventually acted upon Florence's suggestions to create three of her most memorable quilts—*The Quilting Party*, made in 1950; *Toby Lil*, made in 1951; and *Ring and Dove*, made in 1952.

In turn, Bertha introduced her friend Florence to the joy of entering contests, sharing quilts with an appreciative audience, and winning ribbons. The two regularly sent quilts to contests in Florida, Kentucky, Missouri, and Tennessee, and then commiserated with each other over the judges' choices.

In 1954, the Women's International Exposition honored Bertha with a one-woman show in New York. She exhibited thirty-three quilts and took advantage of this opportunity to visit Florence. These two good friends, brought together by their love of quilts, were both inducted into the Quilters Hall of Fame in 1980.

Bertha Stenge died June 18, 1957. Five months earlier, she had donated her Chicago Fair quilt to the Chicago Historical Society. Her daughters each received thirteen quilts, and the Art Institute of Chicago received the gift of her collection of vintage fabrics. Later, her *Lotus* quilt was purchased by the Quilt Conservancy. In 1996, *Victory Quilt* and *The Quilt Show* were acquired by the Art Institute of Chicago, and seven quilts, including *Quilting Party* and *Four Freedoms*, were acquired by the Illinois State Museum, which organized a touring exhibit with additional quilts, *A Cut and Stitch Above: Quilts by Bertha Stenge from the 1930s–1950s.*

In 1999, two of Bertha's Stenge's masterpieces, *The Quilt Show* (c. 1943) and *The Quilting Party* (1950) were selected by a panel of experts for *America's 100 Best Quilts of the 20th Century* exhibit and the accompanying book, securing Bertha's prominent place in quilt history.

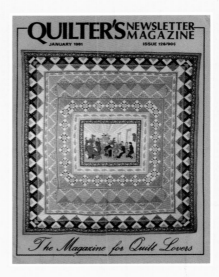

Bertha Stenge's *The Quilting Party*, appeared on the cover of *Quilter's Newsletter Magazine* in January 1981 (no. 128). It is a medallion-style quilt with a faithful reproduction of a painting in the center.

Gail van der Hoof

1943–2004

*"I used to think, sleeping in the same apartment
with the efforts of so many women,
that I could almost hear them speaking and feel them breathing.
They were speaking the language of quilts, and I was listening."*

—Gail van der Hoof, interviewed by Ann Nash in 1997

Gail van der Hoof was inducted into the
Quilters Hall of Fame at the Continental
Quilting Congress in Arlington, Virginia, on
October 27, 1979. *Courtesy of Jonathan Holstein*

by Ann Bodle Nash

IN JULY 1971, An extraordinary exhibition was unveiled in New York City at the prestigious Whitney Museum of American Art. Called *Abstract Design in American Quilts*, the exhibition contained sixty pieced quilts from the collection of Gail van der Hoof and Jonathan Holstein chosen purely for their visual content.

"The showing was unusual for the Whitney," noted Hilton Kramer, a *New York Times* reviewer, on July 3, 1971. "The Whitney has rarely condescended to acknowledge the 'decorative arts,' as they are called, as a significant contribution to American artistic achievements. One can only hope that the current exhibition, which is of an exceptionally high quality, signals a significant change of heart."

Elizabeth Stevens of the *New York Times* reported on July 26, 1971, in the San Francisco edition, that "All the Whitney quilts are 'pieced' and many of them anticipate by as much as 100 years the designs of contemporary optical artists and color painters whose quilt-sized abstract canvases have so often been touted as historic discoveries." Thus the message spread from coast to coast that quilts should now be recognized not merely as bed coverings but as bona fide art with links to contemporary abstract artists.

Gail and Jonathan had spent three years collecting the quilts, primarily in the eastern United States. Their vision and the resulting exhibition marked a dramatic shift in thought by folk art collectors, art patrons, antique dealers, and the general public about those "utilitarian blankets" their grandmothers had made. Their pioneering work helped to spark the resurgence of interest in all aspects of quilt study in the last quarter of the twentieth century.

Gail van der Hoof was born in Berkeley, California, in 1943. Her father was a professor of geology and paleontology, a research geologist for an oil company, and from 1959 until his death in 1964, director of the Santa Barbara Museum of Natural History.

Gail attended high school in Bakersfield and at the Casteleja School in Palo Alto, then entered the University of California–Santa Barbara, where she majored in art and English, receiving her B.A. in 1964. Soon after, she moved to San Francisco to work at the Joseph Magnin clothing store in fashion merchandising and advertising. She combined her art design skills and textile knowledge easily and found this employment most satisfying.

Art Deco Fans | Collected by Gail van der Hoof and Jonathan Holstein | Quiltmaker unknown | Circa 1930 | 82 × 82 inches | Cotton. Gail van der Hoof and Jonathan Holstein purchased this dramatic quilt for their growing collection of pieced quilts in the early 1970s. It was pictured in Jonathan Holstein's book, *The Pieced Quilt: An American Design Tradition* (1973), plate 48, with this caption: "Pure Art Deco design, using striped materials and stylized fan motifs, an indication that the design trends of any era can be assimilated successfully into pieced quilt design." *Courtesy of the International Quilt Study Center and Museum, Jonathan Holstein Collection, University of Nebraska–Lincoln (2003.003.0213)*

The job also served as the foundation for her later interest in the collecting of quilted textiles. Although not a quilter or weaver herself, she designed and constructed "art clothing."

Gail worked for the clothing store until her savings allowed her to travel extensively throughout Europe and West Africa. She lived in Holland and England, holding various jobs, including a stint in a youth hostel. She visited all the major museums and enjoyed her freedom. She took the Orient Express to Istanbul and explored the variety of textiles in Turkey. Her strong attraction to textile art was a constant throughout her life.

"I must have been a rag picker in my last life," exclaimed Gail in a 1997 telephone interview. "I have always haunted thrift shops or used clothes markets and can always find something good."

Eventually she returned to the United States and lived for several years in a small ranching community in Colorado, where she experienced a "back-to-the-earth" lifestyle—no electricity, but abundant land and peace. She recalled, "At the small, local market, the main topic of the conversation, other than kids and gardens, was what new fabrics had come into the local store, what the women were going to sew, and what the others were making. They even discussed what they were going to do with the scraps."

Gail found this a refreshing change from the never-ending chores of the ranchers' wives. "The meals get eaten, the house and clothes get dirty again, the flowers bloom then die, but what they made with their sewing machines, threads and needles, stayed. It was made to be used, admired, maybe put away (to be unfolded and admired again) or given or sent away, with love, to a relative or friend. These things haven't changed in all the years of quiltmaking."

Gail airing, examining, and refolding recently acquired quilts at the home of Roy and Dorothy Lichtenstein in Southampton, New York, in the 1970s. *Courtesy of Jonathan Holstein*

In 1967, Gail met Jonathan Holstein, who was visiting his brother in Aspen, Colorado. She accompanied Jonathan to New York City and began a new stage in her life's journey. They married in 1973, and in 1983 they moved to Cazenovia, New York, where they raised their two children, Cassia and Jared. Gail designed leather and beadwork; her designs were seen in such publications as *Vogue*.

Her passion for quilts began while they were living in New York City, with weekend trips to visit friends outside of the city. Said Gail:

> What an incredible treasure trove of quilts we discovered in the East, but especially in Pennsylvania. . . . There was furniture and folk art, of course, but we were both amazed by the quilts in such glorious profusion! With my art background, I yearned to begin a collection and Jon agreed. We collected in earnest from the start. Our friends delighted in our "show-and-tell" sessions at the end of jaunts to the country. They continued to encourage us and offered us their hospitality on our increasingly long weekends. What a happy time.
>
> Back in New York City, we would unfold, admire, and refold the quilts we had purchased. The increasing number of stacks in the living room eventually overflowed into the extra room. We never lost our enthusiasm for the quilts or the joy they gave us. Our friends, many of them artists, agreed. We were holding an enormous and important body of work, and it should be seen.
>
> All of these unsung artists—creators of such beauty— were not highly regarded in the 1960s and early 1970s, when we were collecting. The quilts were just "merchandise" to the pickers and dealers who sold them. The only valuable quilts then were very early quilts, bought to cover a bed in an historical setting, or appliqué quilts with evidence of much fine needlework.
>
> Fortunately for us, most people showed little interest in everyday quilts, no matter how visually striking they were. These remained relatively inexpensive. Sometimes on our forays into the countryside we'd hear about "that crazy couple from New York who buy all sorts of quilts." . . . The seeds planted earlier for an eventual exhibition were being nourished. The time was coming.

The show at the Whitney Museum was a huge success, leading to others in Europe and America. Both Gail van der Hoof and Jonathan Holstein lectured extensively to artists and quilters alike, influencing the acceptance of Amish quilts, in particular, by mainstream folk art collectors and quiltmakers. The renaissance in quiltmaking began to swell, leading to a bicentennial quilt competition in 1976, state quilt documentation projects in the 1980s, and an expanding field of scholarly research.

The many exhibitions they curated at museums here and abroad, and their lecturing and writing about quilts over the next two decades, were instrumental in broadening interest in quilts as works of art. Gail van der Hoof and Jonathan Holstein were inducted into the Quilters Hall of Fame in 1979, in recognition of their great influence on the Quilt Revival.

Jonathan and Gail were divorced in 1991. Gail moved to a house they owned in Marignana, Italy, and married Nicolo Finocchiaro in 1995. Although far from quilting activities in the United States, she maintained a strong interest in textiles, quilts, and art. Gail van der Hoof passed away at her home in Italy on March 27, 2004, shortly before her sixty-first birthday.

Selected Reading

Holstein, Jonathan. *Abstract Design in American Quilts*. Exhibit catalog. New York: Whitney Museum of American Art, 1971.

————. *Abstract Design in American Quilts: A Biography of an Exhibition*. Louisville, KY: The Kentucky Quilt Project, 1991.

————. *American Pieced Quilts*. Catalog for the exhibition at the Smithsonian Institution, Washington, DC, and other museums throughout the United States. New York: The Viking Press, 1972.

Holstein, Jonathan, and Gail van der Hoof. *Quilts Paris: Musée des Arts Decoratifs*. Exhibit catalog. Paris: Edition des Massons, 1972.

van der Hoof, Gail. "Various Aspects of Dating Quilts." *In the Heart of Pennsylvania: Symposium Papers*. Edited by Jeannette Lasansky. Lewisburg, PA: Oral Traditions Project, 1986.

Coffee Cups | Collected in Colorado | Circa 1920 | 81 × 72 inches | Cotton. This was a favorite of Gail's. She and Jon felt it was an iconic quilt, using an abstracted image of a commonplace object of American life in a sequential pattern to create a mysterious and strangely evocative overall image. It also echoed for them the themes and methods of such New York artists of the time as Andy Warhol. *Courtesy of the International Quilt Study Center and Museum (2003.003.0225)*

Merikay Waldvogel

Merikay Waldvogel was inducted into the Quilters Hall of Fame in Marion, Indiana, on July 17, 2009.

"What is it about quilts that makes them so alluring and enduring? This still-unanswered question has intrigued me ever since I bought that first anonymous quilt."

—Merikay Waldvogel, 2010

by Bets Ramsey

THE MISMATCHED BLOCKS of a North Carolina Lily quilt in the window of an antiques shop in Evanston, Illinois, caught her eye. She was looking for something to decorate her new one-room apartment on the North Side of Chicago. Wondering what unusual circumstances occurred to the quiltmaker to interrupt her work, Merikay Waldvogel decided to give the quilt a home. That was the beginning, in 1974, of Merikay's affair with quilts.

"I doubt that the word *patchwork* had ever crossed my lips," she told me later, adding, "I did not grow up with quilts in my family. However, I was sewing most of my clothes, knitting, and weaving. That one quilt fascinated me; it changed my life and career path."

By 1977, when Merikay moved to Knoxville, Tennessee, she had added several more quilts and was a collector. As program director of the Knoxville Women's Center, she discovered that quilts offered several possibilities for programs and workshops, and she invited me to be a speaker. We found common interests immediately and soon began planning events and exhibitions together. During the 1982 Knoxville World's Fair, Merikay managed a gallery for the Knoxville Arts Council and curated a small exhibit of antique quilts for the Folklife Building on the fair site.

Throughout the 1980s, Merikay came annually to the Southern Quilt Symposium held at the Hunter Museum of American Art in Chattanooga. There, she extended her acquaintance with collectors, quiltmakers, and quilt historians. She met members of the American Quilt Study Group (ASQG) and was encouraged to join their organization.

Merikay is known for the relentless manner in which she pursues missing information concerning a quilt or quiltmaker. Before the resources of the Internet, research was done through interviews, by consulting publications and census and court records, and by networking with other people. The stories of her searches would match many a good detective novel. So how did this determined focus begin?

Century of Progress: World Without End | Designed and made by Aurora See Dyer, Chicago, Illinois | 1933 | 70 × 87 inches. Merikay Waldvogel is known for tracking down quilts entered in the 1933 Sears National Quilt Contest to feature in her *Patchwork Souvenirs of the 1933 Chicago World's Fair*, co-authored with Barbara Brackman. This quilt, found in California with a quiltmaker's descendant, served as the cover for the book and exhibition brochure. The Dyer family still owns the quilt and the tempera drawing of the quiltmaker's design. This original design commemorated the theme of the fair, "1833–1933: A Century of Progress." Unfortunately, it did not win a prize. *Photo by Gary Heatherly, courtesy of Merikay Waldvogel and Barbara Brackman, collection of the Dyer Family Trust*

Soft Covers for Hard Times: Quiltmaking and the Great Depression, published by Merikay Waldvogel in 1990, accompanied the exhibition of the same title and remains one of the earliest and best books on American quilts made during the Depression.

Merikay's first paper for AQSG was only the beginning of presentations on a variety of subjects. "Quilts in the WPA Milwaukee Handicraft Project, 1935–1943" was followed by "Southern Linsey Quilts of the Nineteenth Century" in 1987, "The Marketing of Anne Orr's Quilts" in 1990, "Mildred Dickerson: A Quilt Pattern Collector of the 1960s and 1970s" in 1994, and "The Origin of Mountain Mist Patterns" in 1995. She became a patient mentor to new researchers and assisted with the publication process in several other capacities when she served on the board of directors of AQSG from 1990 to 1995.

The WPA project, the research on Anne Orr, and other investigations led Merikay to write a second book. *Soft Covers for*

For a 1983 exhibition, *Quilt Close-Up: Five Southern Views,* at the Hunter Museum, Merikay was invited to select several Tennessee quilts and write an essay for the catalog. She chose two elderly women who had grown up in the 1920s in rural Sevier County, not far from Knoxville. When she began the interviews, it was like opening a history book for this city girl from St. Louis, Missouri.

Merikay's first quilt essay was the beginning of many research projects, publications, and lectures. It was followed by an investigation of a crib-size sailboat quilt she purchased in 1979. A stamp on the back of the quilt identified it as a Works Progress Administration (WPA) product, which then led to a prolonged and rewarding search for the history of the WPA's Arts & Crafts program. With a little encouragement, Merikay presented these findings in her first paper at AQSG in 1984. From one narrow little quilt she was able to relate an important element of United States history during the Great Depression.

Merikay taught English as a second language at the University of Tennessee and Maryville College from 1983 to 1990. At the same time, we began a survey of Tennessee quilts, recruiting quilt guilds and friends to help us conduct quilt days across the state. We interviewed quilt owners, examined and recorded information about their quilts, and then photographed them. The two-year study resulted in one of the first state quilt survey books, *The Quilts of Tennessee: Images of Domestic Life Prior to 1930,* and an exhibition that toured the state from 1986 to 1988. Now there was no turning back, and quilt research would soon be her full-time occupation.

Merikay led a tour of the exhibit honoring her induction, *Quilts Alive: Some of Merikay Waldvogel's Favorite Quilts,* at the Marion, Indiana, Public Library on July 18, 2009. Here, she is discussing Ida Stow and the Century of Progress quilt she made for the 1933 Chicago World's Fair. *Courtesy of Marian Ann J. Montgomery*

Merikay Waldvogel in her dining room in 1993 with other TQHF honorees and leaders in the quilt history world (clockwise around the table beginning on left): Joyce Gross, Linda Claussen, Eva Earle Kent, Merikay Waldvogel, Bets Ramsey, and Cuesta Benberry. *Photo by Barbara Brackman, courtesy of Merikay Waldvogel*

Hard Times: Quiltmaking and the Great Depression, a thoughtful treatment of quilts and the life and times of the Depression years, was published in 1990. The story of the Tennessee Valley Authority (TVA) quilts designed by Ruth Clement Bond in 1934 for African American quiltmakers whose husbands worked for TVA is among her proudest achievements. One of the Ruth Bond–designed quilts made by Grace Tyler was selected among *America's 100 Best Quilts of the 20th Century.*

Her next book was a collaboration with Quilters Hall of Fame honoree Barbara Brackman about the 1933 Sears National Quilt Contest, *Patchwork Souvenirs of the 1933 World's Fair.* It was much more than an account of the contest and its winners; it dealt with the hopes and ambitions of people struggling to make ends meet who found themselves disillusioned by the quilt judging and the apparent misrepresentation of the grand prize winner.

Research never ends, however. Merikay continues to uncover new information related to Anne Orr, the 1933 Chicago World's Fair Quilt Contest, the TVA quilt of Ruth Clement Bond, and the quilts made by Chicagoans Bertha Stenge and Mary Gasperik.

Merikay married Jerry Ledbetter, an engineer, soon after her arrival in Knoxville. He encourages her activities, and they share interests in sports, travel, and hiking in the Smoky Mountains. He was supportive of her early research, encouraging her to "go on the road" and taking her frequent absences with grace and good

humor, but in 1992 he met an unexpected test of patience. Merikay learned about a rummage sale of patterns from a quilt pattern collector named Mildred Dickerson of Birmingham, Alabama, recently deceased. Merikay could see endless possibilities for quilt study and felt called to save this woman's life work. She drove home with all the boxes she could maneuver into her car and returned for three additional loads. It was Jerry's lot to produce the shelving to house the collection.

Mildred's ambition had been to collect a copy of every quilt pattern, and she shared round robin correspondence with several other pattern collectors, including Cuesta Benberry. Thus Merikay had an enormous gathering of material relating to pattern identification, quilt kits, and quilt marketing. There was enough in Mildred's file boxes for years of research far into the future.

It became apparent that other collectors on the grassroots level were also storing vast amounts of quilt-related information. In 1993, the Alliance for American Quilts was founded to serve as a home for documenting quilts, quiltmakers, and quiltmaking. With the advancement of the Internet, the Alliance's "home" became a website constructed with Michigan State University Museum and MATRIX: Center for the Humane Arts, Letters and Social Sciences Online at Michigan State University.

The Quilt Index, Boxes under the Bed, Quilters Save Our Stories, and Quilt Treasures became the Alliance's featured

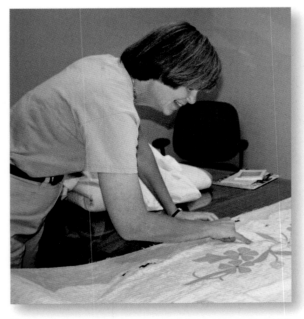

Merikay examines a kit quilt named *Dolly Varden* at a Quilters Hall of Fame Celebration Weekend. *Photo by Karen Alexander, courtesy of Merikay Waldvogel*

Center Medallion Chintz Quilt | Maker
unknown, probably made in North Carolina |
Probably circa 1833 | 110 × 110 inches |
Cotton; hand-pieced and appliquéd; hand-quilted.
With cross-stitched initials *EHR* and the date *1833*,
this is the oldest inscribed quilt in Waldvogel's
collection. The pre-printed circular center panel and
smaller oval panels were imported from England in
the early 1800s. *Photo by Gary Heatherly, courtesy of
Merikay Waldvogel*

Merikay Waldvogel at a May 2000 book signing in Stamford, Connecticut. *Photo by
Linda Koe, courtesy of Merikay Waldvogel*

projects, the first two receiving the attention of Merikay. She
served on the Alliance advisory board (1993–2001) and on the
board of directors for the Alliance (2001–2008). Through her
efforts, the entire Tennessee quilt survey was one of the first state
documentations to go on the Alliance's Quilt Index.

During the survey of Tennessee quilts, a number of quilts made
before or during the Civil War were brought in for documentation
and had amazing stories of concealment, danger, and mystery.
Merikay and I became aware of similar quilts and determined to
write a book about quilts that had survived adversity. Merikay was
relentless in her search for facts and sources of information. *Southern
Quilts: Surviving Relics of the Civil War* was published in 1998.

An outgrowth of the Civil War quilt research was her in-depth
study of early nineteenth-century center medallion chintz appliqué
quilts of the South. Again, one antique quilt she acquired prompted
her to look for other quilts with preprinted panels. The quilt's cross-
stitched date of 1833 and three initials helped narrow the time period
when similar quilts were made in the United States and England.

Although the story is yet to be finalized, the search has shown how a survey of even anonymous quilts can result in important authentication clues to dating and sourcing antique quilts.

Merikay is the author of yet another book, *Childhood Treasures: Doll Quilts by and for Children*, published in 2008. With five books, five papers delivered at AQSG seminars and published in the annuals, numerous magazine articles, and lectures, she became firmly established in the field of quilt history and its social, economic, and cultural implications.

The acquisition of the Mildred Dickerson collection in 1992 led Merikay to expand on the research of Cuesta Benberry and others into the origin and marketing of quilt patterns and kits. With the assistance of Marin Hanson at the International Quilt Study Center at the University of Nebraska, Merikay developed a database of kit information including images of kit quilts and quilt kit packaging. She has been a resident faculty scholar at this institution, where she has twice lectured and taught a graduate-level class derived from the Dickerson material. With the assistance of Michigan State University Museum staff, original quilt pattern materials, many from the Dickerson Collection, will be scanned and added to the Quilt Index.

"The pursuit of the vast amount of information in libraries and on the Internet is exhilarating, but talking directly to people and hearing their accounts firsthand is even more rewarding," says Merikay. As the stories expand, she searches for clues and links to even more information. Her dogged pursuits have become her mark, even as she enlists her family and friends in these activities.

As much as Merikay is known for her splendid and varied publications and her valuable contributions as a quilt consultant in several capacities, her lectures and workshops are her true gifts to people in the quilt world. Her enthusiasm and knowledge captivate the members of her audiences and bring them back for more. Her genuine interest encourages people to broaden their own knowledge of quilt history, just as she was once guided to write her first essay about two quiltmakers in Knoxville and present her first research paper at a quilt seminar. She has brought the vast network of quiltmakers, historians, appreciators, and collectors safely into the twenty-first century.

Quilters Hall of Fame honorees Merikay Waldvogel and Bets Ramsey led the efforts of the Tennessee statewide quilt documentation project and have remained lifelong friends, sharing quilt scholarship efforts and enriching the knowledge of historic American quilts. *Courtesy of Merikay Waldvogel*

Selected Reading

Ramsey, Bets, and Merikay Waldvogel. *The Quilts of Tennessee: Images of Domestic Life Prior to 1930.* Nashville, TN: Rutledge Hill Press, 1986.

———. *Southern Quilts: Surviving Relics of the Civil War.* Nashville, TN: Rutledge Hill Press, 1998.

Waldvogel, Merikay. *Childhood Treasures: Doll Quilts by and for Children.* Intercourse, PA: Good Books, 2008.

———. "The Marketing of Anne Orr's Quilts." *Uncoverings 1990.* San Francisco: American Quilt Study Group, 1991.

———. "Mildred Dickerson: A Quilt Pattern Collector of the 1960s and 1970s." *Uncoverings 1994.* San Francisco: American Quilt Study Group, 1995.

———. "The Origin of Mountain Mist Patterns." *Uncoverings 1995.* San Francisco: American Quilt Study Group, 1996.

———. "Quilts in the WPA Milwaukee Handicraft Project, 1935–1943." *Uncoverings 1984.* Mill Valley, CA: American Quilt Study Group, 1985.

———. *Soft Covers for Hard Times: Quiltmaking and the Great Depression.* Nashville, TN: Rutledge Hill Press, 1990.

———. "Southern Linsey Quilts of the Nineteenth Century." *Uncoverings 1987.* San Francisco: American Quilt Study Group, 1989. Reprinted in *Quiltmaking in America: Beyond the Myths.* Edited by Laurel Horton. Nashville, TN: Rutledge Hill Press, 1994.

Waldvogel, Merikay, and Barbara Brackman. *Patchwork Souvenirs of the 1933 World's Fair.* Nashville, TN: Rutledge Hill Press, 1993.

Marie Webster

1859–1956

*"Among the few home occupations that have survived is quilting. . . .
More quilts are being made at the present time
and over a wider area than ever before."*

—Marie D. Webster, *Quilts: Their Story and How to Make Them* (1915), p. 89

Marie Daugherty Webster was inducted into the Quilters Hall of Fame at the West Coast Quilters Conference in Sacramento, California, on July 18, 1991. *Courtesy of Katherine W. Dwight*

by Katherine Webster Dwight
and Rosalind Webster Perry

AN INFLUENTIAL QUILT DESIGNER of the early 1900s, Marie Webster was the first person to write a history of quilts, and she was also an astute businesswoman. Her floral appliqué designs, created at the height of the Arts and Crafts movement, are still widely appreciated and imitated today.

Born in the town of Wabash in northern Indiana, Marie was the oldest of the six children of Josiah Scott Daugherty and Minerva Harriet Lamoureaux Daugherty. Both of her parents' families had migrated westward from Ohio about 1850 and settled as pioneer farmers in the fertile Wabash River Valley. Josiah became a prosperous businessman and bank president. Minerva was an excellent needlewoman who taught her three daughters those plain and fancy sewing skills so important to domestic life in the nineteenth century.

Marie received her only formal education in the Wabash public schools, graduating from high school in 1878. Her ambition was to acquire a higher education, but her parents considered her too frail to leave home. (She turned out to be anything but frail, outliving all her younger brothers and sisters to reach the age of ninety-seven.) There is no record that she ever took art classes, but she was a voracious reader and studied Greek and Latin at home.

In 1884, she married a young businessman, George Webster Jr., of nearby Marion, Indiana, who would become a respected banker and civic leader. After his death in 1938, Marie continued to live in Marion until 1942, when she retired from her quilt pattern business and went to live with her son's family in Princeton, New Jersey, where she died on August 29, 1956.

Although Marie had made a crazy quilt in 1880, she did not start making appliqué quilts until about 1905. Unable to find a pattern that she liked, she decided to design one of her own. An elaboration of the traditional Rose of Sharon pattern, Marie's first quilt design was later renamed *American Beauty Rose*.

Clematis in Bloom | Evelyn Cammack Clements (1882–1980) | Quilt pattern designed by Marie D. Webster | 1934 | 80 × 89 inches. This beautiful floral appliqué quilt, one of the few known examples of this particular Marie Webster pattern, was made by Mrs. Clements and was found, carefully wrapped, in a cedar chest in her home after her death. She was a prolific quilter who lived in the exclusive Park Cities area of Dallas and made several quilts from Marie Webster kits, probably those for which the fabrics and patterns were provided. *Photo by Brad Flowers, courtesy of Mrs. George Seay*

Poppy | Designed and hand-appliquéd by Marie Webster, Marion, Indiana | Possibly quilted by others, using Marie's designs | 1909 | 83 × 92 inches | **Cotton and linen.** This was one of Marie Webster's first appliqué quilts, with the date 1909 and her initials, *MDW*, in quilting stitches. The quilt was published in color in *Ladies' Home Journal* (January 1912), together with Marie's *White Dogwood*, *Morning Glory*, and *Sunflower* quilts. The center medallion format revived a style that was popular early in the nineteenth century and that would become popular again in the 1920s and 1930s. *Photo by Tony Valainis, private collection*

Marie Webster was incredibly productive during the decade from 1911 to 1921. Five additional articles in *Ladies' Home Journal* showed twelve new quilts and nine pillow designs. She studied the flowers in her garden, creating a naturalism in her appliqué, enhanced by her use of linen fabrics in solid pastel colors. Some of her patterns revived the central medallion style of the mid-nineteenth century, with graceful scalloped borders framing the central design. While most of the quilting was done by others to her specifications, her own appliqué was exquisite.

While creating new designs, she was also busy researching and writing *Quilts: Their Story and How to Make Them*, the first book devoted entirely to the subject, with many photos of antique quilts and of her own designs. The book was published in October 1915 to glowing reviews and an avalanche of enthusiastic letters from quilt lovers around the world. She lectured extensively, often dressed in a period gown.

Her mail-order pattern business thrived. As the quilt revival gained momentum after World War I, Marie decided to sell kits, basted quilts, and finished quilts in addition to the patterns. In 1921, her sister Emma Daugherty, and two friends, Ida Hess and Evangeline Beshore, joined her in a new business venture, the Practical Patchwork Company. Their products were promoted through ads in women's magazines and illustrated catalogs, and were sold by well-known retailers like Eleanor Beard Co., A. M. Caden, and Mary McElwain.

Marie continued to design new patterns until about 1930 and was involved with the business until her retirement in 1942. Hers had been a remarkable thirty-year career of designing, writing, lecturing, judging quilt contests, and conducting a thriving cottage industry.

Marie Webster's influence was far reaching. In 1916, Dr. William Rush Dunton Jr., wrote to her after reading her book, which inspired him to advocate quiltmaking as a form of occupational therapy for his patients. They corresponded again in the 1930s, when Dunton sought her advice about publishing his book *Old Quilts*. Rose Kretsinger also was inspired by Marie Webster, stating in a letter to Ruth Finley in 1929 that she had received "such encouragement from [Mrs. Webster's] kind letters to me." The style of pastel floral appliqué that Marie popularized through *Ladies' Home Journal* articles was widely adopted by professional designers in the 1920s and 1930s.

Quilts: Their Story and How to Make Them also had a significant impact. It legitimized the serious study of quilt history and celebrated the importance of women's artistic efforts. Its success demonstrated the broad appeal of the subject of quilts, not only to quiltmakers, but to a much wider audience that appreciated the artistic and social importance of these artifacts. Furthermore,

She sent the quilt to *Ladies' Home Journal*, the leading women's magazine of the day, which was actively soliciting new ideas from its readers. There her quilt caught the eye of the *Journal's* editor, Arts and Crafts advocate Edward Bok. When he invited her to submit more designs for a full-color page, she created her *Iris*, *Snowflake*, and *Wind Blown Tulip* quilts. Illustrated in the January 1, 1911, issue of the *Journal*, these four innovative designs were viewed by some one and a half million women. Overnight, Marie Webster became a national celebrity.

The demand for her patterns was so great that soon she was filling orders from her home. The pattern packets, costing fifty cents, included a photo of the quilt, brief directions and fabric swatches, and full-size blueprints of the pattern pieces and colored tissue paper guides showing how to arrange the leaves and petals.

A retrospective exhibit of her quilts mounted by the Indianapolis Museum of Art traveled to several venues around the United States from 1991 to 1994. Her quilts were also featured in an exhibit that toured Japan in 1998, *American Quilt Renaissance: Three Women Who Influenced Quiltmaking in the Early 20th Century*, together with work by the Quilters Hall of Fame honorees Rose Kretsinger and Carrie Hall. In 1999, Marie's *Grapes and Vines* quilt was selected as one of *America's 100 Best Quilts of the 20th Century*.

The Quilters Hall of Fame has showcased Marie Webster's quilts in three special exhibits. The organization's very first exhibit, in July 1992, was *The Quilters Hall of Fame Celebrates Marie Webster*. *Marie Webster's Garden of Quilts* was shown in July 2009, celebrating the 150th anniversary of her birth. In 2010, another selection of quilts both old and new, made from her patterns, was exhibited in the Quilters Hall of Fame: *Marie Webster Quilts: A Homecoming*.

In recognition of her pioneering work, Marie Webster was inducted into the Quilters Hall of Fame in 1991. A most modest woman, she did not seek fame for herself. Her legacy, as she would have wished, is inspiring others to create quilts, to appreciate quilting as an art form, and to preserve this heritage for the future. She would have been delighted to know that her home would one day become the Quilters Hall of Fame.

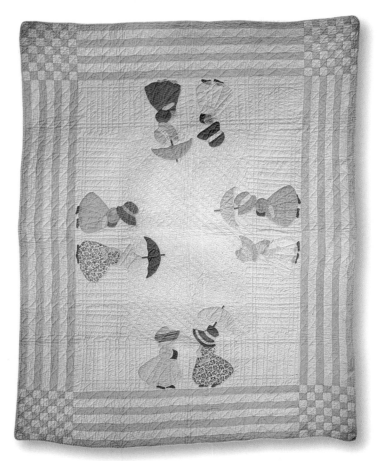

Sunbonnet Lassies | Designed and hand-appliquéd by Marie Webster, Marion, Indiana | Possibly quilted by others, using Marie's designs | 1912 | 37¾ × 48¾ inches | Linen and cotton. This pattern was published in *Ladies' Home Journal* in August 1912 with the following caption: "The sunbonnet lassies . . . suggest an outing or a call from playmates on the morrow. These lassies may be dressed in bits of the gowns of the little maid, and the quilt thus becomes a 'keepsake quilt.'" According to Webster's granddaughter, Rosalind Perry, "The quilted background suggests a peaceful village setting, with a picket fence, nodding sunflowers, and little birds flying overhead. Little girl figures with faces hidden by bonnets were first popularized by the famous illustrator Kate Greenaway, whose designs were often used in embroidery at the turn of the century." *Courtesy of Rosalind Perry*

it was the only quilt book in print until 1929, when Ruth Finley's *Old Patchwork Quilts and the Women Who Made Them* was published. Even in the early 1970s, when the late twentieth-century quilt revival began, Webster's book was one of the few available for use by a new generation of quiltmakers and quilt historians.

Marie Webster's designs appear frequently in quilt magazines, and her book is often cited in contemporary writing on quilt history. Quilt lovers both here and abroad have seen her quilts.

Selected Reading

Benberry, Cuesta. "Marie Webster: Indiana's Gift to American Quilts." *Quilts of Indiana*. Indiana Quilt Registry Project. Bloomington: Indiana University Press, 1991, 88–93.

———. "Marie D. Webster: A Major Influence on Quilt Design in the 20th Century." *Quilter's Newsletter Magazine*, no. 224 (July/August 1990): 32–35.

Perry, Rosalind Webster, and Marty Frolli. *A Joy Forever: Marie Webster's Quilt Patterns*. Santa Barbara, CA: Practical Patchwork, 1992.

———. *Marie Webster's Garden of Quilts*. Santa Barbara, CA: Practical Patchwork, 2001.

Shankel, Carol, ed. *American Quilt Renaissance: Three Women Who Influenced Quiltmaking in the Early 20th Century*. Tokyo: Kokusai Art, 1997.

Webster, Marie D. *Quilts: Their Story and How to Make Them*. Garden City, NY: Doubleday, Page & Co., 1915. Expanded edition with color illustrations, notes, bibliography, and biography of the author by Rosalind Webster Perry. Santa Barbara, CA: Practical Patchwork, 1990.

Jean Wells

"*What an amazing journey it has been,*
being in the quilting business for thirty-five years.
I love what I do! It is never ending—one idea just leads to another.
'Engaging the creative spirit' is the very best part."

—Jean Wells, *Stitchin' Post Class Schedule*, Spring/Summer 2010

Jean Wells (formerly Jean Wells Keenan) was inducted into the Quilters Hall of Fame in Marion, Indiana, on July 17, 2010. *Courtesy of Jean Wells*

by Anne Girod Foster

JEAN WELLS IS KNOWN NATIONALLY not only as a designer and quilter, but also as an author, television personality, teacher, and extremely successful entrepreneur, credited with starting the famous outdoor quilt show in Sisters, Oregon.

Jean graduated from Redmond (Oregon) High School and then from Oregon State University in 1965, with a B.S. degree in home economics education. In 1969, she earned an M.S. in guidance and counseling from Portland State University. She then taught home economics at Beaverton High School. Jean first became interested in quiltmaking when she was searching for a project for her high school class. The geometric shapes of patchwork, she thought, would be a perfect way to include math in the project of making pillows. Her lifelong love of patchwork and quilting was born!

In 1975, Jean and her family moved to Sisters, a small 1880s-style town, with a population at that time of only a few hundred. Jean used her $3,400 teaching retirement money to open a small quilt shop, the Stitchin' Post, one of the first in America. Her grandmother, who taught her to sew, had a pharmacy in the same location in the 1930s. When Jean decided to hang twelve quilts outside her store on a summer Saturday, including some made by her grandmother, that was the start of the Sisters Outdoor Quilt Show.

A few years later, the newly formed East of the Cascades Quilters Guild began helping with the show, which has continued to grow to the present day. From the showing of those few quilts, the Sisters Outdoor Quilt Show has become the world's largest outdoor quilt show. In 2009, it displayed some 1,300 quilts from twenty-eight states, Canada, the United Kingdom, Japan, Ireland, and Rwanda. The show was founded to encourage quilters of all levels of experience, and continues to do so, for the quilts are neither juried nor judged. Quilts wrap downtown, hung on storefronts, fences, walls, and buildings. Volunteers make it successful, spending some three thousand hours hanging the quilts, hosting the event, and then taking down the quilts in the late afternoon of the same day.

Busloads of quilt enthusiasts come from all over the world. Traffic is rerouted away from the center of town so everyone can saunter, take pictures, and admire the quilts. An estimated twenty thousand people visit Sisters on the second Saturday of July each year, where they enjoy this visual feast of beautiful quilts.

The week before the outdoor show, the Around the Block Fiber Arts Stroll brings people to Sisters's stores and galleries to see some thirty local fiber artists demonstrating their craft. And the whole week prior to the show, the Quilter's Affair, launched

The Wedding Garden | Designed, pieced, and quilted by **Jean Wells, Sisters, Oregon** | 2003 | **73 × 63 inches.** Jean created this amazing quilt to celebrate the beauty of her garden on the occasion of her son's and daughter's weddings. In the background, she has placed the Three Sisters mountain peaks (known as Faith, Hope, and Charity) for which the town of Sisters is named. *Courtesy of Jean Wells*

The front of Jean Wells's quilt shop in Sisters, Oregon. *Courtesy of Jean Wells*

Visitors from around the world throng the streets of Sisters, Oregon, during its famous Outdoor Quilt Show. From the first display of 12 quilts in 1975, the show has grown to feature over 1,300 quilts. This photo shows a group of Challenge quilts hanging on the wall of the Stitchin' Post during the 1998 show. *Courtesy of Jean Wells*

in 1978, now holds more than eighty classes for as many as 1,600 quilters. Among the teachers have been Quilters Hall of Fame honorees Jinny Beyer and Georgia Bonesteel. Other teachers have included Gwen Marston, Freddy Moran, Joen Wolfrom, Katie Pasquini Masopust, Velda Newman, Jane Sassaman, and Ruth McDowell.

Jean's dedication to her community is displayed as she hires local high school students to help with the events and invites local churches, clubs, and organizations such as hospice to arrange events and booths to raise money. In all, these activities bring more than three million dollars annually into the economy of Central Oregon. She has truly made the tiny town of Sisters a major tourist destination.

Jean says, "It has been my privilege to help grow this event, and I have long been delighted with the benefit it brings to the community. I am pleased that we have been able to establish the quilt show as a nonprofit organization, hire staff, and develop plans to sustain the event long into the future."

In addition to her leadership of the outdoor show events, Jean has successfully operated the Stitchin' Post since 1975. A major factor in her shop's success is her employees, numbering twenty-three year round, increasing to more than fifty during the quilt show. All are local people whom she has hired and encouraged to develop skills and responsibility. She says she believes in "empowering my staff to do the jobs that they are hired for, and I spend lots of time training them to do it the way I feel is best for the business."

Jean stays on top of the fast-changing retail business by answering the changing needs and desires of her customers. The store website not only features classes, fabrics, and teachers, but also offers free patterns online.

Even before Jean opened her quilt shop, she designed and sold quilted items. She continues to be a prolific designer and teacher of many quilting techniques and styles. Her designs often feature landscape elements: rocks, trees, and flowers. Recently, she has been experimenting with freehand cutting and detail piecing. In 2000, she won the Imagination Award in the Millennium Quilt Contest.

Jean believes in the importance of studying the history of quilting, the preservation of fabrics and quilts, and the need for continuing education of others to ensure that the art and study of quilting be honored. Her lectures and classes always stress not only new techniques and designs but also the study of those of previous years.

Jean Wells has been teaching quilting for thirty-six years and has had an impressive number of titles published, mainly by C&T Publishing Company. She has authored twenty-seven quilt and pattern books, including some coauthored by her daughter Valori Wells Kennedy, who is now her business partner. Jean has also written extensively for magazines, has lectured and taught quilting classes worldwide, and has appeared on numerous television shows. Her workshops on "Quilting Inspirations" and "Tips on Running a Successful Quilt Shop" are especially popular.

Jean is very active in community organizations like the Sisters Chamber of Commerce, the Sisters School Board, and the Oregon State Small Business Development Board, where she often teaches classes. She has taught workshops nationwide, not only in quilting, but also to share her expertise and to encourage other shop owners. "The foundation of my business is education," emphasizes Jean in her Quilt Market business classes.

Jean Wells surrounded by the colorful fabrics she loves in her shop, the Stitchin' Post, which she founded in 1975. *Courtesy of Jean Wells*

Selected Reading

Wells, Jean. *Fans: A Collection of Quilt Designs and Inspirations.* Concord, CA: C&T Publishing Inc., 1987.

————. *Intuitive Color & Design: Adventures in Art Quilting.* Concord, CA: C&T Publishing Inc., 2009.

————. *Machine Appliqué Made Easy: A Beginner's Guide to Techniques, Stitches, and Decorative Projects.* Concord, CA: C&T Publishing Inc., 2005.

————. *Portraits from Nature: 35 Studies of Dimensional Quilts.* Concord, CA: C&T Publishing Inc., 2006.

Wells, Jean, and Valori Wells. *Along the Garden Path: More Quilters and Their Gardens.* Concord, CA: C&T Publishing Inc., 2001.

————. *Through the Garden Gate Quilt Book.* Concord, CA: C&T Publishing Inc., 1992.

Cityscape | Designed, pieced, and quilted by Jean Wells, Sisters, Oregon | 2008 | 25 × 64 inches. This quilt started out as a contemporary sampler with a palette picked from a set shot in a magazine. When Jean took a trip to New York City, the sampler transformed itself into a cityscape, with the city becoming the inspiration. *Courtesy of Jean Wells*

Jean has received many well-deserved honors. In 1997, she was the first person inducted into the Primedia Independent Retailers Hall of Fame. Her shop was the first to be featured in the premier issue of *American Patchwork & Quilting*, in an article called "Top Ten Shops." In 1998, she received the Michael Kile Award for Lifetime Achievement, honoring commitment to creativity and excellence in the quilting industry. The Sisters Chamber of Commerce named the Stitchin' Post "Business of the Year" in 1999, and Jean received their "Citizen of the Year" award in 2007.

Jean's pride in her profession, her skill in sharing knowledge, her commitment to community service, and her significant ethical vision are some of her outstanding qualities. Literally thousands of people have been positively influenced and inspired by Jean during her life. An educator at heart, Jean is an outstanding example of what is happening in the quilting world today—designing and making innovative creative art while preserving our past and recognizing that today's events will become "our past history" in time.

Donna Wilder

*"Quilting evokes a tactile response
that reaches both hand and heart."*

—Donna Wilder, acceptance speech, Silver Star Salute, Houston, Texas,
November 4, 2000

Donna Wilder was inducted into the
Quilters Hall of Fame at the Continental
Quilting Congress in Falls Church, Virginia,
on October 5, 1990.

by Lorraine Covington

DONNA WILDER has been an innovator in the quilting business world for more than thirty years. By promoting the work of contemporary quilters and fabric artists, Donna has inspired thousands to achieve their finest work. As a facilitator of the highest order, she challenges her audience through a fascinating array of contests, fashion shows, TV programs, and exhibits. She was named recipient of the Silver Star Award at the International Quilt Festival in 1998, and in October 2007, as recognition for her contributions and dedication to the art of quilting and fiber arts, Donna was the recipient of the Michael Kile Award of Achievement. This award is presented annually at the International Quilt Market and honors those who have had a significant influence on the quilting industry.

The oldest of three girls, Donna was born in Sacramento, California, and grew up in Clarks Green, Pennsylvania. Her childhood was enriched by unique experiences that set the stage for her high-profile career. She learned to sew at the age of five and appeared on television with her mother, Janet Miller, who was the host of a cooking and sewing program called *At Home with Janet*.

At the age of twelve, Donna was featured on the program giving instructions on how to make a cake.

Donna's first experience with quilting involved cutting apart madras plaid fabrics and sewing the patches back together to form a new pattern. Since then, she has created many quilted wearable art garments and wall hangings.

From the time she was a young girl, Donna knew that she wanted to go to New York City and work in retailing. After graduating from Pennsylvania State University in 1964 with a B.S. in home economics, clothing, and textiles, she began her retail career as an assistant buyer for the costume jewelry department of Abraham & Strauss in Brooklyn. Employment with Simplicity Pattern Company, Fabricland, Riegel Textile Company, and Springs Industries gave Donna fabric merchandising responsibilities at both the retail and mill levels as well as extensive travel throughout the northeastern United States and Japan. Donna married Daniel Wilder in 1973 and raised two sons, Andrew and Matthew, while pursuing her active career.

Hail Thee Stonington Stars | Fabric designed by Donna Wilder, fabric selection coordinated by Donna Wilder and Marsha Evans Moore, machine-pieced and quilted by Marsha Evans Moore | 2002 | 53 × 53 inches | Cotton fabric and batting. With a design adapted from a late-eighteenth-century quilt made in Stonington, Connecticut, this quilt features fabric from the Somersby Collection designed by Donna Wilder for Free Spirit. The floral prints used in this quilt were adapted from early French document fabrics and paintings that Donna purchased, both in France and from antique fabric dealers in New York. The rich colors of the fabric are both authentic in shade and yet mixed in combination for a more updated appearance. Fabric documentation: collection of Free Spirit. *Photo by White Light, courtesy of Donna Wilder*

In 1978, Donna joined Fairfield Processing Corporation, manufacturer of batting products. As vice president of marketing, Donna was responsible for the promotion of the company's products as well as all communications and product development. Donna also collected contemporary quilts for Fairfield's Corporate Art Collection in the company's headquarters in Danbury, Connecticut.

Through her positions at Fairfield, Donna was the catalyst and coordinator for many quilt block contests, quilt contests, and quilt shows. Fairfield's quilt block contests began in 1980, with themes like "These Are a Few of My Favorite Things" and "Quilting through the Century." The winning blocks were made into quilts and exhibited at major quilting events across the country. These quilts now reside in the company's permanent collection.

The famous Fairfield Fashion Show, an invitational designer show of wearable art, started in 1979 at the suggestion of Donna Wilder, with help from Karey Bresenhan, president of Quilts, Inc.; Priscilla Miller, then of Concord Fabrics; and Anita Wellings of Fairfield. This extravaganza provided a showcase for the most creative and innovative designers in the quilted clothing world of the day. More than one thousand articles of clothing by more than four hundred designers were featured. Donna issued invitations to approximately fifty designers for each year's show and served as show moderator.

The unveiling of these innovative creations at the International Quilt Festival and Market in Houston, Texas, was eagerly awaited each fall. The collection then traveled across the United States and overseas for a year, where it was exhibited and modeled at major quilt shows. The garments were also featured in quilt magazines

Donna Wilder on the set of *Sew Creative. Courtesy of Donna Wilder*

and in a video version of the fashion show. In 2001, Bernina began sponsorship of the fashion show, with Donna continuing as commentator until 2003.

In addition to the block contests and the fashion show, Donna created other well-known quilt events. One of the most popular was the *State Quilt Flags* show exhibited at the Great American Quilt Festival II held in New York City in April 1986 to celebrate the centennial of the Statue of Liberty.

Her years of promoting quilt products and creating contests and shows have made Donna a popular choice for judging quilt shows. Among the many shows she has judged are the Vermont Quilt Festival, New England Images, American Quilter's Society Fashion Show and Quilt Contest, shows for *Better Homes and Gardens* and *American Patchwork & Quilting*, and the International Quilt Festival show in 2000.

In 1988, she served as judge with fellow Hall of Fame honorees Jeffrey Gutcheon, Carter Houck, and Bonnie Leman for the Memories of Childhood crib quilt contest sponsored by Fairfield, Coats & Clark, and the Museum of American Folk Art (now the American Folk Art Museum). In 1989 she was a juror for the *Fabric Gardens* exhibition at the International Garden and Greenery Exposition in Osaka, Japan. Her quilt expertise and research have also taken her to Holland, France, and England.

Also an author, Donna wrote "Quilts at an Exhibition" for *America's Glorious Quilts*, published in 1987, providing a concise history of quilts in shows, contests, and state documentation projects. She has also written for consumer magazines and trade

Donna Wilder was the driving force behind the Fairfield Fashion Show when she worked for Fairfield. This fashion show of quilted garments was prestigious and very popular at the International Quilt Festival. Quilt artists were invited to participate, and the invitation was highly coveted. This book, published in 1988, was an overview of the best garments made for the Fairfield Fashion Show over a decade.

publications on contemporary trends in quilting. She penned more than a dozen books based on techniques taught on the television show she hosted and produced, *Sew Creative*. This series of half-hour shows began in 1991 on public broadcasting stations. Covering a variety of sewing and quilting topics, the show's format was designed for all levels of ability, with simple directions for the novices and innovative ideas for the experts.

With Janie Donaldson, Donna cohosted three series of the TV program *Quilt Central*, focusing on sophisticated techniques and long-arm quilting. It won a 2003 Telly award for outstanding television production.

Donna has served on the boards of many organizations, including the International Quilt Study Center, the New England Quilt Museum, and the Hobby Industry Association (now CHA). She was a member of the advisory board for Quilt Market and served on the acquisitions committee and as vice president of the board of trustees for the National Quilt Museum.

In 2000, Donna started a new fabric company, FreeSpirit, a division of Fabric Traditions, to manufacture fabric specifically for independent fabric and quilt shops, utilizing talented artists to create unique designs. Honorees Jean Ray Laury and Michael James are a few of the popular quilters who have designed for FreeSpirit.

In December 2008, Donna retired from full-time work. She continues to consult for fabric companies and designers and creates a line of quilting fabrics for Fabric Traditions under the umbrella of the Stonehill Collection.

Selected Reading

Wilder, Donna. *Classics Revisited: A Collection of Patchwork and Applique*. Danbury, CT: FPC Media, 1999.

———. *Dimensions: A New Approach to Piecing and Applique*. Danbury, CT: FPC Media, 1999.

———. *Fabric Garden: A Bouquet of Patchwork and Applique*. Danbury, CT: FPC Media, 1998.

———. *Folk Art: A Sampler of Patchwork and Applique*. Danbury, CT: FPC Media, 2000.

———. *The Masterpiece Sampler Quilt*. San Marcos, CA: American School of Needlework, 1996.

Wilder, Donna, ed. *Art to Wear. Diamond Extravaganza: A Decade of Design*. Danbury, CT: FPC Media, 1998.

Donna Wilder has been the catalyst for thousands of quilts and quilted fashions. Inspired by her mother and with dreams of a big city career in fashion merchandising, she found a comfortable match for her talents in the expanding textile craft industry. Her innovative themes and design ideas have inspired quilters to explore new territory, and her exhibits have provided artists with opportunities to showcase their quilts and quilted clothing for a broad audience.

Plain and Fancy fabric line designed by Donna Wilder for Free Spirit.
Courtesy of Donna Wilder

Fiesta Fabric line designed by Donna Wilder for Free Spirit.
Courtesy of Donna Wilder

About the Contributors

Rosalind Webster Perry, Editor, First Edition

Rosalind Webster Perry, author, publisher, and granddaughter of Marie Webster, lives in Santa Barbara, California. Her passion for quilts began in 1988, when she started to research her grandmother's life for the expanded Practical Patchwork edition of *Quilts: Their Story and How to Make Them*. Rosalind has also coauthored two books featuring Marie Webster's quilt patterns, *A Joy Forever* and *Marie Webster's Garden of Quilts*.

Marian Ann J. Montgomery, Ph.D., Editor, Second Edition

Marian Ann Montgomery, an independent museum and textile consultant with expertise in quilt history, lives in Dallas, Texas, where she coordinated *Quilt Mania I* and *Quilt Mania II*, collaborative exhibitions bringing together twenty cultural institutions exhibiting quilts related to their institutional missions. Former board member of the American Quilt Study Group and contributor to the organization's scholarly journal *Uncoverings*, Marian Ann has worked for thirty years in the museum field. Through her work as the curator of fashion and textiles for the Tennessee State Museum, her attendance at the major quilt festivals, and her membership and contributions to one of the largest and oldest guilds (the Quilters Guild of Dallas, Inc.), she has been mentored and taught by many of those featured in this volume.

For more information on honorees Virginia Avery, Georgia Bonesteel, Barbara Brackman, Jonathan Holstein, Bets Ramsey, and Merikay Waldvogel, please see their profiles within the book.

Karen B. Alexander joined the American Quilt Study Group in 1981, served on the board of the Quilters Hall of Fame from 2001 to 2008 (as president from 2005 to 2008), and created the Quilters Hall of Fame blog (thequiltershalloffame.blogspot.com).

Virginia Butz Amling, who first took an interest in quilting at the age of nine, served as national president of the Valparaiso (Indiana) University Guild, which supports scholarships and supplies classroom enhancements for the students of "Valpo."

Nancy Bavor served as the curatorial intern for the Joyce Gross exhibition at the San Jose Museum of Quilts and Textiles.

Dr. Julia (Judy) Berg, a public school administrator, focused her doctorate degree on organization and research, which she then applied to her interest in quilts and quiltmakers by serving as a member of Michigan Quilt Network and a chairperson for Michigan's state preservation committee, lecturing statewide on the importance of quilt documentation.

Debra Bissantz, who worked in the pharmaceutical industry and now is a technical writer in the computer systems industry, has been quilting since 1983 and has found inspiration in Bonnie Leman's entrepreneurial spirit and energy.

Carol Bosshardt's master's degree studies involved comparing the work of Nebraskan quilters to literary texts of plains writers. She currently works with Red Cross disaster services in Kearney, Nebraska, and still lectures on Nebraska quilts and quilters.

Debora Clem lives in Atlanta where, as a member of the Phoenix Quilt Guild, she quilts, collects fabric and antique quilts, and continues her research into the history of quiltmaking, in particular as it relates to women's history.

Lorraine Covington, a former schoolteacher and tutor, has judged quilt shows, has taught at the Academy of Sewing, and is active in several quilt guilds in the Columbus, Ohio, area.

Vickie L. Douglas has been designing and making quilts as well as teaching about quilts for more than twenty years and belongs to several quilt guilds.

Katherine Webster Dwight and **Rosalind Webster Perry,** granddaughters of honoree Marie Webster, were born in Marion, Indiana, but spent most of their childhood years in Princeton, New Jersey, where their grandmother and her sister shared the family home. Both sisters served on the board of directors of the Quilters Hall of Fame.

Susan Fiondella, a quilt appraiser certified by the American Quilters Society, is a teacher, lecturer, and quiltmaker who served on the board of directors of the Connecticut Quilt Search Project and coauthored *Quilts and Quiltmakers Covering Connecticut*.

With a master's degree in home economics, **Anne Girod Foster** judged county and state fairs in Oregon, California, and Montana; taught clothing and textiles classes at Portland Community

---

Baskets | **Maker unknown, possibly made in Ohio** | **Circa 1930–1950** | **79½ × 66 inches.** Once Ardis and Robert James understood the genius of Pennsylvania Amish quilts, it was a great revelation for them to discover that unique creative ability was embodied also in the quilts of the Midwestern Amish. According to Jonathan Holstein, this *Baskets* quilt said it all for them: " . . . an arresting, compelling, and strangely moving image created through simple forms and color manipulations." *Courtesy of the International Quilt Study Center, Jonathan Holstein Collection (2003.003.0107)*

College; and coordinated and supervised the "Balancing Work and Family" program in the Oregon community colleges.

The essay on Jeffrey Gutcheon was updated by the son of Jeffrey and Beth Gutcheon, **David Gutcheon**. David is a writer living in New York City.

Retired reference librarian **Diane Hammill** designs her own patterns and creates art quilts while managing the Crawfordsville District Public Library's Mary Bishop Memorial Art Gallery.

Former public schoolteacher and librarian **Mary Sue Hannan,** a personal friend of Cuesta Benberry, is a quiltmaker, quilt researcher, writer, and scholar.

Author of the award-winning book *Mary Black's Family Quilts* and numerous other publications, **Laurel Horton** founded Quilters of South Carolina, was a member of the American Quilt Study Group board of directors from 1986 to 1996, and served as editor of *Uncoverings* from 1987 to 1993 and 2008 to 2011.

Christina Fullerton Jones, granddaughter of Ruby McKim, collaborates with her cousin, Merrily McKim Tuohey, to further Ruby's legacy through adaptations of her work in needlework and quilting. Ruby's original designs and other artwork may be found at www.mckimstudios.com.

Registered psychiatric nurse **Eileen "Bunnie" Jordan** is also a quilter and quilt appraiser accredited by the American Society of Appraisers, is active in her local guild (Quilters Unlimited), serves on the board of directors of the American Quilt Study Group, and is on the staff of the Jinny Beyer Hilton Head Seminar.

Former English teacher **Amy Korn** is an American Quilter's Society certified quilt appraiser and currently serves on the board of the American Quilt Study Group while passionately pursuing quiltmaking, quilt history, and antique fabric.

Stacie McIntyre Seeger Matheson, formerly a quilt appraiser, quilt historian, and board member of the American Quilt Study Group, now works in the medical field and coordinates conferences on women's issues.

Suellen Meyer, professor of English at St. Louis Community College–Meramec, has collected antique quilts and written about them since the early 1970s, with articles appearing in *Uncoverings*, *Country Living*, *Quilter's Newsletter Magazine* and other publications.

Ann Bodle Nash is currently involved in quilt appraising, collecting, historical study, and experimentation with alternative new quilt construction materials and techniques, as well as serving as a board member of the Quilters Hall of Fame and the La Conner Quilt Museum.

Public relations specialist **Pamela Neiwirth** was inspired by Jinny Beyer's *Ray of Light* quilt to become a quilter and, later, a quilting teacher.

Sunburst quilt | Quiltmaker unknown, made in Central Texas | Circa 1870 | 74½ × 80½ inches (blocks measure 37 × 37 inches) | Cotton, possibly linen; hand-pieced and hand-quilted using six stitches per inch. A large, bold, four-block design in the collection of Karey Bresenhan, this quilt was made in red and gold, and hand-pieced and quilted in the difficult Sunburst pattern. The small, red square in the center of the gold sashing and the feather design quilted into the block corners and two borders are special touches. The backing fabric appears to be homespun. *Courtesy of the International Quilt Festival Collection*

Pat L. Nickols writes, lectures, occasionally teaches, and makes wall-hanging-size quilts but actively continues her passionate study of the history of quilts and the wonderful fabrics they contain.

Formerly a museum curator, **Dorothy Osler** has since focused her attention on textiles, gaining international recognition for her books, articles, lectures, and classes. Dorothy was the first Heritage Officer for the Quilters' Guild of the British Isles (1983–1989) and also the first international representative on the advisory board of the International Quilt Study Center at the University of Nebraska–Lincoln (1998–2001).

Elizabeth Palmer-Spilker, a quiltmaker, pattern designer, and curator of art quilt exhibits, credits Jean Ray Laury with helping her understand that inspiration does not come from quilting tools but from hard work.

Kathlyn Ronsheimer, former board member of the American Quilt Study Group and the Northern California Quilt Council, helped Joyce Gross organize the annual Point Bonita Getaway for many years and became its principal organizer upon Joyce's retirement before it was turned over to the YMCA.

Bob Ruggiero, manager of publications and public information for Quilts, Inc., also serves as editor of the *International Quilt Association Journal.*

When the call came for volunteers to research Quilters Hall of Fame honorees, **Robin L. Rushbrook,** Ph.D. and quilter, jumped at the chance and has subsequently exhibited and sold quilts before beginning her next formal career—library science.

Nancy Shamy has attended numerous quilt classes, lectures, and seminars over the years and has spent the last ten years teaching a variety of classes on quilts and wearable art. She is working on a pattern line to debut in 2011.

With both a bachelor's and master's degree in English, **Amy Bonesteel Smith,** Georgia's daughter, has contributed to *Time*, the *New York Times Magazine, Atlanta Magazine, Parenting*, and many other publications.

For the first eight years of the Quilters' Guild of the British Isles, **Tina Fenwick Smith** curated the Guild Collection and even based her dissertation on Averil Colby's scrap bag.

Alyson B. Stanfield, a former museum curator and educator, served on the Ultimate Quilt Search committee as a representative for the Alliance for American Quilts, helping to select the one hundred best American quilts of the twentieth century.

A retired college professor and librarian, **Linda Wilson** loves quilting, printmaking, and collecting vintage silk kimono fabric that she uses to make one-of-a-kind silk scarves.

Sawtooth | Maker unknown, possibly made in Massachusetts | Circa 1890–1910 | 89½ × 76 inches | Cotton; hand-pieced and hand-quilted. Gail van der Hoof and Jonathan Holstein expanded their initial search across the country and soon found this *Sawtooth* quilt in Massachusetts. It helped confirm their notion that the type of quilt they liked was not just a regional phenomenon but had been made across the United States. Its simplicity, boldness, complete use of the surface, and two-color palette made it an icon for them and, through its exposure in many exhibitions over the years, for many others. *Courtesy of the International Quilt Study Center, Jonathan Holstein Collection (2003.003.0024)*

Index